JOSSEY-BASS TEACHER

Jossey-Bass Teacher provides K–12 teachers with essential knowledge and tools to create a positive and lifelong impact on student learning. Trusted and experienced educational mentors offer practical classroom-tested and theory-based teaching resources for improving teaching practice in a broad range of grade levels and subject areas. From one educator to another, we want to be your first source to make every day your best day in teaching. *Jossey-Bass Teacher* resources serve two types of informational needs—essential knowledge and essential tools.

Essential knowledge resources provide the foundation, strategies, and methods from which teachers may design curriculum and instruction to challenge and excite their students. Connecting theory to practice, essential knowledge books rely on a solid research base and time-tested methods, offering the best ideas and guidance from many of the most experienced and well-respected experts in the field.

Essential tools save teachers time and effort by offering proven, ready-to-use materials for in-class use. Our publications include activities, assessments, exercises, instruments, games, ready reference, and more. They enhance an entire course of study, a weekly lesson, or a daily plan. These essential tools provide insightful, practical, and comprehensive materials on topics that matter most to K–12 teachers.

MATH ESSENTIALS

HIGH SCHOOL LEVEL

Lessons and Activities for Test Preparation

FRANCES McBROOM THOMPSON, Ed.D.

JOSSEY-BASS
A Wiley Imprint
www.josseybass.com

Additional Objectives

Additional objectives typically covered on high school exit exams are provided in another book in this series, *Math Essentials*, *Middle School Level*, and are listed here with their section and objective numbers shown respectively in brackets:

Add Integers to Solve Word Problems [2.2]

Subtract Integers to Solve Word Problems [2.3]

Multiply and Divide Integers to Solve Word Problems [2.4]

Model Situations with Linear Equations of the Form: $aX + b = c$, where a, b, and c Are Integers or Decimals and X Is an Integer [2.5]

Sketch Side Views (Orthogonal Views) of Solids and Identify Different Perspectives of Solids That Satisfy the Side Views [3.1]

Identify Transformations or Graph Reflections (Flips), Rotations (Turns), and Translations (Slides) on a Coordinate Plane (That Is, Find Congruent Shapes Under Certain Conditions) [3.2]

Use Dilations (Reductions or Enlargements) to Generate Similar Two-Dimensional Shapes, and Compare Their Side Lengths, Angles, and Perimeters; Find Missing Measurements Using Proportional Relationships [3.3]

Apply Nets and Concrete Models to Find Total or Partial Surface Areas of Prisms and Cylinders [3.8]

Construct and Interpret Circle Graphs [4.2]

Compare Different Numerical or Graphical Models for the Same Set of Data, Including Histograms, Circle Graphs, Stem-and-Leaf Plots, Box Plots, and Scatter Plots [4.3]

Find the Mean of a Given Set of Data, Using Different Representations such as Tables or Bar Graphs (Reviews Mode and Median) [4.4]

Notes to the Teacher

Math Essentials, High School Level consists of thirty key objectives arranged in four sections. These objectives have been selected from the standard mathematics curriculum for grades 9 to 11 and from the high school curriculum recommended by the National Council of Teachers of Mathematics. Because of the cumulative nature of mathematics, some objectives from grade 8 are also covered in the text. Other appropriate grade 8 objectives, which are frequently included in exit-level exams, are listed in the "Additional Objectives" section and described in detail in *Math Essentials, Middle School Level* (2005). Each objective has three activities (two developmental lessons and one independent practice), along with a list of common errors students make with respect to problems related to the objective. A worksheet and answer key are provided for most activities. Each of the four sections also contains a practice test with an answer key.

Description of Activities

Two developmental activities have been included for each objective: the first at the manipulative stage and the second at the pictorial stage. Detailed steps guide the teacher through each of these two activities. Activity 1 usually requires objects of some kind. Materials are described in detail, and necessary building mats, pattern sheets, and worksheets with answer keys are provided. Activity 2 involves pictures or diagrams that closely relate to the actions performed in Activity 1. Worksheets and answer keys are also available for this second activity. Activity 3 provides an opportunity for students to practice the objective independently and at the abstract level of thinking. Worksheet exercises for this third stage often have multiple-choice responses to provide students with additional testing experience. The exercises have been kept to a minimum (five to eight exercises) to reduce or prevent frustration in at-risk students. Having fewer exercises also allows more class time for student discussions about their answers and the methods they used to find those answers. The communication of mathematical ideas is an essential classroom experience.

These three activities may be presented as a connected set, with the manipulative activity leading naturally to the pictorial activity and then the independent practice, or each activity may be used separately, depending on the learning needs of the students. All students, however, regardless of intellectual ability or diversity of background, need to experience each of the three stages of learning at some point. The natural learning progression that moves from hands-on action to paper-and-pencil drawing and finally to abstract notation is essential for all students to experience and should not be excluded from classroom instruction. Therefore, it is recommended that the three activities be used together.

Common Errors Made by Students

When studying any mathematical objective, students will have errors in their work. Test developers know this and usually select item response choices that reflect these errors. Hence, it is helpful if the classroom teacher also is aware of these common errors and can identify them when they occur in an individual student's work.

To assist teachers with this process, a list of typical errors is given with each objective in this text. Various studies have found that if students are made aware of their particular mistakes in mathematics, they are more likely to replace them with correct procedures or conceptual understanding. When such errors are not specifically addressed, students are likely to continue making them, no matter how many times the teacher demonstrates the correct steps to use.

Section Practice Tests

A practice test, along with an answer key, is provided at the end of each section. For each objective in a section, two multiple-choice test items are provided on the section's practice test. The format and level of difficulty of these items are similar to those found in state or national standardized tests or on exit-level tests for high school students. Where appropriate, the activity worksheets for an objective reflect the types of problems included in the practice test. Otherwise the activities are designed to give students the conceptual foundation they need to understand the test items.

Instructional Accountability

Teachers must be accountable for what they are teaching to students. The alternative instructional methods and assessment techniques presented in this text will greatly assist teachers as they try to align their classroom instruction with their district and state mathematics guidelines and seek to measure the progress their students make.

About the Author

Frances M^CBroom Thompson, Ed.D., has taught junior high and senior high mathematics in Anaheim, California, and Dallas, Texas. She has also served as an educational consultant for grades K–12 in both Georgia and Texas. Frances currently is professor of mathematics at Texas Woman's University in Denton, where she focuses on the preparation of elementary and secondary teachers in mathematics. She is also actively involved as a staff development trainer for in-service teachers throughout North Texas.

Frances's teaching methods, based on many years of research with classroom teachers and their students, incorporate manipulatives and diagrams for the development of new concepts. These methods have been successful with all types of learners, including the gifted and the learning disabled. Besides the Math Essentials series, she has written two other resource books for teachers and parents that reflect these methods: *Hands-on Math! Ready-to-Use Games and Activities for Grades 4–8* (1994), and *Hands-on Algebra! Ready-to-Use Games and Activities for Grades 7–12* (1998). Her professional goal is to help students enjoy mathematics while they grow in their abilities to understand and reason with new mathematical ideas.

Contents

SECTION 1: ALGEBRAIC THINKING AND APPLICATIONS   1

Objectives

SECTION 2: GRAPHS, STATISTICS, AND PROBABILITY   93

Objectives

SECTION 3: LINEAR AND QUADRATIC FUNCTIONS AND THEIR PROPERTIES   173

Objectives

SECTION 4: GEOMETRY AND MEASUREMENT WITH APPLICATIONS 245

Objectives

ALGEBRAIC THINKING AND APPLICATIONS

Objective 1: Simplify Algebraic Expressions Involving One or Two Variables

Students have great difficulty recognizing the differences among linear, quadratic, and constant terms in algebraic form. Exponents seem insignificant to them. Viewing each type of term as an area helps students visualize the role each term plays in an expression. The following activities provide experience with such visualization in the combining of like terms. It is assumed that students have already mastered the four operations with integers.

Activity 1
Manipulative Stage

Materials

Packets of variable and unit tiles (described in step 1 below)
Worksheet 1–1a
Legal-sized plain paper or light tagboard (for building mats)
Regular paper and pencils

Procedure

1.   Give each pair of students a packet of tiles, two copies of Worksheet 1–1a, and a sheet of plain paper or tagboard (approximately 8.5 inches by 14 inches) for a building mat. If preferred, laminate the mats to make them more durable. Mats define a specific space on which to represent a problem being solved. If teacher-made tiles are used, each packet should contain the following in different colors of laminated tagboard: 8 square (quadratic) variable tiles, each 3 inches by 3 inches (color #1); 8 square variable tiles, each 3.25 inches by 3.25 inches (color #2); 12 rectangular (linear) variable tiles, 0.75 inches by 3 inches (color #1); 12 rectangular variable tiles, 0.75 inch by 3.25 inches (color #2); and 20 unit tiles, 0.75 inch by 0.75 inch (color #3). Each tile should have a large X drawn on one side to show the inverse of that tile. Use tagboard that is thick enough so that the X will not show through to the other side. Commercial tiles are also available for two different variables, but a large X must be drawn on one of the largest faces of each tile in order to represent the inverse of that tile when the X faces up.

2.   The meaning of a large square tile needs to be connected to a long rectangular tile of the same color. Have students place a rectangular variable tile of color #1 (call it variable A) horizontally on the mat. Then have them place two more variable tiles below and parallel to the first tile on the mat. Ask: "If a single variable tile A is considered to cover an area of 1 by A, or A, how can we describe the arrangement indicated by these tiles on the mat?" ("3 rows of A.") "What product or area is this?" ("$3A$.") Ask: "How can we show A rows of A on the mat if we do not know what the value of A is?" Show students how to build several rows of one variable tile each, using one variable tile A as the multiplier, or "ruler," that indicates when to stop putting tiles in the product on the mat (see the illustration below). When the product is finished, the multiplier tile should be removed from the mat. Depending on the dimensions used to make the tiles, whether commercial or teacher-made, the width across several rectangular tiles placed with their longer sides touching may or may not match the length of the longer side of the same type of tile. Such a match is not important and should be deemphasized since the variable tile A is not considered to have a specific length or value in unit tiles. Therefore, although the width of 4 of the variable tile A may appear to match to one variable tile length as shown on the mat below, do not allow students to say that 4 rows of A equal $4A$.

3.   Ask: "Is there another single block that will cover the same surface area on the mat that the product A of A, or $A(A)$, covers?" ("Yes. The large square tile in color #1; its side length equals the length of the variable tile A.") Again, discuss the idea that the large square tile in color #1 may or may not fit perfectly on top of the "A rows of A" tile arrangement; it will be close enough. Since both the square and rectangular tiles in color #1 are representing variables without known values, we want to maintain their variable nature as much as possible. Physical models like the tiles naturally have specific dimensions that affect or limit areas being built with the tiles, but for our purpose, we will assume that *only the unit tiles may be used to represent exact amounts of area.* We will now assign the large square tile in color #1 the name of A-squared, or A^2. Hence, A rows of A equal A^2. From now on, whenever A rows of A are needed, the large square tile will be used to show that amount of area on the mat.

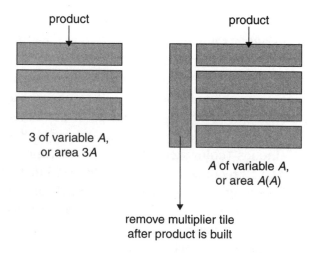

product

product

3 of variable A,
or area $3A$

A of variable A,
or area $A(A)$

remove multiplier tile
after product is built

4.   Similarly the areas of the square and long rectangular variable tiles in color #2 might be described as B-squared, or B^2, and B, respectively. If an X appears on the top side of a variable tile, the <u>inverse</u> or <u>opposite</u> of the tile's area will be indicated. For

example, a B-squared tile with X on top will be called "the <u>opposite</u> or <u>inverse</u> of B-squared" and written as $(-B^2)$. Each small square tile in color #3 represents an area of 1 by 1, or 1 square unit of area. If a given set of unit tiles all have an X showing—for example, 5 tiles with X—then the tile value will be the "<u>negative</u> of 5 square units of area" and written as (-5). Note that area itself is an absolute measure, neither positive nor negative. Area, however, can be assigned a direction of movement in real applications; hence, we can consider the opposite or negative of a given area.

5. After the area of each type of tile is identified, have students do the exercises on Worksheet 1–1a. For each exercise, they should place a set of tiles on the building mat to show the first expression. Then they will either add more tiles to this initial set or remove some tiles from the set according to the second expression of the exercise.

6. After combining tiles that have the same amount of area, students should record an expression for the total or remaining area on the worksheet.

7. Discuss an addition exercise and a subtraction exercise with the class before allowing students to work the other exercises independently.

Consider Exercise 1 on Worksheet 1–1a for addition: $\left(3A^2+2A-5\right)+\left(-A^2+3A+2\right)$: Use color #1 variable tiles with the color #3 unit tiles.

Have students place 3 large square (quadratic) variable tiles, 2 long rectangular (linear) variable tiles, and 5 negative unit tiles on the building mat to represent the first expression. Any such group of tiles is called a *polynomial*, that is, a combination of variable tiles and/or unit tiles. Leaving this set of tiles on the mat, have students place additional tiles on the mat below the initial tiles to represent the second expression. The second set should contain a quadratic variable tile with X showing, 3 linear variable tiles, and 2 unit tiles:

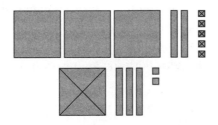

Ask: "Can any 0-pairs be made through joining, then removed from the mat?" (One 0-pair of the large quadratic tiles and two 0-pairs of the small unit tiles should be formed and removed from the building mat.) "Can you now describe the total in tiles still on the mat?" Since tiles for two of A-squared, 5 of A, and -3 remain on the mat, students should complete the recording of Exercise 1 on Worksheet 1–1a: $\left(3A^2+2A-5\right)+\left(-A^2+3A+2\right)=2A^2+5A-3$.

Now consider Exercise 2 on Worksheet 1–1a for subtraction: $\left(4A^2-3A+4\right)-\left(A^2+2A-2\right)$. Again, use color #1 variable tiles with the unit tiles.

Have students place tiles on their mats to show the first group. There should be 4 of the quadratic variable tile, 3 of the linear variable tile with the X-side showing for the inverse variable, and 4 positive unit tiles on the building mat. Discuss the idea that the subtraction symbol between the two polynomial groups means to *remove* each term in the second group from the first group. Ask: "Can we remove one quadratic variable tile from the original four? ("Yes; 3 quadratic variable tiles, or $3A^2$, will remain.") "Can $2A$ be removed from –3A?" Since only inverse variable tiles are present initially, 0-pairs of A and –A tiles will need to be added to the mat until two of the variable A are seen. Then 2A can be removed, leaving 5 of –A on the mat. Similarly, –2 will be removed from +4 by first adding two 0-pairs of +1 and –1 to the mat. Then –2 can be removed from the mat, leaving +6. The mat arrangement of the initial tiles and the extra 0-pairs of tiles is shown here <u>before</u> any tile removal occurs. Have students complete Exercise 2 on Worksheet 1–1a by writing an expression for the tiles left on the mat: $\left(4A^2 - 3A + 4\right) - \left(A^2 + 2A - 2\right) = 3A^2 - 5A + 6$.

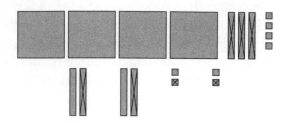

Remind students that when they use 0-pairs of a tile and remove one form of the tile (for example, positive), then the other form (for example, negative) remains to be added to the other tiles on the mat. Show students that when they needed to remove 2A from the mat earlier, two 0-pairs of A and –A were placed on the mat. After 2A was removed to show subtraction, the two inverse variable tiles, –2A, still remained on the mat to be <u>combined</u> with the other tiles for the final answer. Hence, a <u>removal</u> of a tile from the mat is equivalent to <u>adding the inverse or opposite</u> of that tile to the mat.

To confirm this, have students place the original group of tiles $\left(4A^2 - 3A + 4\right)$ on the mat again. The opposites needed $(-A^2, -2A, \text{ and } +2)$ should then be placed on the mat and <u>combined</u> with the original tiles. See the illustration below. Remove any 0-pairs formed, leaving tiles for $3A^2$, –5A, and +6 on the mat as the answer. Finally, have students write another equation below Exercise 2 on Worksheet 1–1a, this time showing the alternate method that uses addition: $\left(4A^2 - 3A + 4\right) + \left(-A^2 - 2A + 2\right) = 3A^2 - 5A + 6$. Encourage students to use whichever of these two methods seems comfortable to them.

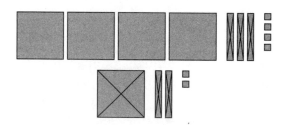

In the answer key for Worksheet 1–1a, when the coefficient of a final variable is 1, the number 1 will be written with the variable. This approach seems to be helpful to many students. Nevertheless, discuss the idea with the class that the 1 in such cases is often not recorded but simply understood as being there.

Answer Key for Worksheet 1–1a

1. $2A^2 + 5A - 3$

2. $3A^2 - 5A + 6$; alternate: $(4A^2 - 3A + 4) + (-A^2 - 2A + 2) = 3A^2 - 5A + 6$

3. $3B^2 + 2$; alternate: $(5B^2 + 3) + (-2B^2 - 1) = 3B^2 + 2$

4. $2A^2 + 1A - 4$

5. $1B^2 + 2A - 8$

6. $3A + 1A^2 + 5$; alternate: $3A + (A^2 + 5) = 3A + 1A^2 + 5$

7. $1A^2$; alternate: $(5B^2 - 4) + (-5B^2 + 4 + A^2) = 1A^2$

8. $3A + 1A^2 - 13 + 1B$

6

Worksheet 1–1a

Name _____

Building Sums and Differences
with Tiles

Date _____

Build each polynomial exercise with tiles. Different variables require different tiles. Record the result beside the exercise. For each subtraction exercise, also write the alternate addition equation below the subtraction equation.

1. $\left(3A^2 + 2A - 5\right) + \left(-A^2 + 3A + 2\right) =$

2. $\left(4A^2 - 3A + 4\right) - \left(A^2 + 2A - 2\right) =$

3. $\left(5B^2 + 3\right) - \left(2B^2 + 1\right) =$

4. $\left(2A^2 - 3A + 1\right) + \left(4A - 5\right) =$

5. $\left(4A - 2 + B^2\right) + \left(-6 - 2A\right) =$

6. $3A - \left(-A^2 - 5\right) =$

7. $\left(5B^2 - 4\right) - \left(5B^2 - 4 - A^2\right) =$

8. $3A - 2A^2 - 5 + B - 8 + 3A^2 =$

Activity 2
Pictorial Stage

Materials

Worksheet 1–1b
Regular paper and pencil

Procedure

1. Give each student a copy of Worksheet 1–1b. Have students work in pairs, but they should draw the diagrams separately on their own worksheets. Large squares will be drawn for the quadratic variable, a long rectangle whose length equals an edge length of the large square will be drawn for the linear variable, and a small square will represent the integral unit. A large X should be drawn in the interior of a shape to show the inverse of that shape. If an exercise involves two different variables, letters need to be written on the drawn shapes to identify the different variables. The product of two different variables, for example, A and B, should be shown as a large rectangle similar in size to the quadratic squares and labeled as AB. The notation AB simply means A rows of B, or the area AB.

2. For addition exercises, students should draw the required shapes and connect any two shapes that represent a 0-pair. The remaining shapes will be recorded in symbols to show the sum.

3. For subtraction exercises, students will be asked to use either the removal method or the alternate method, which involves addition of inverses. To remove a shape, students should mark out the shape. When needed, two shapes should be drawn together as a 0-pair. For the alternate method, inverses of the subtrahend expression should be drawn and combined with the first expression to produce a sum. The result will be recorded symbolically.

4. When checking students' work after all are finished, allow time for students to explain their steps; do not just check for answers. Students need to practice expressing their ideas mathematically. Such verbal sharing is also very beneficial to *auditory learners*.

5. Discuss Exercises 1 and 2 on Worksheet 1–1b with the class before allowing partners to work together on their own.

Consider Exercise 1: $(-3B^2+B+2)+(B^2-4B+1)$. Students should draw the necessary shapes on their papers to represent each polynomial group. The shapes for the first polynomial group may be drawn in a row from left to right following the order of the given terms. The shapes for the second polynomial group should be drawn as a second row below the first row, but students may rearrange the shapes and draw them below other like shapes in the first row. Since only one variable is involved, no labeling is needed for the shapes. Any 0-pairs should be connected. Remaining shapes will then be counted and recorded as the answer. A sample drawing is shown here:

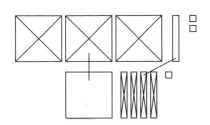

The final equation will be as follows and should be recorded on Worksheet 1–1b: $\left(-3B^2+B+2\right)+\left(B^2-4B+1\right)=-2B^2-3B+3$. At this point, begin to encourage students to record the terms of a polynomial with their exponents in decreasing order.

Now consider Exercise 2: $\left(A^2+5A-3\right)-\left(2A^2+3A+2\right)$. Since the removal process is required for this exercise, students should draw shapes for the first polynomial group and then draw any 0-pairs below that group, which will be needed in order to mark out the shapes shown in the second group. The shapes remaining or not marked out in the finished diagram will be the difference. Here is the completed diagram:

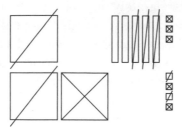

The final equation should be recorded on Worksheet 1–1b as follows: $\left(A^2+5A-3\right)-\left(2A^2+3A+2\right)=-A^2+2A-5$. It may be helpful for some students to write $-1A^2$ instead of $-A^2$. This is acceptable notation.

Answer Key for Worksheet 1–1b

Only symbolic answers may be given.

1. $-2B^2-3B+3$ (see sample diagram in text)

2. $-A^2+2A-5$ (see sample diagram in text)

3. $5A^2-2A+6$

4. $-3A-2B+1$

5. $2A^2+3B^2-2$

Sample diagram for Exercise 5:

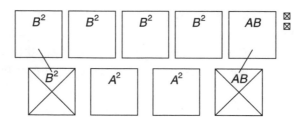

6. $B^2-3AB-A+1$

Worksheet 1–1b   Name _____

Drawing Sums and Differences   Date _____

Use shapes to simplify each polynomial exercise according to the directions. Label shapes to identify different variables when necessary. Record the algebraic result beside the exercise.

1. $\left(-3B^2 + B + 2\right) + \left(B^2 - 4B + 1\right) =$

2. $\left(A^2 + 5A - 3\right) - \left(2A^2 + 3A + 2\right) =$

    [use removal]

3. $\left(6A^2 - A + 3\right) - \left(A^2 + A - 3\right) =$

    [use addition of inverses]

4. $\left(A - 5B + 6\right) + \left(3B - 4A - 5\right) =$

5. $\left(4B^2 + AB - 2\right) + \left(2A^2 - B^2 - AB\right) =$

6. $\left(2B^2 - 3AB + A\right) - \left(B^2 + 2A - 1\right) =$

    [use either method]

Activity 3
Independent Practice

Materials
Worksheet 1–1c
Regular paper and pencil

Procedure
Give each student a copy of Worksheet 1–1c. After all students have completed the worksheet, ask various students to show their solutions or any illustrations they might have used to the entire class. In particular, select students to share their work who have solved the same problem in different ways.

Answer Key for Worksheet 1–1c
1. C

2. D

3. A

4. A

5. C

Possible Testing Errors That May Occur for This Objective
- When combining polynomials, students fail to recognize 0-pairs among the terms; for example, they write the sum $(+3x) + (-3x)$ as $(+6x)$ instead of 0.

- When finding differences by the alternate method of adding inverses of the subtrahend group to the original minuend group, students do not exchange all the terms for their inverse forms; hence, they add the wrong terms together. For example, in $(2N + 5) - (N + K - 3)$, they actually add $(2N + 5)$ to $(-N + K + 3)$ instead of to $(-N - K + 3)$.

- Students make computational errors when combining like terms. For example, $(+4y) + (-7y)$ is incorrectly written as $(+11y)$ instead of $(-3y)$.

Worksheet 1–1c   Name _____

Finding Sums and Differences of   Date _____
Polynomials

Solve the exercises provided and be ready to discuss your methods and answers with the entire class.

1. The following diagram represents the product of $2N$ rows of $(3N + 2)$. Which expression is equivalent to the total area, $2N(3N + 2)$, of the product diagram?

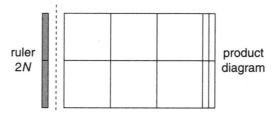

    A. $6N^2 + 2$ B. $6N + 2$ C. $6N^2 + 4N$ D. $6N + 4$

2. Which expression is equivalent to $\left(\frac{2}{3}\right)(6x - 3y) + (4y - 7x)$?

    A. $-x + y$ B. $-3x + y$ C. $4x - 2y$ D. $-3x + 2y$

3. Which expression is equivalent to $(5k - 2)(3k) - (5k - 2)(k - 1)$?

    A. $10k^2 + k - 2$ B. $10k^2 - 4k - 2$ C. $10k^2 - 2$ D. $5k^2 + 2$

4. Simplify the expression and evaluate for $T = -5$: $(2T^2 + 3T) + (5T - 2T^2 + 3) = ?$

    A. –37   B. 38   C. –43   D. Not here

5. Which expression is equivalent to $(5y^2 - 3xy - 4) - (5y^2 - y - 3xy - 4)$?

    A. 0   B. $-6xy - 4$ C. y D. $-y$

Objective 2: Solve a Linear Equation Involving One Variable with a Fractional Coefficient

Fraction operations are difficult for most students to comprehend. Extending fraction multiplication to partial sets of a variable is even more complicated. Rote methods are often taught and students seemingly master them, yet they do not attain a deeper understanding of the method. Students need experiences with partial sets that will lead to discovering what the whole set will contain. The following activities provide such experiences.

Activity 1
Manipulative Stage

Materials

> Tile sets (minimal set: 1 variable tile with its inverse tile, 30 positive unit tiles with their inverse tiles)
> Building Mat 1–2a
> Pieces of colored yarn (approximately 12 inches long) or flat coffee stirrers
> Extra construction paper (use colors that match the variable tiles in the sets)
> Scissors
> Regular paper and pencils

Procedure

1.   Give each pair of students a set of tiles, a copy of Building Mat 1–2a, a piece of yarn or coffee stirrer, scissors, and a sheet of construction paper (the same color as their variable tiles).

2.   To make fractional variable tiles, have students cut out 6 rectangular strips from their sheet of construction paper. The paper strips should be the same size and color as one of their variable tiles. Show them how to fold the paper strips, mark the creases, and label the parts with fractional names. Two strips should be folded and labeled for halves, yielding 4 half-variables total. Two more strips should be folded and labeled for thirds, and another 2 strips for fourths. Use the ratio format for labeling the fractional parts, for example, $\frac{1}{2}$, $\frac{1}{3}$, and $\frac{1}{4}$. On one side of each fractional part made, have students mark a thin, large X to represent the *inverse* of the fractional part. Be sure that the X does not show through on the other side of the paper. Additional paper strips may be cut out as needed.

3.   Have students place tiles on Building Mat 1–2a to build each equation shown on Worksheet 1–2a. Below each equation on Worksheet 1–2a, they should record the symbolic steps they used to solve the equation.

4.   For each equation solved, students should confirm their solution. Have them rebuild the original equation with tiles and then substitute the variable's discovered value in unit tiles for the variable tile itself to show the true equality. Students should write a check mark beside the solution on the worksheet after the correct value has been confirmed.

5.   Discuss Exercises 1 and 2 on Worksheet 1–2a with the class before allowing students to work the rest of the exercises independently.

Consider Exercise 1 on Worksheet 1–2a: $\frac{2}{3}K - (+3) = -7$. Have students build this equation with tiles. A paper variable folded into thirds should be cut apart and 2 of the thirds placed on the left side of Building Mat 1–2a. The subtraction sign on the left side of the equation indicates that +3 must be removed from the mat. Since there are not 3 positive unit tiles on the left side, three 0-pairs of positive and negative unit tiles should be placed on the left side of the mat, followed by removal of the 3 positive unit tiles. Some students may realize that subtracting +3 is equivalent to adding –3; if so, they may simply place –3 on the left side of the mat with the fractional variable tiles instead of working with the 0-pairs first. Finally, 7 negative unit tiles should be placed on the right side of the mat.

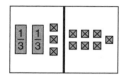

Ask: "What changes can we make to the mat that will leave the variable tiles by themselves on the left?" ("Either take away –3 or bring in +3 on the left.") The students must then repeat whichever action they choose on the right side of the mat and record their steps with symbolic notation below Exercise 1 on Worksheet 1–2a.

(a) Take-Away Model

$$\frac{2}{3}K - (+3) = -7$$

$$\frac{2}{3}K + (-3) = -7$$

$$\underline{-(-3) \quad -(-3)}$$

$$\frac{2}{3}K = -4$$

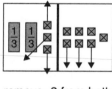
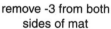

remove -3 from both
sides of mat

(b) Add-On Model

$$\frac{2}{3}K - (+3) = -7$$

$$\frac{2}{3}K + (-3) = -7$$

$$\underline{+(+3) \quad +(+3)}$$

$$\frac{2}{3}K = -4$$

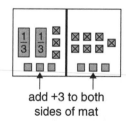

add +3 to both
sides of mat

Ask: "Two of the thirds of a variable remain on the left by themselves. What do we need to do to find a whole variable tile now?" ("First find a single third of the variable by separating the 2 variable parts or by finding 'half' of the present variable group; 3 of this single third will make a whole variable tile.") Remember that you need to use *multiplication* language here, not *addition* language. That is, you want *3 of* the third-variable in order to make a whole variable, not *2 more of* the third-variable.

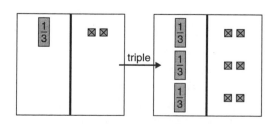

After students perform these two actions, halving and then tripling, on both sides of the mat, have them record their new actions as shown below:

(a) Take-Away Model

$\frac{2}{3}K - (+3) = -7$

$\frac{2}{3}K + (-3) = -7$

$\qquad \underline{-(-3) \quad -(-3)}$

$\qquad \frac{2}{3}K = -4$

$\frac{1}{2}\left(\frac{2}{3}K\right) = \frac{1}{2}(-4)$

$\qquad \frac{1}{3}K = -2$

$3\left(\frac{1}{3}K\right) = 3(-2)$

$\qquad K = -6$

(b) Add-On Model

$\frac{2}{3}K - (+3) = -7$

$\frac{2}{3}K + (-3) = -7$

$\qquad \underline{+(+3) \quad +(+3)}$

$\qquad \frac{2}{3}K = -4$

$\frac{1}{2}\left(\frac{2}{3}K\right) = \frac{1}{2}(-4)$

$\qquad \frac{1}{3}K = -2$

$3\left(\frac{1}{3}K\right) = 3(-2)$

$\qquad K = -6$

Note: The hope is that most students will realize that the halving-tripling process used above can be combined and shown in the recording as follows:

$\frac{2}{3}K = -4$

$\frac{3}{2}\left(\frac{2}{3}K\right) = \frac{3}{2}(-4)$

$\qquad K = -6$

If the students do not easily accept this combination of steps, allow them to continue recording the two separate steps of division and multiplication. Also notice that when we previously needed "half of the 2-thirds of the variable K," the factor $\frac{1}{2}$ was used with multiplication, rather than using 2 as a divisor, or dividing by 2. This helps students connect to the reciprocal method more easily.

The solution, $K = -6$, should be confirmed on the mat by exchanging variable parts for units. Have students rebuild the original equation on their mats and place 6 negative unit tiles on the mat just above the variable tiles. Since thirds are involved, –6 should be separated into 3 equal groups of –2 each. Each variable part on the mat should be replaced with one of the groups of –2. The unused –2 should be removed from the top of the mat. Now 2 groups of –2, along with another group of –3, can be seen on the left side, and –7 appears on the right. Since the two sides have the same total value, $K = -6$ is the correct solution. A check mark should be written beside the solution equation on the worksheet.

Now discuss the equation for Exercise 2 on Worksheet 1–2a: $(-1) - \frac{1}{4}p = -4$.

Have students build the equation on Building Mat 1–2a, using paper fourths of a variable. Each fourth-variable should have an X marked on one side. First have students place –4 in unit tiles on the right side of the mat and –1 in unit tiles on the left side. Discuss the idea that just as with unit tiles earlier, subtraction of a variable group is equivalent to the addition of the inverse variable group. Hence, after showing a 0-pair of fourths of a variable (one plain fourth and one fourth with an X-side facing up) on the left side of the mat with –1 and then removing $+\frac{1}{4}p$, students will have $-\frac{1}{4}p$ and –1 still remaining on the left side.

Students should now isolate the fourth of an inverse variable by either the take-away or the add-on method. The tiles on each side of the mat should then be quadrupled to yield 4 variable parts that are equivalent to a whole inverse variable, $-p$. If students prefer, they may replace the 4 variable parts on the mat with a whole inverse variable tile.

Since a solution usually involves a value for the regular variable p, not its inverse, $-p$, a coffee stirrer or piece of yarn should be placed below the last row of tiles on the mat: $-p = -12$. The inverse of $-p$ is p and the inverse of -12 is $+12$; therefore, the regular, whole variable tile should be placed on the mat below the coffee stirrer or yarn and the 4 fourths of the inverse variable, and 12 positive units should be placed below the negative units and coffee stirrer or yarn on the right. The building and recording are as follows:

(a) Add-On Method	**(b) Take-Away Method**

(a) Add-On Method

$$(-1) - \frac{1}{4}p = -4$$

$$(-1) + \left(-\frac{1}{4}p\right) = -4$$

$$\underline{+(+1) \quad +(+1)}$$

$$-\frac{1}{4}p = -3$$

$$4\left(-\frac{1}{4}p\right) = 4(-3)$$

$$-p = -12$$

So, $p = +12$

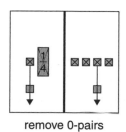

remove 0-pairs

(b) Take-Away Method

$$(-1) - \frac{1}{4}p = -4$$

$$(-1) + \left(-\frac{1}{4}p\right) = -4$$

$$\underline{-(-1) \quad -(-1)}$$

$$-\frac{1}{4}p = -3$$

$$4\left(-\frac{1}{4}p\right) = 4(-3)$$

$$-p = -12$$

So, $p = +12$

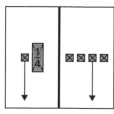

remove -1 from both
sides of mat

Here are the final steps for both methods:

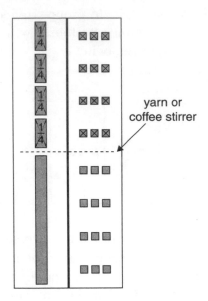

yarn or
coffee stirrer

Finally, the solution needs to be confirmed. The original equation should be rebuilt on the mat, including one of the fourths of the inverse variable tile. If $p = +12$, then $-p$ must equal -12; hence, -12 should be placed on the mat above the tiles on the left side. Since a fourth of the variable is needed, -12 should be separated into four equal groups of -3 each. One group of -3 should be exchanged for the variable part and the other three groups of -3 removed from the mat. A single, negative unit tile, as well as the group of -3, are now seen on the left side of the mat, and a group of -4 is seen on the right. Both sides of the mat have the same total value, so the solution, $p = +12$, is correct. A check mark should be written beside the solution equation on the worksheet.

Answer Key for Worksheet 1–2a
Only solutions are provided; no mats are shown.

1. $K = -6$

2. $p = +12$

3. $C = +10$

4. $m = -4$

5. $B = +4$ [use 3 half-variable tiles; then isolate the variable tiles on the left side of the mat; separate each side of the mat into 3 equal groups to find the value for one half-variable tile]

6. $w = -12$

Building Mat 1–2a

Worksheet 1–2a

Solving Linear Equations with Tiles

Name _____

Date _____

Solve the equations with tiles on a building mat. Below each equation, record the steps used with symbolic notation. Confirm each solution found by exchanging the appropriate amount of unit tiles for the variable tiles given in the original equation. Write a check mark beside any solution equation shown to be correct with tiles.

1. $\frac{2}{3}K - (+3) = -7$

4. $+4 = -\frac{3}{4}m - (-1)$

2. $(-1) - \frac{1}{4}p = -4$

5. $\frac{3}{2}B + 6 = +12$

3. $7 = 2 + \frac{1}{2}C$

6. $(-5) + \left(-\frac{2}{4}w\right) = +1$

Activity 2
Pictorial Stage

Materials

Worksheet 1–2b
Regular pencils
Red pencils

Procedure

1. Give each student a copy of Worksheet 1–2b and a red pencil. Have students work in pairs.

2. Have students draw a small square to represent each unit integer. For a negative unit, they should draw diagonals inside the square. Tall, narrow rectangles will represent whole variable bars. To show a fractional amount of a variable, have students draw a short rectangle (but slightly taller than the squares drawn for integral units) and write the fractional label inside the rectangle. A large but light X should be drawn inside the rectangle to show the inverse form of the variable.

3. For each equation on Worksheet 1–2b, students should draw a diagram for the equation on the worksheet. They should transform the diagram in order to find the solution to the equation.

4. After each new step has been performed on the diagram, have students record that step in symbols beside the diagram on Worksheet 1–2b.

5. After a solution is found, students should confirm the solution by drawing in red pencil the appropriate number of small squares on each variable shape in the diagram. The total number of small squares on the left side of the frame should equal the total number of small squares on the right side. Also have them confirm their solutions by writing a number sentence below the symbolic steps to show the substitutions used.

6. Discuss Exercise 1 on Worksheet 1–2b with the class before allowing students to work independently.

Consider the equation for Exercise 1: $-\frac{1}{3}M + 5 = +7$. To make a diagram of this equation, ask students to draw a short rectangle (but slightly taller than the squares drawn for integral units) on the left side of a pair of parallel line segments (the equal sign). Have them draw a light but large X (to show the inverse) in the interior of the rectangle and write the fraction, $\frac{1}{3}$, over the X. This will represent $-\frac{1}{3}M$, read as "one-third of the inverse of the variable M." Avoid the language "negative one-third M" until later. Also draw 5 small, plain squares on the left side with the variable rectangle. Seven small, plain squares should then be drawn on the right side to represent +7. The diagram should be drawn on the left half of Worksheet 1–2b below the equation.

To isolate the variable by itself, students have the usual two methods available: remove +5 from both sides of the diagram, or bring in –5 to both sides of the diagram to form 0-pairs of the units. The transformed diagrams will appear as follows:

(a) Removal Method   **(b) Add-On Method**

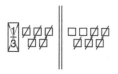   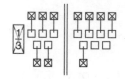

A horizontal bar should be drawn below the initial diagram that shows the removal or add-on step, and the shapes remaining for $-\frac{1}{3}M$ on the left and +2 on the right should be redrawn below that bar. Students now need to form a whole variable. This is done by drawing more rows of shapes on the second diagram until there are <u>3 rows in all</u>; each row shows a $-\frac{1}{3}M$ on the left of the vertical bars and +2 on the right. Remind students that they now have *3 times as many* $-\frac{1}{3}M$'s and *3 times as many groups of +2* as they did before they drew the extra amounts on the diagram. "3 times as many" is multiplicative language, which is needed for this type of equation.

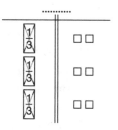

By this time, students should recognize the three inverse thirds of a variable, one drawn above another, as a whole variable, and they should not need to draw a new, longer rectangle to show the whole inverse variable. It might be helpful, however, to have students draw a larger rectangle around the three smaller rectangles to show them grouped together. Since the diagram shows $-M = +6$, a horizontal bar should be drawn below this diagram and a plain rectangle for M drawn below the bar on the left side and 3 rows of –2 drawn below the bar on the right. That is, inverses have to be taken of $-M$ and +6 in order to solve for the regular variable, M.

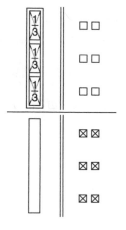

   Students should record their pictorial steps in symbolic notation on the right half of the worksheet below the equation. Depending on the method used, their recordings should appear as follows:

(a) Removal-Multiplication Method   **(b) Add-On/Multiplication Method**

$-\frac{1}{3}M + (+5) = +7$

$$\underline{-(+5) \quad -(+5)}$$

$-\frac{1}{3}M = +2$

$3\left(-\frac{1}{3}M\right) = 3(+2)$

$-M = +6$

So, $M = -6$

$-\frac{1}{3}M + (+5) = +7$

$$\underline{+(-5) \quad +(-5)}$$

$-\frac{1}{3}M = +2$

$3\left(-\frac{1}{3}M\right) = 3(+2)$

$-M = +6$

So, $M = -6$

   To confirm the solution as $M = -6$, have students first draw in red pencil two plain unit squares above the small rectangle for $-\frac{1}{3}M$ in the initial diagram; that is, if $M = -6$, the fractional amount must equal $+2$. The left side of the initial diagram now contains $+7$ in small plain squares and the right side contains $+7$, which confirms the solution. Below the symbolic steps, students should write the number sentence that shows their substitution: $-\frac{1}{3}M + (+5) = \frac{1}{3}(+6) + (+5) = (+2) + (+5) = +7$ [viewing $-\frac{1}{3}M$ as "a third of the inverse variable, $-M$," or $\frac{1}{3}$ of $+6$]; or $-\frac{1}{3}M + (+5) = -\frac{1}{3}(-6) + (+5) = (+2) + (+5) = +7$ [viewing $-\frac{1}{3}M$ as "the opposite of $\frac{1}{3}$ of the variable, M," or $-\frac{1}{3}$ of -6]. The $+7$, found after substitution to be the value of the left side of the original equation, agrees with the $+7$ given for the right side of the equation. Thus, $M = -6$ is confirmed again to be the correct solution.

Answer Key for Worksheet 1–2b
Only solutions and possible substitution number sentences are provided here. No diagrams are shown except for a partial diagram from Exercise 2.

   1. $M = -6$; $-\frac{1}{3}M + (+5) = \frac{1}{3}(+6) + (+5) = (+2) + (+5) = +7$

   [The complete diagram and recordings are shown in the text.]

   2. $A = +12$; $\frac{2}{4}A - 8 = \frac{2}{4}(+12) - 8 = (+6) - 8 = -2$

   [When multiple fractional parts of a variable are present in an equation and the variable parts are isolated by removing appropriate unit squares, rings should be drawn around the remaining shapes to form the same number of equal groups on each side of the diagram. Each fractional variable represents one group, so in this exercise, there will be two groups on the right side; this requires two groups of +3 to be formed on the left side. One group from each side is then redrawn and will be repeated to form the equivalent of a whole variable amount. Part of the diagram is shown here.]

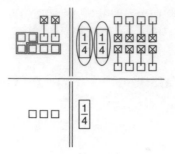

3. $c = +8;\ \frac{1}{4}c - 4 = \frac{1}{4}(+8) - 4 = (+2) - 4 = -2$

4. $A = -10;\ (+5) + \left(-\frac{3}{5}A\right) = (+5) + \frac{3}{5}(+10) = (+5) + (+6) = +11$

Worksheet 1–2b   Name _____

Solving Linear Equations by   Date _____
Drawing Diagrams

Solve each equation by drawing a diagram below the equation. Beside each diagram, record the steps used with symbolic notation. Confirm each solution found by drawing in red pencil the appropriate number of unit squares for each fractional variable above that variable shape in the initial diagram. Also, below the symbolic steps, write a number sentence that shows the substitutions made in the original equation.

1. $-\frac{1}{3} M + (+5) = +7$

3. $-2 = \frac{1}{4} c - 4$

2. $-2 = \frac{2}{4} A - 8$

4. $(+5) + \left(-\frac{3}{5} A\right) = +11$

Activity 3
Independent Practice

Materials
> Worksheet 1–2c
> Regular pencils

Procedure
Give each student a copy of Worksheet 1–2c to complete independently. After all have finished, have them share their methods and answers with the class.

Answer Key for Worksheet 1–2c
1. C

2. A

3. $n = +15$

4. $X = +16$

5. $c = -30$

Possible Testing Errors That May Occur for This Objective

- Students do not correctly interpret the subtraction sign in an equation and use addition instead; for example, for the expression $N - (-8)$ they will use $N + (-8)$. Other sign errors also occur.

- When an equation involves a fractional coefficient with the variable, students attempt to use the reciprocal method, but do not multiply by the correct fraction. For example, when trying to solve $\frac{3}{4} K = +6$, they will use either $\frac{1}{3}\left(\frac{3}{4} K\right)$ or $4\left(\frac{3}{4} K\right)$ instead of the combination step, $\frac{4}{3}\left(\frac{3}{4} K\right)$.

- When applying the reciprocal method to solve an equation, students will multiply the variable group by the reciprocal of the variable's coefficient, but fail to multiply the equivalent constant by the same value. As an example, for $\frac{2}{5} A = -4$ students will compute $\frac{5}{2}\left(\frac{2}{5} A\right)$, but will continue to use -4 instead of $\frac{5}{2}(-4)$.

Worksheet 1–2c   Name _____

Solving Linear Equations   Date _____

Complete each exercise provided. Be ready to explain to other students the steps or reasoning you used to work each exercise.

1. If $A = +22$ is a solution for the equation $-\frac{1}{2}A + 9 = -2$, which expression may be used to confirm the solution?

  A. $-\frac{1}{2}(+11) + 9$ C. $\frac{1}{2}(-22) + 9$

  B. $-\frac{1}{2}(-22) + 9$ D. $\frac{1}{2}(+22) + 9$

2. Which expression is not a correct interpretation of the expression $-\frac{2}{3}p$?

  A. $-3\left(\frac{1}{2}p\right)$ B. $-2\left(\frac{1}{3}p\right)$ C. $\frac{2}{3}(-p)$ D. $2\left(-\frac{1}{3}p\right)$

3. Solve for n: $+7 = \frac{1}{3}n - (-2)$.

4. Solve for X: $-18 = (-6) - \frac{3}{4}X$.

5. Solve for c: $8 + \frac{2}{6}c = -2$.

Objective 3: State an Equation with One or More Variables That Represent a Linear Relationship in a Given Situation; Apply the Equation to Solve the Problem, If Appropriate

Practical applications of mathematics require that students be able to translate the actions of a situation into an equation. Students may know how to solve a linear equation written in symbolic language, but this in no way guarantees that they can translate a word problem into an equation. This lesson focuses on the translation, but some actual solving may be required for additional practice. It is assumed that students already have a basic knowledge of how to solve simple linear equations involving integers. Objective 2 provides specific training with fractional coefficients if a review is necessary.

Activity 1
Manipulative Stage

Materials

Sets of tiles (minimum set: 8 linear variable tiles of equal length, 30 unit tiles, and
   the fractional variable tiles from Objective 2; inverse tiles should be included
   for each type of tile)
Building Mat 1–3a
Worksheet 1–3a
Regular pencils

Procedure

1. Give each pair of students a set of tiles, a copy of Building Mat 1–3a, and two copies of Worksheet 1–3a.

2. Using the tiles, students should build equations on the building mat to represent the situations described in each exercise on Worksheet 1–3a.

3. For each exercise modeled with tiles, have students write the initial equations in symbols below the word problem. Then have them solve the equations with the tiles. The solutions should also be recorded beside the equations on Worksheet 1–3a.

4. Discuss Exercises 1 and 2 on Worksheet 1–3a with the class before allowing students to work independently with their partners.

Consider Exercise 1 on Worksheet 1–3a: "Three consecutive positive integers have a sum of 24. Find the three consecutive integers."

Discuss examples of consecutive positive integers like 2, 3, and 4, or 25, 26, and 27. Guide students to recognize that each new number is one more than the previous number. Since the actual numbers are not yet known, have students place one variable tile on the left side of Building Mat 1–3a to represent the first number. The second number is one more than the first number, so students should place another variable tile (same color or tile length as the first variable tile), along with 1 unit tile, on the left side of the mat. Finally, they should place an additional variable tile and 2 unit tiles on the left side to represent the third number. The collective set of tiles on the left is the sum of the 3 numbers. Since the sum equals 24, students should place 24 unit tiles on the right side of Building Mat 1–3a. Here is the initial appearance of the building mat:

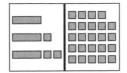

Have students record the following unsimplified equation below Exercise 1, using N for the variable tile: $N + (N + 1) + (N + 2) = 24$.

Students should then solve the equation with the tiles. Remind them that the variable tiles need to be isolated, which requires that the 3 unit tiles be removed from the left side of the mat. To keep the building mat balanced, 3 unit tiles must also be removed from the right side. Continuing, the remaining variable tiles must be separated into 3 groups (each variable tile forms a "group"), which forces the 21 unit tiles on the right side to be separated into 3 groups as well. The groups on the mat should now have this appearance:

Each variable tile determines a row on the right side of the mat. Hence, the value of one variable tile equals +7, which becomes the first number of the three consecutive numbers being sought. The next two numbers are represented by $N + 1$ and $N + 2$, so their values are $7 + 1 = 8$ and $7 + 2 = 9$. Students should record the following three equations beside their initial equation for Exercise 1 on Worksheet 1–3a: $N = 7$, $N + 1 = 7 + 1 = 8$, and $N + 2 = 7 + 2 = 9$.

Now consider Exercise 2 on Worksheet 1–3a: "Three-fourths of the Math I class and five students from the Math II class are planning to go to the museum. Seventeen students in all will go on the field trip. How many students total attend the Math I class?"

Have students use their paper strips from Objective 2 to show fractional amounts of a variable tile. The whole variable tile equals the number of students in Math I, so 3 of the fourth-variable tiles should be placed on the left side of Building Mat 1–3a to represent the students from Math I going on the field trip. Five unit tiles should also be placed on the left side to show the 5 students from Math II who will be going. Since the combined groups equal 17, students should place 17 unit tiles on the right side of the building mat. The building mat will have the following initial appearance:

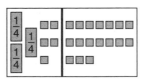

Using the variable M as the total number of students in Math I, have students record the following equation below Exercise 2 to represent the tiles shown on the building mat: $\frac{3}{4}M + 5 = 17$.

Now have students use the tiles on the mat to solve for the value of the whole variable, M. At first they must remove 5 unit tiles from both sides of the mat to isolate the fourth-variable group on the left side. Then the fourth-variables should be separated into three equal groups (a fourth-variable forms a "group" this time), which forces the 12 remaining unit tiles on the right side to be separated into three equal groups as well. The new tile arrangement will be as shown:

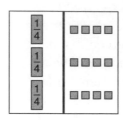

Discuss the idea that one row on the building mat shows that a fourth-variable tile equals +4. To make a whole variable tile, four of the fourth-variable tiles will be needed on the left side of the mat. Similarly, four rows of +4 will be needed on the right side to keep the mat balanced. Have students place more tiles on the building mat in order to have the four rows needed. The solution to the initial equation is now found. Four fourth-variable tiles or 1 whole variable tile equals 4 rows of +4 each. Have students record the following statement beside the original equation below Exercise 2: $M = 16$ students in Math I.

Answer Key for Worksheet 1–3a

1. $N + (N + 1) + (N + 2) = 24$; $N = 7$, $N + 1 = 7 + 1 = 8$, $N + 2 = 7 + 2 = 9$

2. $\frac{3}{4} M + 5 = 17$; $M = 16$ students in Math I

3. $4p - 6 = 10$; $p = 4$ cents per piece of gum

4. $\frac{1}{2} R - 3 = 4$; $R = 14$ rings in a full box

5. $T + (T + 4) + 3T = 19$; $T = 3$ movie passes for Toni

6. $\frac{1}{3} G = 8$; $G = 24$ gallons in a full drum

Building Mat 1–3a

Worksheet 1–3a   Name _____

Modeling Linear Relationships   Date _____
with Tiles

For each exercise, build an equation with tiles on Building Mat 1–3a to represent the situation. Write the equation in symbols below the exercise. Solve the equation with tiles, and write the solution beside the symbolic equation.

1. Three consecutive positive integers have a sum of 24. Find the 3 consecutive integers.

2. Three-fourths of the Math I class and 5 students from the Math II class are planning to go to the museum. Seventeen students in all will go on the field trip. How many students are in the Math I class?

3. Kate bought 4 pieces of chewing gum at the school store. After a discount of 6 cents was applied to the total purchase, she paid 10 cents in all. What was the original price for each piece of gum?

4. Jorge won one-half of a box of rings at the carnival, but on the way home lost 3 of the rings. Later at home, he still had 4 rings left. How many rings were originally in a full box?

5. Maria has 4 more movie passes than Toni. Angela has 3 times as many passes as Toni. Together the three girls have a total of 19 movie passes. How many movie passes does Toni have?

6. Two-thirds of the oil in an oil drum has leaked out. Eight gallons of oil are left in the drum. How many gallons total can the drum hold?

Activity 2
Pictorial Stage

Materials

Worksheet 1–3b
Regular pencils
Regular paper

Procedure

1. Give each student a copy of Worksheet 1–3b. Have students work in pairs.

2. For each exercise on Worksheet 1–3b, have students draw on regular paper a diagram for each relationship described in the given situation. If more than one type of variable is needed, students will need to label each variable shape with a letter they select for that variable.

3. Beside each diagram, students should record an equation in symbolic language that is equivalent to the diagram.

4. For practice in solving equations, students might also be instructed to solve for the variables in the equations they find for Exercises 2 through 5 and Exercise 8.

5. Discuss Exercises 1 and 2 on Worksheet 1–3b before allowing students to work independently with a partner.

Consider Exercise 1 on Worksheet 1–3b: "Eddie's Dogwalking Service charges \$3 for each walk plus \$2 per hour for each hour the dog is walked. Find an equation that shows the relationship between the number of hours walked, H, and the total cost, C, for one walk."

Discuss the idea that the total cost is the combination of the single fee of \$3 and the charges based on time. Each hour is worth \$2, so H hours indicates how many of the \$2 are needed. That is, the H hours serves as the multiplier, or counter of sets, and \$2 is the multiplicand, or the set being repeated. Have students draw an equation frame that shows a variable C on the left side and shapes for the sum of the two kinds of charges on the right side. A pair of vertical parallel bars should be drawn to indicate equality of the two sides of the diagram. Because the multiplier in this case is a variable or an unknown amount, an exact amount of \$2 sets cannot be shown; rather, a *countable amount* will be indicated in the diagram through special labeling. Here is a possible final diagram for the situation in Exercise 1. The following equation should be recorded beside the diagram: $C = \$3 + H\,(\$2)$. Since H serves as the multiplier, it is written in the multiplier position, which is the first factor of the product.

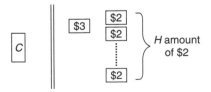

Now consider Exercise 2 on Worksheet 1–3b: "Marian took cookies to a party. She gave a third of her cookies to Adam. Adam then gave a fourth of his cookies to Charles. Charles gave half of his cookies to Barbara. If Barbara received two cookies in all, how many cookies did Marian have in the beginning? Show the initial equations. Then try to combine them into one equation that involves only the variable for Marian's amount of cookies."

Since several relationships are involved in this situation, have students draw a diagram for each one. A horizontal bar should be drawn between each touching pair of diagrams. Here is a possible sequence of diagrams to use, along with their recorded equations:

$$\frac{1}{3}M \quad \| \quad A \qquad \frac{1}{3}M = A$$

$$\frac{1}{4}A \quad \| \quad C \qquad \frac{1}{4}A = C$$

$$\frac{1}{2}C \quad \| \quad B \qquad \frac{1}{2}C = B$$

$$B \quad \| \quad \square\square \qquad B = 2$$

Exercise 2 asks students to find a single equation that relates Marian's amount of cookies to the 2 cookies that Barbara received. Guide students to apply backward thinking to their diagrams, beginning with the last diagram. Through a substitution process, the diagrams can be stacked on each other. Looking only at the left side of each diagram and moving upward, one-half C replaces the B in the last diagram, then one-fourth A replaces C, and finally one-third M replaces A. It might be helpful for students to draw arrows on their diagrams to show where the substitutions occur. Here is a possible example, along with the combined equation that results:

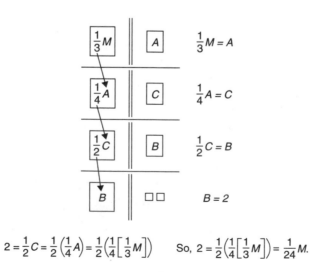

$$2 = \frac{1}{2}C = \frac{1}{2}\left(\frac{1}{4}A\right) = \frac{1}{2}\left(\frac{1}{4}\left[\frac{1}{3}M\right]\right) \qquad \text{So, } 2 = \frac{1}{2}\left(\frac{1}{4}\left[\frac{1}{3}M\right]\right) = \frac{1}{24}M.$$

Answer Key for Worksheet 1–3b
Suggested diagrams and their equations are provided; other formats are possible.

1. $C = \$3 + H\,(\$2)$ [The diagram is shown in the text.]

2. [See the diagrams and sequence of equations in the text.]

3. C = number of jelly beans in whole cup; $35 - \frac{1}{3}C = 28$

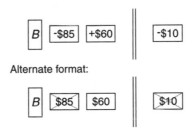

4. B = initial balance in bank account; $B - \$85 + \$60 = -\$10$

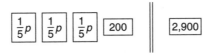

Alternate format:

5. p = size of parking lot in square feet; $\frac{3}{5}p + 200 = 2900$

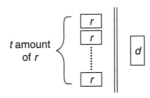

6. $d = t(r)$. [Note: The factor t in this case is the *multiplier*, so it is written first in the product; later, the commutative property might be applied to rewrite the equation in the more familiar form, $d = rt$.]

t amount
of r

7. G, L, and A: Number of tokens each person has:

$G = 4 + L$; $A = \frac{1}{2}G$; $A = \frac{1}{2}(4 + L) = 2 + \frac{1}{2}L$

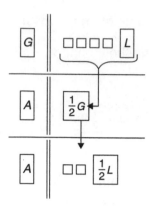

8. N, $N + 2$: consecutive odd integers; $N + (N + 2) = 76$

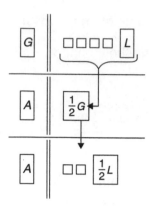

Worksheet 1–3b   Name _____

Drawing Diagrams for Linear   Date _____
Relationships

For each exercise, draw a diagram on another sheet of paper to represent each relationship in the situation. Write equations in symbols beside the diagrams.

1. Eddie's Dogwalking Service charges $3 for each walk plus $2 per hour for each hour the dog is walked. Find an equation that shows the relationship between the number of hours walked, H, and the total cost, C, for 1 walk.

2. Marian took cookies to a party. She gave a third of her cookies to Adam. Adam then gave a fourth of his cookies to Charles. Charles gave half of his cookies to Barbara. If Barbara received two cookies in all, how many cookies did Marian have in the beginning? Show the initial equations. Then try to combine them into one equation that involves only the variable for Marian's amount of cookies.

3. Jaime removed one-third of a cup of jelly beans from a jar that held 35 jelly beans at first. She recounted and found that there were still 28 jelly beans in the jar. Approximately how many jelly beans would fill a whole cup?

4. On Friday, Sam wrote a check for $85. The following Monday, he deposited $60 into his bank account. On Wednesday, he checked his bank's Web site and learned that he had overdrawn his account by $10. If Sam made no other transactions between Friday and Wednesday, what was his balance before he wrote the check on Friday?

5. Three-fifths of a parking lot is scheduled to be resurfaced with new asphalt. Another 200 square feet of driveway will also be resurfaced at that time. The contractor has agreed to repave 2,900 square feet total. What is the size of the parking lot in square feet? Hint: To show a large quantity in a diagram, write the number inside a rectangle.

6. Let r represent the average speed in miles per hour that a car traveled on a trip. Let d represent the distance in miles that the car had traveled t hours after the beginning of the trip. Find an equation that relates the distance traveled to the speed and the time traveled.

7. Gary has 4 more game tokens than Leo has. Angie has half as many tokens as Gary. Find an equation that relates Angie's tokens to Leo's tokens.

8. Two consecutive odd integers have a sum of 76. What are the two integers?

Activity 3
Independent Practice

Materials
Worksheet 1–3c
Regular pencils

Procedure

Give each student a copy of Worksheet 1–3c to complete independently. After all have finished, ask various students to explain the steps they used to get their answers.

Answer Key for Worksheet 1–3c
1. D

2. A

3. C

4. B

5. B

Possible Testing Errors That May Occur for This Objective
- When writing equations for several relationships in a word problem, students will omit one or more of the relationships.

- When one variable is described as twice as much as another variable, students will reverse the relationship. For example, if A should be twice as much as B, students will write the equation as $B = 2A$ instead of $A = 2B$.

- When one variable is described as some amount less than another variable, for example, X is 3 less than Y, students will write $X = 3 - Y$, instead of $X = Y - 3$.

Worksheet 1–3c   Name _____

Translating Situations into Linear   Date _____
Equations

Solve the exercises provided. Be ready to share your answers and procedures with others in the class.

1. David's Grocery Mart sells 3 cans of soup for $1.45 total. The total cost, C, of buying N cans of this same soup can be found by which of the following procedures?

   A. Multiplying N by $1.45   C. Dividing N by $1.45

   B. Dividing N by the cost of one can   D. Multiplying N by the cost of one can

2. A situation involves relationships that lead to the equation: $3m - 4 + 5m = 4m + 8$. Solve for the value of m.

   A. 3   B. 2   C. 1.5   D. 1

3. Susan has a third as many movie passes as Joe. Angie has 2 fewer passes than Joe. Together the 3 students have a total of 19 movie passes. Which equation can be used to find how many movie passes Joe has?

   A. $J + 3J + (J - 2) = 19$ C. $\frac{1}{3}J + (J - 2) + J = 19$

   B. $\frac{1}{3}J + J + (J + 2) = 19$ D. $3J + (J + 2) + J = 19$

4. A person of normal weight has a wrist circumference, w, equal to half of his or her neck circumference, n. Which equation best describes this relationship?

   A. $w = \frac{1}{2} + n$ C. $w = n - \frac{1}{2}$

   B. $w = \frac{1}{2}n$ D. $w = 2n$

5. A student needs to find three consecutive whole numbers whose sum is 72. He writes the equation: $(n - 1) + n + (n + 1) = 72$. What does the variable n represent in the equation?

   A. The greatest of the 3 numbers   C. The least of the 3 numbers

   B. The middle of the 3 numbers   D. None of the 3 numbers

Objective 4: Apply Number Properties to Solve Word Problems

There are various number properties that students need to master, such as common multiples and consecutive even or odd integers. They also need the logical reasoning and the language involved in working with Venn diagrams. These topics are covered in the following activities.

Activity 1
Manipulative Stage

Materials

    Set of 30 small counters per pair of students
    Building Mat 1–4a per pair of students
    Worksheet 1–4a
    Regular pencils

Procedure

1. Give each pair of students one set of counters, two copies of Worksheet 1–4a, and one copy of Building Mat 1–4a.

2. Have each pair of students use their counters to model each exercise on Worksheet 1–4a on Building Mat 1–4a. They should use the quantities found on the building mat to complete the table below the exercise.

3. For each exercise on Worksheet 1–4a, guide students to write several statements about their results on the back of the worksheet.

4. Discuss Exercise 1 with the class before allowing students to work Exercise 2 independently.

Consider Exercise 1 on Worksheet 1–4a: "Let the circles on Building Mat 1–4a represent these characteristics: Circle A, 'things that have four legs'; Circle B, 'things that eat meat'; and Circle C, 'things that climb trees.' Place counters in the mat's disjoint regions to locate the following groups: 2 rabbits, 4 squirrels, 2 cats, 1 dog, 3 caterpillars, 8-year-old Kate, Kate's hat, Grandpa who loves hot dogs, and Grandma the vegetarian. After placing the counters, find the region(s) described in each row of the table below, and record the total counters for that row. How many things were counted in all?"

Guide students to identify each group by the three characteristics in order to locate the appropriate region on Building Mat 1–4a for the necessary counters. For example, the 4 squirrels have 4 legs AND climb trees AND do NOT eat meat. So 4 counters should be placed in the region that belongs to Circle A and to Circle C, but not to Circle B. Since Grandma is a vegetarian and assuming she can no longer climb trees, a counter for her should be outside all three circles. One counter for Kate's hat will also be outside all three circles. Grandpa's counter will be in Circle B but not in Circle A or Circle C (too old to climb trees). We will assume that Kate is a good tree climber.

After all counters have been placed, students should complete the totals for the table as follows:

Four Legs	Eats Meat	Climbs Trees	Total
yes	yes	yes	2 cats
yes	yes	no	1 dog
yes	no	yes	4 squirrels
yes	no	no	2 rabbits
no	yes	yes	1 Kate
no	yes	no	1 Grandpa
no	no	yes	3 caterpillars
no	no	no	1 Grandma and 1 hat

Using the table or the counters on the building mat, students should find the total objects involved (without repeats). For Exercise 1, there are 16 people or things found in the disjoint regions of the building mat or the rows of the table.

Also on the back of Worksheet 1–4a, have students write sample descriptions for objects that share one characteristic, share two characteristics, or share three characteristics. Language can be confusing at this point. We are not consistent with when "having 4 legs" is intended to be exclusive (that is, "only having 4 legs" but not "eating meat" or "climbing trees"), or inclusive (that is, "having 4 legs" whether or not it "eats meat" or "climbs trees"). Generally with this type of logic problem, writers intend for the inclusive meaning to be used, and we will use that here. Here are sample descriptions and totals that students might use for the following combinations with A, B, and C:

Circle A: 2 rabbits, 4 squirrels, 2 cats, and 1 dog have four legs.
Circles A and B: 1 dog and 2 cats have 4 legs and eat meat.
Circles A, B, and C: 2 cats have 4 legs, eat meat, and climb trees.
Not Circles A, B, or C: Grandma and Kate's hat do not have 4 legs, do not eat meat, and do not climb trees.

Other combinations of characteristics are possible. For example, students might use B, and (B and C), along with (A, B, and C) and Not (A, B, or C). Remind students that Not (A, B, or C) is logically equivalent to (Not A, Not B, and Not C).

Answer Key for Worksheet 1–4a
1. Table, total, and sample descriptors are shown in the text.

2. Total = 5 + 2 + 2 + 3 + 4 + 1 + 5 = 22 students surveyed

Sample descriptors [others are possible]:

Circle C: (5 + 2 + 2 + 1) or 10 students are Service Club members.
Circles B and C: (2 + 1) or 3 students are Service Club members and music students.

Circles A, B, and C: 2 students are juniors, music students, and Service Club members.

Not Circles A, B, or C: 0 students are not juniors, not music students, and not Service Club members.

Junior Class	Music Student	Service Club	Total
yes	yes	yes	2
yes	yes	no	3
yes	no	yes	2
yes	no	no	5
no	yes	yes	1
no	yes	no	4
no	no	yes	5
no	no	no	0

Building Mat 1–4a

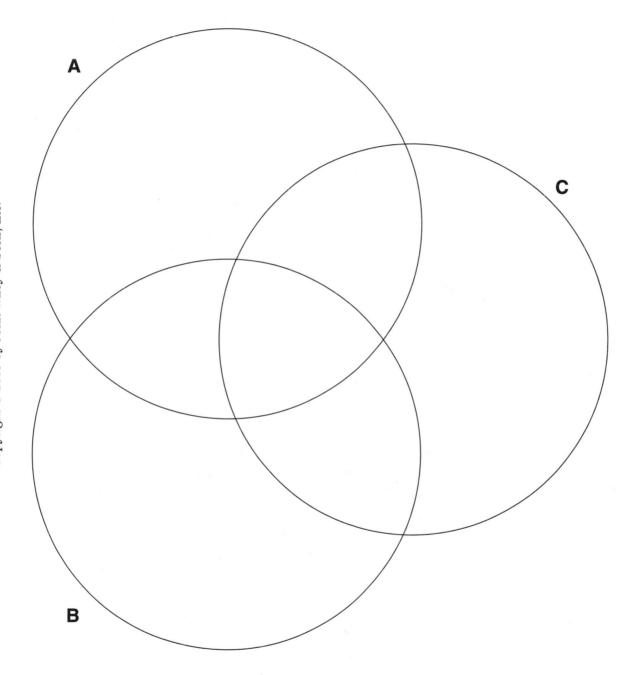

A

C

B

42

Use counters on Building Mat 1–4a to solve the exercises provided.

1. Let the circles on Building Mat 1–4a represent these characteristics: Circle A, "things that have 4 legs"; Circle B, "things that eat meat"; and Circle C, "things that climb trees." Place counters in the mat's disjoint regions to locate the following groups: 2 rabbits, 4 squirrels, 2 cats, 1 dog, 3 caterpillars, 8-year-old Kate, Kate's hat, Grandpa who loves hot dogs, and Grandma the vegetarian. After placing the counters, find the region(s) described in each row of the table below and record the total counters for that row. How many things were counted in all?

Four Legs	Eats Meat	Climbs Trees	Total
yes	yes	yes	
yes	yes	no	
yes	no	yes	
yes	no	no	
no	yes	yes	
no	yes	no	
no	no	yes	
no	no	no	

2. Repeat the steps of Exercise 1 with the following: Circle A, "junior class"; Circle B, "music students"; Circle C, "Service Club members." The survey included 12 juniors, 10 music students, and 10 Service Club members. Use totals given in the table to place counters in the regions of Building Mat 1–4a. Find the missing totals in the table. How many students were actually in the survey?

Junior Class	Music Student	Service Club	Total
yes	yes	yes	2
yes	yes	no	3
yes	no	yes	
yes	no	no	
no	yes	yes	1
no	yes	no	
no	no	yes	5
no	no	no	0

Activity 2
Pictorial Stage

Materials

Worksheet 1–4b
Regular pencils

Procedure

1. Give each student a copy of Worksheet 1–4b. Have students work in pairs.

2. Below each exercise on Worksheet 1–4b, have students draw a diagram to represent the word problem. The diagram should help students decide which equations are needed. They should then write the equation(s) beside the diagram and solve them. It is assumed that students have the necessary skills to solve the simple equations involved in this activity.

3. When all have finished, have various students draw their diagrams on the board and discuss the different approaches used, along with the results found.

4. Discuss Exercise 1 on Worksheet 1–4b before allowing students to work the other exercises with their partners.

Consider Exercise 1 on Worksheet 1–4b: "A low brick wall is to be built along a portion of one edge of a terrace. The wall must be over 5 feet long. Five-inch-long tan bricks will form the top layer of the wall, and 8-inch-long brown bricks will form the second layer. What is the minimal length the wall must be so that the bricks in the top two layers align with each other at both ends of the wall without partial bricks being used?"

The length of the top layer of bricks must be a multiple of 5 inches since 5-inch bricks are used. The second layer must be a multiple of 8 inches since 8-inch bricks are used. For the two layers to match, the two multiples must equal each other. Have students draw the following diagram below Exercise 1 to represent the multiples involved:

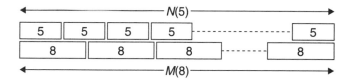

The diagram leads to the equation: $N(5) = M(8)$. Students need to find values for N and M, so that $N(5) = M(8)$. One possible solution would be $N = 8$ and $M = 5$. These choices, however, would produce a wall 40 inches long, and the wall must be over 5 feet or 60 inches long. The next possible solution will be $N = 16$ and $M = 10$. Therefore, the minimal wall length will be 80 inches long. Have students record this minimal wall length beside the diagram, along with the equation and solution selected.

Answer Key for Worksheet 1–4b

Suggested diagrams are shown; other forms are possible.

1. $N(5) = M(8)$; $N = 16$ and $M = 10$ [a possible diagram is shown in the text]

2. $3N + (3N + 1) = 31$; $N = 5$, so $3N = 15$, the fifth multiple of 3

Possible diagram:

3. $N(c) = M(C)$, so $N(2)(3.14)(2) = M(2)(3.14)(7)$; $N = 7$ and $M = 2$ for the first possible solution, so the small gear will rotate 7 times while the large gear rotates 2 times before the 0-marks coincide again.

4. $5N – 2N = 51$; $N = 17$, the number needed.

Worksheet 1–4b   Name _____

Solving with Diagrams   Date _____

Draw diagrams to model the exercises provided. Then find their equations and solutions.

1. A low brick wall is to be built along a portion of one edge of a terrace. The wall must be over 5 feet long. Five-inch-long tan bricks will form the top layer of the wall, and 8-inch-long brown bricks will form the second layer. What is the minimal length the wall must be so that the bricks in the top two layers align with each other at both ends of the wall without partial bricks being used?

2. Two consecutive integers have a sum of 31. The first number is a multiple of 3. Is the first integer the fourth, fifth, or sixth multiple of 3?

3. In a machine, a small gear wheel of radius 2 centimeters turns along the rim of a large gear wheel of radius 7 centimeters. The gears are initially positioned with their 0-marks touching. How many complete revolutions will the small gear make and the large gear make before the 0-marks touch again?

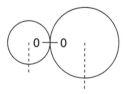

4. Five times a number minus two times that same number equals 51. Find the number.

Activity 3
Independent Practice

Materials
  Worksheet 1–4c
  Regular pencils

Procedure
Give each student a copy of Worksheet 1–4c to complete independently. Encourage students to draw diagrams to help them set up any needed equations. When all have finished, have various students share the diagrams and equations they used to solve the different exercises.

Answer Key for Worksheet 1–4c
  1. D

  2. B

  3. C

  4. B

  5. A

Possible Testing Errors That May Occur for This Objective
  • When seeking the least common multiple of a set of numbers, students will find a common multiple by multiplying all the given numbers together, but will fail to find the least multiple possible.

  • When using a Venn diagram to analyze the quantities resulting from a survey, students will use the quantity listed for a single characteristic in the exclusive sense rather than in the inclusive sense. That is, if 20 people are identified as "eating a hot dog," students will view them as "only eating a hot dog." The 20 people are excluded from "drinking a cola" or "eating ice cream," for example. This causes students to find the wrong total involved in the survey.

  • When the sum of two consecutive even or two consecutive odd numbers is required, students will use $N + (N + 1)$ for the sum instead of $N + (N + 2)$.

Worksheet 1–4c   Name _____

Solving Numerical Problems   Date _____

Solve the exercises provided. Be ready to share your steps and your reasoning with others in the class.

1. A bag of wieners contains 10 wieners. A bag of hot dog buns contains 8 buns. If enough bags are bought so that there are equal numbers of wieners and buns, what is the least number of hot dogs that can be made that will use all the wieners and buns bought?

   A. 8   B. 10   C. 18   D. 40

2. Two positive integers have a sum of 57. The lesser number is an even number, and the difference between the two integers is 5. What is the even number?

   A. 5   B. 26   C. 31   D. 57

3. Henry and Georgia both leave campus at the same time to begin a driving marathon. Henry drives at 55 mph, and Georgia drives at 60 mph. If each driver records the total distance traveled only at full hour intervals, what is the least distance at which they both will record the same mileage?

   A. 115 mi.   B. 132 mi.   C. 660 mi.   D. 3,300 mi.

4. Some vacationers were exiting a tour bus, so Mary and her friends decided to count them in various ways. Each looked for something different. Here are the results: 18 people wore jeans; 15 wore tennis shoes; 10 wore hats; 6, tennis shoes and hat; 9, jeans and tennis shoes; 7, hat and jeans; and 4, hat, jeans, and tennis shoes. Five people did not wear a hat, jeans, or tennis shoes. How many people actually were counted leaving the bus?

   A. 43   B. 30   C. 25   D. 18

5. Maude bought a bag of 5 dozen assorted cookies at the bakery. When she opened the bag, she found the following amounts: 10 cookies had only pecans; 10 had only raisins; 15, only cinnamon; 15, raisins and pecans; and 5, pecans and cinnamon without raisins. How many cookies had cinnamon and raisins without pecans?

   A. 5   B. 10   C. 30   D. 60

Objective 5: Apply Ratio and Proportion to Solve Numeric Problems or Problems Involving Variables

Proportional thinking allows several major ideas to be placed into a larger family of concepts. These ideas include probability, percents, and rates. For example, given the rate of 30 mph, students are typically taught to multiply the given rate by a new time to find a new corresponding distance in miles. Using the *proportion* approach, however, students may equate the ratio of 30 miles to 1 hour to the ratio of the new distance to the new time. Similarly, probability and percent problems may be set up as proportions. The concept of proportions and its applications will be developed in the following activities.

Activity 1
Manipulative Stage

Materials

Building Mat 1–5a per pair of students
Bag of small counters (2 colors, 20 counters per color) per pair of students
Worksheet 1–5a
Regular pencil

Procedure

1.   Give each pair of students two copies of Worksheet 1–5a, a copy of Building Mat 1–5a, and a bag of small counters (2 colors, 20 counters per color). The top level on the mat will be for the *basic ratio* (a ratio that uses the smallest whole numbers possible), and the bottom level on the mat will be for the *secondary ratio* (the larger amounts formed by multiple amounts of the basic ratio's numbers, each amount being arranged as an array). One color of counter will be used to show the first amount in each ratio, and the second color of counter will show the second amount in each ratio.

2.   Have students build basic ratios and their corresponding secondary ratios on Building Mat 1–5a with the counters, using the exercises on Worksheet 1–5a.

3.   After students complete each exercise, have them write a word sentence below the exercise that describes their results.

4.   Discuss Exercise 1 on Worksheet 1–5a before allowing students to work independently.

Consider Exercise 1 from Worksheet 1–5a: "At the store, 3 mechanical pencils cost $2. What will 12 pencils cost?"

Have students place 3 color #1 counters (the 3 pencils) in a row in the left empty region of the top level of Building Mat 1–5a and 2 color #2 counters (the $2 price for the 3 pencils) in the right empty region of the top level. The pencils will be represented in the left region since they were mentioned first, before the cost in the exercise. Now have the students randomly place 12 color #1 counters in the left empty region of the lower level of the mat.

Students must find how many color #2 counters go in the lower right region of Building Mat 1–5a. Since the secondary ratio consists of repeats of the basic ratio, the color #1 counters in the lower left region must be rearranged into an array having 3 counters per row to match the row of color #1 counters in the top left region; 4 rows will be formed. The 4 rows indicate that 4 of the basic ratio have been used to make the secondary ratio. Thus, 4 rows of color #2 counters must be used in the lower right region of the mat.

Since two color #2 counters have been used in the basic ratio, two color #2 counters must be used in each of the four rows in the secondary ratio. The final mat arrangement yields 8 color #2 counters in the right region of the secondary ratio. This indicates that 12 pencils will cost $8. Have students record the results on Worksheet 1–5a below Exercise 1 as follows: "3 pencils compare to $2 like 12 pencils compare to $8. So 12 pencils cost $8." The initial and final stages of mat work are shown below. The final completed building mat represents a proportion (two equivalent ratios):

Initial Mat:

Basic ratio:	●●●	●●
Secondary ratio:	(12 counters)	

Final Mat:

Basic ratio:	●●●	●●
Secondary ratio:	●●● ●●● ●●● ●●●	●● ●● ●● ●●

There are four regions to fill on Building Mat 1–5a. The word problems in the exercises of Worksheet 1–5a will vary, so that different regions need to be filled. In Exercise 1, the lower right region was needed; that is, the value for that region was the unknown for the problem. Whenever one region is needed, the numbers for the other 3 regions must be given in the word problem. The placement in the left and right regions of the building mat should follow the initial order given for the ratios in each exercise. For example, if the exercise states "3 girls for every 5 boys," then "3 girls" should be shown in the upper left region and "5 boys" in the upper right region.

Answer Key for Worksheet 1–5a
Here are possible sentences to use.

1. 3 pencils compare to $2 like 12 pencils compare to $8. So 12 pencils cost $8.

2. 4 people compare to 3 dogs like 16 people compare to 12 dogs. So 16 people attended the dog show.

3. 12 girls compare to 15 boys like 4 girls compare to 5 boys. There are 5 boys in the class for every 4 girls.

4. 1 red marble compares to 3 blue marbles like 3 red marbles compare to 9 blue marbles. So there are 3 red and 9 blue marbles in 12 marbles total.

5. 12 cans compare to $16 like 3 cans compare to $4. The basic ratio is 3 cans for $4.

6. 5 miles compare to 1 hour like 15 miles compare to 3 hours. It will take 3 hours to ride 15 miles on the bike.

Building Mat 1–5a

Basic ratio:	
Secondary ratio:	

Worksheet 1–5a   Name _____

Building Ratios   Date _____

Solve the word problems provided by placing counters on Building Mat 1–5a. Below each exercise, write a word sentence that states as a proportion the results found for that exercise.

1. At the store, 3 mechanical pencils cost $2. What will 12 pencils cost?

2. At the dog show, there are 4 people for every 3 dogs. If there are 12 dogs in the show, how many people are present at the show?

3. Mr. Jordan's eighth-grade class has 12 girls and 15 boys. How many boys are in the class for every 4 girls?

4. There is 1 red marble for every 3 blue marbles in a box. If there are 12 marbles total in the box and each marble is either red or blue, how many marbles are red and how many are blue?

5. Jan bought 12 cans of stew for $16. What is the basic ratio of cans to dollars?

6. If George rides his bike at 5 mph, how many hours will it take him to ride 15 miles if his speed remains constant?

Activity 2
Pictorial Stage

Materials
Worksheet 1–5b
Red pencil and regular pencil

Procedure
1. Give each student a copy of Worksheet 1–5b and a red pencil.
2. Students should complete Exercises 1 to 4 by drawing small shapes in the ratio frames. The finished ratio frames should look much like the completed building mat illustrated in the Manipulative Stage. Because of larger numbers used in Exercise 4, students might draw rectangles and write a value inside each rectangle instead of using unit counters.
3. Beside each completed ratio frame, have students record equations that describe the proportion represented. A variable will be recorded for the missing part of the proportion. It is assumed that students can solve simple equations like $2N = 16$. The discussion of Exercise 1 will include the types of equations to use.
4. For Exercises 5 and 6, students will graph on a grid several ratio pairs that come from the same situation. On the grid, the points for the ratio pairs will then be connected in red pencil. In each case, a red line should be formed, which indicates that the proportional situations are linear relationships.
5. Discuss Exercise 1 on Worksheet 1–5b with the class before allowing students to finish the worksheet independently. Also review graphing techniques before having them work Exercises 5 and 6.

Consider Exercise 1: "There are 15 cats and 9 dogs at the pet shop. How many cats are there for every 3 dogs?"

Students should draw circles on the ratio frame to represent the cats and triangles to represent the dogs. At first, 3 triangles will be drawn in the upper right region of the ratio frame to represent the 3 dogs. The upper right region is used since "dogs" was stated second in the initial ratio of *cats* to *dogs*. Having "3 triangles in one row" then determines the number <u>per row</u> in the lower right region. This requires 3 <u>rows</u> of triangles to be drawn in order to show the 9 dogs total. Remind students that rows in an array are left to right, not up and down.

Students should now be aware that 3 <u>rows</u> of circles will have to be drawn in the lower left region of the frame when representing all the cats. Since 15 circles must be drawn to represent the 15 cats total and these circles must be drawn in 3 rows, this forces 5 circles to be in each row. In turn, this causes 5 circles to be drawn in the upper left region of the ratio frame. The initial and final stages of the ratio frame are shown here.

Initial Frame:

Basic ratio:		△ △ △
Secondary ratio:		△ △ △ △ △ △ △ △ △

Final Frame:

Basic ratio:	○ ○ ○ ○ ○	△ △ △
Secondary ratio:	○ ○ ○ ○ ○ ○ ○ ○ ○ ○ ○ ○ ○ ○ ○	△ △ △ △ △ △ △ △ △

Have students record their results beside the ratio frame that is now completed. Be sure that the two ratios keep the same order, that is, "cats to dogs." Have the students use the following formats where N represents the unknown amount of cats in the basic ratio:

15 cats to 9 dogs = N cats to 3 dogs

$$\frac{N}{3} = \frac{3\,\text{rows} \times N}{3\,\text{rows} \times 3} = \frac{15}{9}, \text{so } 3N = 15\,\text{cats and } N = 5\,\text{cats.}$$

Notice that $\frac{15}{9}$ represents the secondary ratio, and $\frac{N}{3}$ represents the basic ratio, with N as the part to be found (read as "15 to 9" and "N to 3"). The left factor in the numerator and in the denominator of the expression, $\frac{3 \times N}{3 \times 3}$, indicates the number of <u>rows</u> that were drawn in each region of the secondary ratio. Since each of the denominators equals 9, students only need to compare the numerators, $15 = 3N$, in order to solve for N as 5 cats. Discuss the idea that finding equivalent ratios in a proportion is similar to finding equivalent fractions.

In preparation for Exercises 5 and 6 on Worksheet 1–5b, review the graphing of ordered pairs. Also discuss how to determine the step or interval sizes for the horizontal and vertical scales of a grid. In each of the two exercises, the three ordered pairs plotted will have collinear points. The red path connecting the three points will be straight. Equivalent ratios have a linear relationship. After students have completed Exercises 5 and 6, help them make these observations.

Answer Key for Worksheet 1–5b
Suggested equations are shown; other equivalent forms are possible.

1. 15 cats to 9 dogs = N cats to 3 dogs

    $$\frac{N}{3} = \frac{3 \times N}{3 \times 3} = \frac{15}{9}, \text{so } 3N = 15 \text{ and } N = 5 \text{ cats.}$$

2. $4 to 1 hour = $20 to N hours

$$\frac{\$4}{1} = \frac{5 \times \$4}{5 \times 1} = \frac{\$20}{N} \quad \text{So, } N = 5 \times 1, \text{ or 5 hours.}$$

3. 2 blue to 5 total marbles = N blue to 20 total marbles

$$\frac{2}{5} = \frac{4 \times 2}{4 \times 5} = \frac{N \text{ blue marbles}}{20 \text{ total marbles}} \quad \text{So, } N = 4 \times 2, \text{ or 8 blue marbles.}$$

4. $3 discount to N% discount = $15 total price to 100% total

$$\frac{\$3}{N\%} = \frac{5 \times \$3}{5 \times N\%} = \frac{\$15}{100\%} \quad \text{So, } 5 \times N\% = 100\% \text{ and } N\% = 20\% \text{ discount off total price.}$$

Basic ratio:	$3	20%
Secondary ratio:	$3	20%
	$3	20%
	$3	20%
	$3	20%
	$3	20%

5. Ordered pairs graphed: (1 hour, $4), (5 hours, $20), (7 hours, $28); connecting red path is straight

6. Ordered pairs graphed: (5 total, 2 blue), (15 total, 6 blue), (20 total, 8 blue); connecting red path is straight

Worksheet 1–5b   Name _____

Drawing and Graphing Ratios   Date _____

Solve the word problems by drawing shapes on a ratio frame provided. Beside Exercises 1 to 4, write equations that state as proportions the results found for each exercise. Solve for each variable or unknown part. For Exercises 5 and 6, graph ordered pairs for ratios on the grids as directed.

1. There are 15 cats and 9 dogs at the pet shop. How many cats are there for every 3 dogs?

Basic ratio:		
Secondary ratio:		

2. Lynn earns $4 per hour at her weekend job. How many hours must she work to earn $20?

Basic ratio:		
Secondary ratio:		

3. There are 2 blue marbles for every 5 marbles in a jar. If there are 20 marbles total, how many marbles are blue?

Basic ratio:		
Secondary ratio:		

Worksheet 1–5b Continued

Name _____

Date _____

4. Mario bought a music CD for $3 off the original price of $15. What was the percent of discount on the CD? Hint: Use "discount amount to discount %" for the basic ratio, and "total price to total %" for the secondary ratio.

Basic ratio:		
Secondary ratio:		

On each grid for Exercises 5 and 6, plot points for the three ratios found, and draw a path in red pencil to connect the three points. What do you notice about the red path drawn on each grid?

5. Find another secondary ratio for Exercise 2, using 7 hours for the time. Then plot points for the 3 ratios found, using (hours worked, amount earned) as the ordered pair. Number the grid axes as needed.

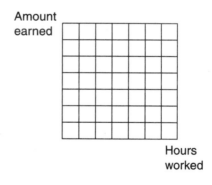

Amount earned

Hours worked

6. Find another secondary ratio for Exercise 3, using 15 marbles total. Then plot points for the 3 ratios found, using (# total, # blue) as the ordered pair. Number the grid axes as needed.

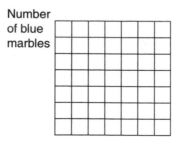

Number of blue marbles

Number of total marbles

Activity 3
Independent Practice

Materials
>   Worksheet 1–5c
>   Regular pencil

Procedure

Give each student a copy of Worksheet 1–5c. Encourage students to set up proportions similar to those equations used in Exercises 1 to 4 on Worksheet 1–5b of Activity 2. For example, in Exercise 3 of Worksheet 1–5c, they might write the following:

$$\frac{13}{20} = \frac{5 \times 13}{5 \times 20} = \frac{N}{100},$$ where N equals 65 shots made.

Since N is compared to 100, finding N as 65 is equivalent to finding that 65% of the attempted shots were successful. Although Exercises 3 and 7 involve percents, students should focus on the proportion method to solve the problems and not on an alternative method often used for percents.

Also, in problems like Exercise 7, students may have difficulty finding the correct factor to use to form the new or equivalent ratio. In such cases, simple integral factors do not work. Show students how to <u>construct</u> the factor in the following way. The proportion needed is $\frac{\$24}{N} = \frac{40}{100}$, where the numerators are the dollars and the percent amount for the *discount*. The denominators N and 100 represent the dollars and percent amount for the *total* cost or regular price. The numerator and denominator of one ratio should multiply by the same factor to produce the numerator and denominator of the other ratio. To construct the factor, consider the two numerators with known values. How can 40 be changed to $24? A factor can be constructed so that 40 is divided out and $24 is brought in; that is, $\left(\frac{\$24}{40}\right)$ becomes the chosen factor. Then $40 \times \left(\frac{\$24}{40}\right)$ will equal $24. Then the denominators must use the same factor: $100 \times \left(\frac{\$24}{40}\right)$ must equal N. Students should not *compute* $\frac{\$24}{40}$ until this last equation is set up. So they will have $100 \times \left(\frac{\$24}{40}\right) = \$60$ for N, which is the regular price (total cost) of the jacket.

Answer Key for Worksheet 1–5c
1. B

2. D

3. A

4. B

5. C

6. D

7. B

8. C

Possible Testing Errors That May Occur for This Objective

- Students multiply the numerator of the initial ratio by one factor and the denominator by another factor when changing the initial ratio to an equivalent ratio.

- The initial ratio's numerator and denominator are changed to the new ratio's numerator and denominator by *adding* a constant instead of *multiplying* by a constant. For example, to compare $\frac{3}{8}$ to $\frac{N}{12}$ to find N, students incorrectly use $\frac{(3+4)}{(8+4)} = \frac{7}{12}$ instead of $\frac{(1.5 \times 3)}{(1.5 \times 8)} = \frac{4.5}{12}$.

- Students do not maintain the same <u>order</u> in the two ratios being compared in a proportion. For example, they will equate cats/dogs to dogs/cats, instead of using cats/dogs = cats/dogs.

Worksheet 1–5c   Name _____

Using Ratios to Solve   Date _____
Word Problems

Solve the word problems, using proportions.

1. On the first day of his vacation, Thomas counted the car license plates he saw from different states. Of the 80 plates he counted, 45 were from Ohio, 23 were from Illinois, and 12 were from other states. If he sees 160 license plates on his return trip home, how many of these could he expect to be from Illinois?

   A. 24   B. 46   C. 80   D. 90

2. The Disco Shop is selling CDs at $7.50 per package of 3 CDs. What will it cost to purchase 12 CDs?

   A. $7.50   B. $15   C. $22.50   D. $30

3. Carrie made 13 out of 20 shot attempts during a recent basketball game. To find the percent of shots that Carrie made, how many successful shots out of 100 attempts would be equivalent to her score?

   A. 65   B. 72   C. 78   D. 85

4. A car is traveling at an average speed of 62 miles per hour. At this rate of speed, which is the best estimate for how long it will take the car to travel 356 miles?

   A. 5 hours   B. 6 hours   C. 7 hours   D. 8 hours

5. A box contains 24 colored cubes. There are 6 blue cubes, 3 red cubes, and 7 yellow cubes. The rest of the cubes are green. The ratio of green cubes to total cubes is equivalent to which probability for drawing out a green cube at random?

   A. $\frac{1}{8}$ B. $\frac{1}{4}$ C. $\frac{1}{3}$ D. $\frac{7}{24}$

Worksheet 1–5c Continued

Name _____

Date _____

6. Leo reported the following data on his time sheet at work: (2 hours, $10), (5 hours, $25), (8 hours, $40), (7 hrs, $30), and (4 hours, $20). If his hourly rate was constant, which data pair was incorrect?

A. (2, 10) B. (5, 25) C. (8, 40) D. (7, 30)

7. Myshondi saved $24 when she bought a jacket on sale. If the discount was 40% of the regular price, what was the regular price of the jacket?

A. $52 B. $60 C. $75 D. $80

8. A package of three Brand B batteries costs $4.95, and a package of three Brand C batteries costs $3.75. Which proportion can be used to determine the percent, N, of the cost of the Brand B batteries that will be saved if the Brand C batteries are purchased?

A. $\dfrac{(4.95 - 3.75)}{3.75} = \dfrac{N}{100}$

C. $\dfrac{(4.95 - 3.75)}{4.95} = \dfrac{N}{100}$

B. $\dfrac{3.75}{4.95} = \dfrac{N}{100}$

D. $\dfrac{4.95}{3.75} = \dfrac{N}{100}$

Objective 6: Identify Two Given Linear Equations, Given in Algebraic Form or Graphic Form, as Parallel, Perpendicular, or with the Same *x*- or *y*-Intercept

Students need experience with certain properties of lines and should be able to recognize these properties in the algebraic equations of the lines. Of particular interest are the parallel and perpendicular properties of a pair of lines, along with their possible sharing of an intercept point. For the following activities, it will be assumed that students are familiar with the $y = mx + b$ format for a line, even though their understanding may be somewhat limited.

Activity 1

Manipulative Stage

Materials

Worksheet 1–6a
Building Mat 1–6a
Rulers or straightedges
Index cards (3 inches by 5 inches; any color but white)
Regular pencils

Procedure

1. Give each pair of students two copies of Worksheet 1–6a, one copy of Building Mat 1–6a, a ruler, and one colored index card. The lower left corner of the building mat will be considered the origin of the grid.

2. For each exercise on Worksheet 1–6a, students must use the measuring edge of the ruler to locate line A on Building Mat 1–6a. The ruler's edge must pass through the points of the two ordered pairs given for line A. Students should identify the vertical change and the horizontal change as they move from one point to the other point given for line A, then record these changes as the ratio for line A's slope on Worksheet 1–6a. The ratio may be simplified, but should be kept in *a/b* format.

3. While holding the ruler in place on the grid, students should align the short edge of the index card with the ruler's edge and slide the card along the ruler's edge until the card's <u>long</u> edge touches the points given for line B. As with line A, students should find the vertical change and the horizontal change between the two points, then record the slope for line B on Worksheet 1–6a. Again, simplify the ratio if necessary, but keep the *a/b* format.

4. Have students estimate what the *y*-intercept might be for each line and write an equation for each line on the worksheet, using the $y = mx + b$ format.

5. Because of the alignment of the index card with the ruler, lines A and B in each exercise will be perpendicular to each other. Guide students to realize that line A's slope is the inverse or opposite of the reciprocal of line B's slope. Have students write a statement on the back of Worksheet 1–6a about two perpendicular lines and the relationship between their slopes.

6. Discuss Exercise 1 on Worksheet 1–6a with the class before allowing partners to work the exercises on their own.

Consider Exercise 1 on Worksheet 1–6a:

Line A: (0,5) and (2,2); slope = _____; equation: _____

Line B: (3,1) and (6,3); slope = _____; equation: _____

Have students position a ruler on Building Mat 1–6a so that its edge passes through the points for (0,5) and (2,2) to represent line A. There will be a vertical change of –3 and a horizontal change of +2, so students should record a slope of $\frac{-3}{+2}$ for line A on Worksheet 1–6a. Since (0,5) is the actual y-intercept, have students record the equation for line A as $y = \frac{-3}{+2}x + 5$, following the $y = mx + b$ format.

Holding the ruler in place on the grid, students should align the short edge of the index card with the ruler, then slide the card along the ruler's edge until the long edge of the card passes through the points for (3,1) and (6,3). This new position of the card's long edge will represent line B. The vertical change will be +2, and the horizontal change will be +3, so a slope of $\frac{+2}{+3}$ should be recorded for line B. Using the slope to extend to new points off the grid, the y-intercept is found to be at (0, –1). Students should now record the equation for line B on the worksheet as $y = \frac{+2}{+3}x + (-1)$.

Discuss the idea that the lines represented by the ruler's edge and the index card's long edge are perpendicular to each other (that is, they form a 90 degree angle with each other). Guide students to compare the slopes of line A and line B and to notice that each slope is the inverse of the reciprocal of the other slope. For this comparison, it is helpful to show the signs on the numerator and the denominator of each slope ratio. The ruler and the index card might be arranged as follows on the grid, with the bold arrows indicating the two lines being represented by the ruler's edge and the card's long edge:

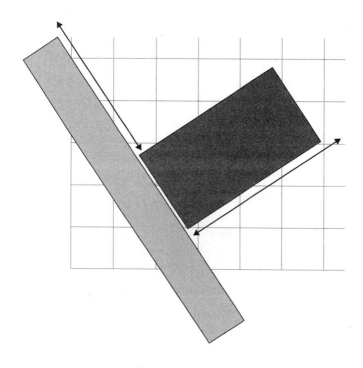

When students have completed all four exercises, have them write a statement on the back of Worksheet 1–6a that describes two perpendicular lines and the special relationship between their slopes. Note that the y-intercepts of perpendicular lines may or may not be equal. The lines will share the same y-intercept if the two lines intersect on the y-axis.

Answer Key for Worksheet 1–6a

1. [The answer is given in the text.]

2. Line A: slope $= \frac{+4}{+2} = \frac{+2}{+1}$; $y = \frac{+2}{+1}x + 0$

   Line B: slope $= \frac{-2}{+4} = \frac{-1}{+2}$; $y = \frac{-1}{+2}x + 5$

3. Line A: slope $= \frac{-1}{+1}$; $y = \frac{-1}{+1}x + 5$

   Line B: slope $= \frac{+1}{+1}$; $y = \frac{+1}{+1}x + (-1)$

4. Line A: slope $= \frac{+3}{+1}$; $y = \frac{+3}{+1}x + 3$

   Line B: slope $= \frac{-1}{+3}$; $y = \frac{-1}{+3}x + 5\frac{1}{3}$

Building Mat 1–6a

Worksheet 1–6a

Comparing Slopes of
Perpendicular Lines

Name _____

Date _____

For each exercise, use a ruler to locate line A on Building Mat 1–6a and use a colored index card to locate line B. Find their slopes and compare them. Estimate the y-intercepts of the two lines. Then write equations for the lines, using the $y = mx + b$ format.

1. Line A: (0, 5) and (2, 2); slope = _____; equation: _____

   Line B: (3, 1) and (6, 3); slope = _____; equation: _____

2. Line A: (1, 2) and (3, 6); slope = _____; equation: _____

   Line B: (2, 4) and (6, 2); slope = _____; equation: _____

3. Line A: (1, 4) and (2, 3); slope = _____; equation: _____

   Line B: (4, 3) and (5, 4); slope = _____; equation: _____

4. Line A: (0, 3) and (1, 6); slope = _____; equation: _____

   Line B: (1, 5) and (4, 4); slope = _____; equation: _____

Activity 2
Pictorial Stage

Materials
Worksheet 1–6b
Worksheet 1–6c
Rulers or straightedges
Colored pencils (2 bright colors; not yellow)
Regular pencils

Procedure
1.   Give each pair of students 4 copies of Worksheet 1–6b, 2 copies of Worksheet 1–6c, a ruler or straightedge, and 2 colored pencils (2 different colors). On each grid, students should position the origin in the center of the grid and draw the horizontal and vertical axes.

2.   Each exercise on Worksheet 1–6c should be drawn on its own copy of the grid on Worksheet 1–6b. For each exercise, have students draw line A through its two given points, using pencil color #1 on the grid. Then they should translate A's two points as directed to find two new points for line B. Line B should be drawn through its two points with pencil color #2 on the same grid.

3.   After line A and line B are drawn, have students measure the perpendicular distance between the two lines at several different locations to confirm that the two lines are the same distance apart, no matter where the measurement is made. This indicates that the two lines are parallel to each other.

4.   Then for each line of the same exercise, have students find the slope and y-intercept and write an equation for the line, using the $y = mx + b$ format. This information should be recorded below the exercise on Worksheet 1–6c.

5.   After all exercises are completed, discuss the idea that in each exercise, line A and line B have the same slope but different y-intercepts. These are properties of parallel lines. Have students write a statement on the back of Worksheet 1–6c about parallel lines and the relationship between their slopes.

6.   Discuss Exercise 1 on Worksheet 1–6c with the class before allowing partners to work the other exercises on their own.

Consider Exercise 1 on Worksheet 1–6c:

Line A: (–2, 1) and (3, –2); slope = _____; equation: _____
Translation: Move vertically by +4.
Line B: (___, ___) and (___, ___); slope = _____; equation: _____

Have students number a copy of Worksheet 1–6b as grid #1 to correspond to Exercise 1, then draw and label a pair of coordinate axes, placing the origin in the center of the grid. In pencil color #1, have them locate the two points (–2, 1) and (3, –2) given for line A, then draw line A through the points on the grid.

The two points given for line A should be translated according to the given rule: Move vertically by +4. This means that the y-value of each ordered pair should be increased by 4. So (–2, 1) becomes (–2, 5), and (3, –2) becomes (3, 2). The two new points should be recorded on Worksheet 1–6c for line B. Students should use pencil color #2 to locate the two new points on grid #1 and draw a line through those points to show line B. Here is a graph of line A and line B shown on a partial grid #1:

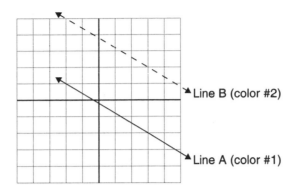

Line B (color #2)

Line A (color #1)

Using the ruler, students should measure the perpendicular distance between line A and line B at various locations to confirm that the two lines remain the same distance apart at all points. The actual numerical measurement is not important here. In fact, in lieu of a ruler, the edge of an index card might be used to mark off the perpendicular distance between the two lines. Then the marked-off length might be used to test other positions along the two lines.

After graphing the two lines, students should find the vertical and horizontal changes between each line's two stated points and compute the slope, or estimate the changes directly from the graph of the line. For line A, the slope will be $\frac{(-2)-1}{3-(-2)} = \frac{-3}{+5}$, and for line B, the slope will be $\frac{2-5}{3-(-2)} = \frac{-3}{+5}$. Other equivalent forms are possible. For later comparisons, it is helpful to students to continue to show the signs in both the numerator and the denominator of the slope ratio. The slopes should be recorded in the appropriate blanks below Exercise 1 on Worksheet 1–6c.

In order to find the equation for each line, students need to estimate the y-intercept graphically or use substitution of the slope and one point of the line in $y = mx + b$ to find the value of b. Practice with both methods is valuable. For line A, a graphical estimate for b might be 0, and for line B, it might be +4. If substitution is used, a more accurate value for line A's y-intercept is $\frac{-1}{5}$, and for line B, it is $3\frac{4}{5}$. Students should record the equations for either or both methods below Exercise 1 on Worksheet 1–6c. The equations will be as follows: (A) $y = \frac{-3}{+5}x + \left(\frac{-1}{5}\right)$, or $y = \frac{-3}{+5}x + 0$; and (B) $y = \frac{-3}{+5}x + 3\frac{4}{5}$, or $y = \frac{-3}{+5}x + 4$.

When students have completed all four exercises, guide them to notice that each pair of parallel lines has the same slope, but their y-intercepts differ. Have students write a statement on the back of Worksheet 1–6c that describes two parallel lines and the special relationship between their slopes. They should also note that the y-intercepts of distinct parallel lines will not be equal.

Answer Key for Worksheet 1–6c

Slope ratios and y-intercepts are shown as initially computed; equivalent forms are possible; estimates of y-intercepts may also be used.

1. Line A: $(-2, 1)$ and $(3, -2)$; $m = \dfrac{-3}{+5}$; $y = \dfrac{-3}{+5}x + \left(\dfrac{-1}{5}\right)$

    Line B: $(-2, 5)$ and $(3, 2)$; $m = \dfrac{-3}{+5}$; $y = \dfrac{-3}{+5}x + 3\dfrac{4}{5}$

2. Line A: $(-3, -2)$ and $(4, -2)$; $m = \dfrac{0}{+7} = 0$; $y = 0x + (-2)$

    Line B: $(-3, -5)$ and $(4, -5)$; $m = \dfrac{0}{+7} = 0$; $y = 0x + (-5)$

3. Line A: $(0, 0)$ and $(-5, -4)$; $m = \dfrac{-4}{-5}$; $y = \dfrac{-4}{-5}x + 0$

    Line B: $(3, 0)$ and $(-2, -4)$; $m = \dfrac{-4}{-5}$; $y = \dfrac{-4}{-5}x + \left(-2\dfrac{2}{5}\right)$

4. Line A: $(5, 1)$ and $(-5, -1)$; $m = \dfrac{-2}{-10} = \dfrac{-1}{-5}$; $y = \dfrac{-1}{-5}x + 0$

    Line B: $(4, -1)$ and $(-6, -3)$; $m = \dfrac{-2}{-10} = \dfrac{-1}{-5}$; $y = \dfrac{-1}{-5}x + \left(-1\dfrac{4}{5}\right)$

Worksheet 1–6b

Name _____

Date _____

Worksheet 1–6c   Name _____

Comparing Slopes of Parallel Lines   Date _____

For each exercise, use a ruler to draw line A in color #1 on a copy of Worksheet 1–6b. Translate A's points to find line B's points; then draw line B in color #2 on the same grid. Measure the perpendicular distance between the two lines at several locations. Find the slopes, and find or estimate the y-intercepts of the two lines. Then write equations for the lines, using the $y = mx + b$ format.

1. Line A: (–2, 1) and (3, –2); slope = _____; equation: _____

   Translation: Move vertically by +4.

   Line B: (__, __) and (__, __); slope = _____; equation: _____

2. Line A: (–3, –2) and (4, –2); slope = _____; equation: _____

   Translation: Move vertically by –3.

   Line B: (__, __) and (__, __); slope = _____; equation: _____

3. Line A: (0, 0) and (–5, –4); slope = _____; equation: _____

   Translation: Move horizontally by +3.

   Line B: (__, __) and (__, __); slope = _____; equation: _____

4. Line A: (5, 1) and (–5, –1); slope = _____; equation: _____

   Translation: Move vertically by –2 and horizontally by –1.

   Line B: (__, __) and (__, __); slope = _____; equation: _____

Activity 3
Independent Practice

Materials
    Worksheet 1–6d
    Regular pencils

Procedure
Give each student a copy of Worksheet 1–6d. After all have completed the worksheet, ask various students to explain their methods and their answers for the different exercises.

Answer Key for Worksheet 1–6d
   1. B

   2. C

   3. A

   4. B

   5. D

   6. C

   7. A

Possible Testing Errors That May Occur for This Objective
  - Students do not understand the role of the slope when identifying pairs of lines as parallel or perpendicular, so they use the same slope for both lines or randomly select slopes that are not related in any way when asked to find equations for such lines.

  - When finding the slopes needed to produce two perpendicular lines, students will find reciprocals but fail to use inverses or opposites of the reciprocals. For example, they will use +3 and $\frac{+1}{3}$ for the required slopes, instead of using +3 and $\frac{-1}{3}$, or –3 and $\frac{+1}{3}$.

  - When asked to match a pair of equations to their graphs, students incorrectly find or graph ordered pairs for the equations, thereby matching to the wrong pair of lines.

Worksheet 1–6d   Name _____

Applications of Parallel and   Date _____
Perpendicular Lines

Solve the exercises. Be ready to discuss your answers with the entire class.

1. A portion of trapezoid NPRT is shown on the grid. Through what coordinates
    should line RT be drawn to make side NP parallel to side RT in the trapezoid?

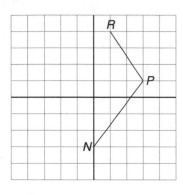

    A. (–2, 3)   C. (0, 2)

    B. (–2, 0)   D. (–1, –1)

2. Which equation describes the line that passes through the point (1,3) and is
    parallel to the line represented by the equation $-2x + y = -5$?

    A. $y = -2x + 1$ B. $y = \frac{1}{2}x - 5$ C. $y = 2x + 1$ D. $y = -\frac{1}{2}x + 3$

3. What is the slope of a line that is perpendicular to the line having the equation
    $2x + 3y = 15$?

    A. $\frac{+3}{+2}$ B. +5   C. $\frac{-2}{+3}$ D. –5

Name _____

Date _____

4. Which pair of equations represents the perpendicular lines shown on the graph?

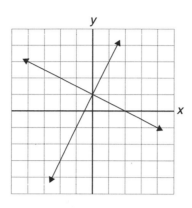

   A. $y = 4x + 1$ and $y = -4x + 1$

   B. $y = -\frac{1}{2}x + 1$ and $y = 2x + 1$

   C. $y = -x + 2$ and $y = x - \frac{1}{2}$

   D. $y = 2x$ and $y = -\frac{1}{2}x$

5. Given the function $y = 2.6x - 35.4$, which statement best describes the graphical effect of increasing the y-intercept by 18.6, but making no other changes in the function?

   A. The new line is perpendicular to the original.

   B. The new line has a greater rate of change.

   C. The x-intercept increases.

   D. The new line is parallel to the original.

6. Which of the following best describes the graph of the two equations $4y = 2x - 4$ and $2y = -3x + 6$?

   A. The lines have the same y-intercept.

   B. The lines are perpendicular.

   C. The lines have the same x-intercept.

   D. The lines are parallel.

Worksheet 1–6d Continued

Name _____

Date _____

7. Which graph best represents the line passing through the point (0, –3) and perpendicular to $y = -\frac{1}{2}x$?

A.

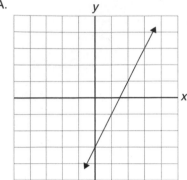

C.

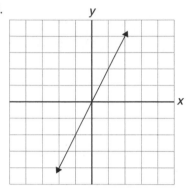

B.

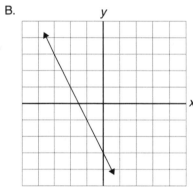

D.

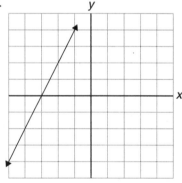

Objective 7: Identify Algebraic Equations or Graphs Needed to Represent a System of Linear Equations Described in a Given Situation; Solve the System by a Substitution Method or a Graphical Method

Systems of equations are difficult for students. They do not understand that two different conditions or relationships are existing concurrently for the same situation. Several methods are available for solving such systems, but the following activities will focus on the substitution method and the graphical method, which seem to be more intuitive for students. It is assumed that students have already mastered the solving of linear equations in one variable, and that in equations having two variables they are able to solve for one variable in terms of the other variable.

Activity 1
Manipulative Stage

Materials

> Sets of algebra tiles per pair of students (see step 1 under "Procedure" for details)
> Building Mat 1–7a
> Worksheet 1–7a
> Regular pencils and paper

Procedure

1.   Give each pair of students a set of algebra tiles, one copy of Building Mat 1–7a (system building mat), and two copies of Worksheet 1–7a. The set of tiles should contain 30 unit tiles, along with 12 variable tiles in each of two different sizes or colors. Consider the shorter variable tile as variable A and the longer variable tile as variable B for notation purposes. If teacher-made tiles are used, each packet should contain the following in different colors of laminated tagboard: 12 rectangular (linear) variable tiles, 0.75 inch by 3 inches (color #1); 12 rectangular variable tiles, 0.75 inch by 3.25 inch (color #2); and 30 unit tiles, 0.75 inch by 0.75 inch (color #3). Each tile should have a large X drawn on one side to show the inverse of that tile. Use tagboard that is thick enough so that the X will not show through to the other side. Commercial tiles are also available for two different variables, but a large X must be drawn on one of the largest faces of each tile in order to represent the inverse of that tile when the X faces up.

2.   For each exercise on Worksheet 1–7a, have students represent the two equations with tiles on Building Mat 1–7a. Equation (a) should be shown in the upper half of the mat and equation (b) in the lower half of the mat. Discuss the idea that if two groups of tiles are considered equal in value, either one of the groups can replace the other on an equation mat. Also, since equations in a system have the same solutions, the replacement of equivalent groups can occur in any equation within the same system.

3.   In one of the equations of an exercise, students will use the tiles to solve for one variable tile in terms of the other. The new group of tiles found for this first variable will then be substituted for that same variable in the other original equation. This results in a new equation involving only one variable. Students will solve this equation for its variable.

4.   After the value of one variable has been found, its value will be substituted into the symbolic form of the first equation transformed, and that equation will be solved to find the value of the second variable. The substitution equation and the values of the two variables should then be recorded below the exercise on Worksheet 1–7a.

5.   Now have students verify that their solutions for the two variables will satisfy both equation (a) and equation (b). Have them rebuild the original equations on the building mat, and then replace each variable tile with its value in unit tiles. The amounts on each side of an equation should be equal in value. Since the equality holds for both equations, this verifies that the values found for variable *A* and variable *B* form the solution pair for the given system of equations.

6.   Discuss Exercise 1 on Worksheet 1–7a with the class before allowing partners to work on the other exercises on their own. Consider Exercise 1 on Worksheet 1–7a: "(a) $A - B = 1$ and (b) $2A + B = -4$."

Have students show each equation with tiles on Building Mat 1–7a. Build equation (a) on the top half of the building mat, and build equation (b) on the bottom half of the mat. The initial mat and tiles should have the following appearance (variable *A* is represented by the plain rectangle and variable *B* by the shaded rectangle):

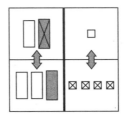

Students should now solve one of the equations for one of the variables in terms of the other variable. For discussion purposes, we will use equation (a) on the top half of the mat, since it is easy to solve for variable *A*. Have students add one variable *B* tile to each side of the equation mat and remove the 0-pair formed on the left side. The building mat will then have the following appearance:

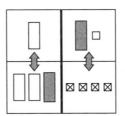

Since *A* equals *B* + 1 in the top equation, have students replace each variable *A* in the bottom equation with tiles for *B* + 1. The top half of the mat should be cleared of any remaining tiles. After the substitution is completed, the building mat will appear as follows:

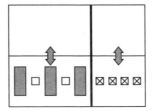

The two positive unit tiles on the left side of the equation should be removed by bringing in two negative unit tiles to both sides of the equation. Two 0-pairs will be formed on the left side and should be removed from the mat. A total of –6 will be on the right side of the equation. Students should separate the three variable B tiles on the left and form three rows. The same separation or division process should be shown with the –6 on the right side. Each complete row across the mat will show $B = -2$. The building mat will then appear as follows:

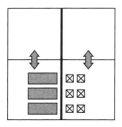

Have students remove two of the three rows of tiles from the building mat. The remaining row will show the solution for B in the original system of equations; that is, $B = -2$. This solution should be recorded below Exercise 1 on Worksheet 1–7a. Below Exercise 1, students should also rewrite equation (a), but substitute –2 for the variable B: $A - (-2) = 1$. They should solve for A in this equation, obtaining $A = -1$ and recording this result below Exercise 1.

Now have students rebuild the original two equations on Building Mat 1–7a, then substitute the values found for variable A and variable B into the equations, using unit tiles. The solutions for A and B are verified when the left and right sides of each equation equal each other. This also reinforces the idea that in a system of equations, all equations have the same solution pair for (A,B). Here is a possible mat arrangement that shows the verification:

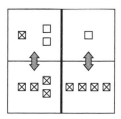

Answer Key for Worksheet 1–7a

1. $A = -1, B = -2$

2. $A = -3, B = +5$

3. $A = +2, B = +3$

4. $A = -2, B = -1$

5. $A = -4, B = -2$

Building Mat 1–7a

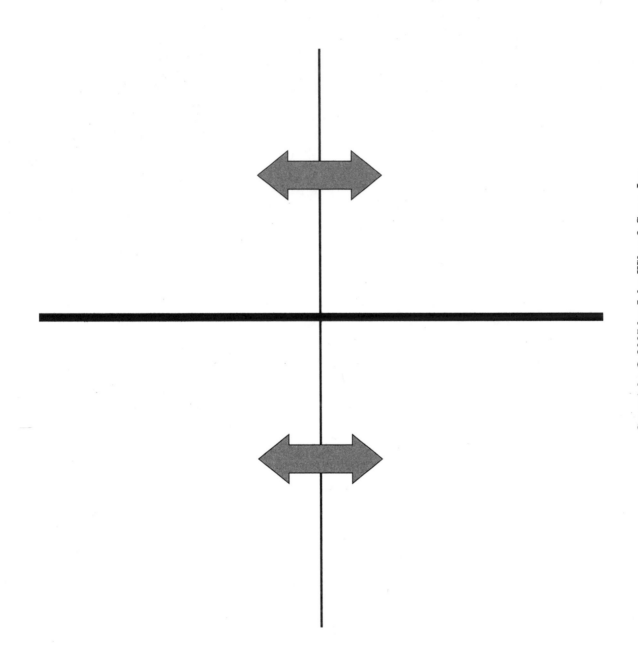

Worksheet 1–7a

Solving Systems of Equations
with Algebra Tiles

Name _____

Date _____

For each exercise, build each equation with tiles on Building Mat 1–7a. Follow your teacher's instructions to solve the two equations for the two variables involved. Record the value of each variable below the exercise.

1. (a) $A - B = 1$, and (b) $2A + B = -4$

2. (a) $A - B = -8$, and (b) $B = 2 - A$

3. (a) $3B - 2A = 5$, and (b) $2A - B = 1$

4. (a) $A + B = -3$, and (b) $2B - 3A = 4$

5. (a) $A - 3B = 2$, and (b) $-2A + 2B = 4$

Activity 2
Pictorial Stage

Materials
    Worksheet 1–7b
    Worksheet 1–7c
    Rulers or straightedges
    Regular pencils

Procedure
1. Give each pair of students two copies of Worksheet 1–7c, a ruler, and eight copies of Worksheet 1–7b (four copies per person).
2. For each exercise on Worksheet 1–7c, have students draw the necessary graphs on a copy of Worksheet 1–7b. It may be necessary in some exercises for students to identify the equations needed before they can graph them. Any equations found should be recorded below the exercise on Worksheet 1–7c. Some exercises will need the origin for the graphs to be in the lower left corner of the grid, while others will need the origin to be in the center of the grid. Students will need to decide how to number each scale on the grid, based on the data given in the exercise.
3. Students will use the pair of lines graphed for an exercise to find the solution to the system of equations involved. They will graphically estimate the coordinates of the intersection point of the two lines, then substitute the chosen coordinates into the system equations to verify the solution. If an intersection point lies between grid marks, the first estimate for a coordinate may not work in the given equations. Students will then need to adjust their estimate until it works. The numerical substitutions verifying the solution should be recorded below the exercise on Worksheet 1–7c.
4. After students have found the ordered pair that is the solution to the system of linear equations, they should use that information to answer any specific questions included in the exercise.
5. Discuss Exercise 1 with the class before having students work on other exercises with their partners.

Consider Exercise 1 on Worksheet 1–7c: "At a restaurant the cost for a breakfast taco and a carton of milk is $2.50. The cost for 2 tacos and 3 cartons of milk is $6.00. Write equations for the relationships described, then use graphs of the equations to find the cost of one taco and the cost of one carton of milk."

The two relationships include the 1 taco–1 milk combination and the 2 tacos–3 milks combination. Using T for the taco cost and M for the milk cost, guide students to write the following equations below Exercise 1 on Worksheet 1–7c: (a) $T + M = \$2.50$, and (b) $2T + 3M = \$6.00$. Have students graph each equation on the same copy of Worksheet 1–7b. Ordered pairs for each equation will need to be found by trial and error. Discuss the idea that each algebraic equation may represent a general set of ordered pairs that may or may not make sense in the given situation. For example, students might be able to purchase 2 cartons of milk for $2, but they might not be able to buy 1 taco for $0.50 at the same time, yet ($2, $0.50) is a solution for equation (a). So only specific points on each line might actually relate to the given situation. The graphs might appear as shown:

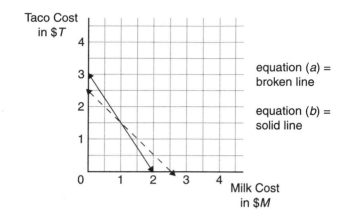

Have students identify the ordered pair for the intersection point of the two lines. It will be $(M, T) = (\$1, \$1.50)$. The intersection point should be circled on the graphs and its ordered pair recorded below Exercise 1. This point belongs to both lines; therefore, it represents the solution to the system of the two equations. That is, it satisfies both relationships in the given situation. Note that it is the only solution shared by both equations.

Students should also verify the solution by substituting the values for M and T into the two equations. The substitutions should be shown on Worksheet 1–7c below Exercise 1 as follows:

(a) $T + M = \$1.50 + \$1 = \$2.50$
(b) $2T + 3M = 2(\$1.50) + 3(\$1) = \$6.00$

Answer Key for Worksheet 1–7c
Only solutions/answers and substitutions are provided; (a) and (b) assignments may vary; no graphs are shown.

1. $(M,T) = (\$1, \$1.50)$; (a) $T + M = \$1.50 + \$1 = \$2.50$, and (b) $2T + 3M = 2(\$1.50) + 3(\$1) = \$6.00$

2. $(x, y) = (3, 1)$; (a) $y = \frac{5}{3}x - 4 = \frac{5}{3}(3) - 4 = 1$, and (b) $y = \frac{-2}{3}x + 3 = \frac{-2}{3}(3) + 3 = 1$

3. $(t, a) = (16, 1200)$; (a) $a = -100t + 2800 = -100(16) + 2800 = 1200$, and (b) $a = 50t + 400 = 50(16) + 400 = 1200$; planes have same altitude 16 minutes after initial siting

4. $(a, c) = (50, 35)$; (a) $a + c = 50 + 35 = 85$ people, and (b) $a(\$5) + c(\$2) = 50(\$5) + 35(\$2) = \$320$; 50 adult tickets were sold

Worksheet 1–7b

Name _____

Date _____

Worksheet 1–7c

Solving Systems of Equations
by Graphing

Name _____

Date _____

Use graphing to find the solution to each system of linear equations or the answer to the exercise. Verify that an ordered pair is a solution to a system by substituting its coordinate values into each equation of the system.

1. At a restaurant, the cost for a breakfast taco and a carton of milk is $2.50. The cost for 2 tacos and 3 cartons of milk is $6.00. Write equations for the relationships described, then use graphs of the equations to find the cost of one taco and the cost of one carton of milk.

2. Graph the line for the equation $y = \frac{5}{3}x - 4$. Graph $y = \frac{-2}{3}x + 3$ on the same grid. What is the solution to this system of equations?

3. At Miami International Airport, plane A is sited at an altitude of 2,800 feet as it descends toward runway 3 at a rate of 100 feet per minute. At the same moment, plane B is sited at 400 feet as it climbs at a rate of 50 feet per minute after taking off from runway 4. In about how many minutes after the initial siting will the two planes be at the same altitude?

4. At a spaghetti supper, band members served 85 people and raised $320. If each adult's ticket was $5 and each child's ticket was $2, how many adult tickets were sold to the supper?

Activity 3
Independent Practice

Materials

Worksheet 1–7d

Grid paper

Regular pencils and regular paper

Procedure

Give each student a copy of Worksheet 1–7d and a sheet of grid paper. Remind students that the solution to a system of equations may be found either by substitution or graphing. When all have finished the worksheet, ask various students to share their solutions and the methods they used to find the solutions.

Answer Key for Worksheet 1–7d

1. D

2. A

3. C

4. B

5. A

Possible Testing Errors That May Occur for This Objective

- When substitution is used to solve a system of equations, students fail to use the distributive property correctly. For example, if $y = 2x + 5$ is substituted in the equation $5x - 3y = 4$, $(-3)(2x + 5)$ is replaced with $-6x + 5$ instead of $-6x - 15$, thereby leading to the wrong solution.

- When the solution to a system of equations is to be found graphically, students incorrectly read the vertical or horizontal scale of the graph when finding the ordered pair for the intersection point of the two lines.

- When given a word problem, students set up linear equations that incorrectly reflect the conditions of the situation.

Worksheet 1–7d

Solving Systems of Equations by Graphing and Substitution

Name _____

Date _____

Solve each exercise provided. Be ready to share your reasoning and your answers with the entire class.

1. What is the x-coordinate of the solution to the system of linear equations $5x + 4y = 8$ and $-3x + 2y = -18$?

    A. -4　　　　B. -3　　　　C. $+3$　　　　D. $+4$

2. In the system of equations $9x + 3y = 6$ and $7x + 3y = 10$, which expression can be correctly substituted for y in the equation $7x + 3y = 10$?

    A. $y = 2 - 3x$　　B. $y = 2 + 3x$　　C. $y = 6 - 3x$　　D. $y = 6 + 3x$

3. In the movie theater parking lot, there are 57 cars and motorcycles altogether. If the wheels are counted on all the vehicles, there are 194 wheels total. How many cars and how many motorcycles are in the parking lot?

    A. 35 cars, 22 motorcycles　　　　C. 40 cars, 17 motorcycles

    B. 28 cars, 29 motorcycles　　　　D. 48 cars, 9 motorcycles

4. At the bakery, Carol bought 5 pieces of fudge and 3 chocolate chip cookies for a total of $5.70. Her friend Juan bought 2 pieces of fudge and 10 chocolate chip cookies, for a total of $3.60. Which system of equations could be used to determine the cost, f, of 1 piece of fudge, and the cost, c, of 1 chocolate chip cookie?

    A. $f + c = 20$　　　　　　　　C. $5f + 2f = \$3.60$

    　　$7f + 13c = \$9.30$　　　　　　　$3c + 10c = \$5.70$

    B. $5f + 3c = \$5.70$　　　　　　D. $5f + 3c = \$3.60$

    　　$2f + 10c = \$3.60$　　　　　　$2f + 10c = \$5.70$

Worksheet 1–7d Continued

Name _____

Date _____

5. Jimmy purchased a math book and a paperback novel for a total of $54 without tax. If the price, M, of the math book is $8 more than 3 times the price, N, of the novel, which graph of a system of linear equations could be used to determine the price of each book?

A.

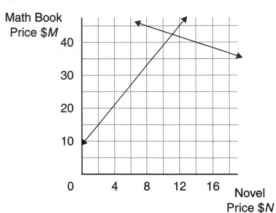

B.

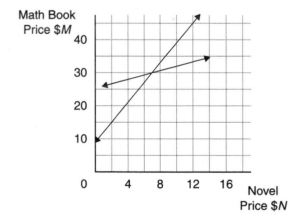

C.

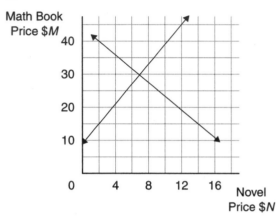

D.

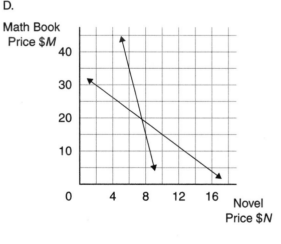

Section 1

Name _____

Date _____

ALGEBRAIC THINKING AND APPLICATIONS: PRACTICE TEST ANSWER SHEET

Directions: Use the answer sheet to darken the letter of the choice that best answers each question.

1. ◯ A ◯ B ◯ C ◯ D   8. ◯ A ◯ B ◯ C ◯ D

2. ◯ A ◯ B ◯ C ◯ D   9. ◯ A ◯ B ◯ C ◯ D

3. ◯ A ◯ B ◯ C ◯ D   10. ◯ A ◯ B ◯ C ◯ D

4. ◯ A ◯ B ◯ C ◯ D   11. ◯ A ◯ B ◯ C ◯ D

5. ◯ A ◯ B ◯ C ◯ D   12. ◯ A ◯ B ◯ C ◯ D

6. ◯ A ◯ B ◯ C ◯ D   13. ◯ A ◯ B ◯ C ◯ D

7. ◯ A ◯ B ◯ C ◯ D   14. ◯ A ◯ B ◯ C ◯ D

Section 1: Algebraic Thinking and Applications: Practice Test

1. The following diagram represents the product of $2N$ rows of $(3N + 5)$. Which expression is equivalent to the total area, $2N(3N + 5)$, of the product diagram?

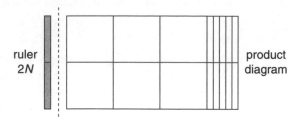

   A. $6N^2 + 5$ B. $6N + 5$ C. $6N^2 + 10N$ D. $6N + 10$

2. Which expression is equivalent to $\left(\dfrac{2}{3}\right)(3x - 6y) + (5y - 8x)$?

   A. $-6x + y$ B. $-2x - y$ C. $-6x - y$ D. $-5x + y$

3. If $A = -21$ is a solution for the equation $-\dfrac{1}{3}A - 10 = -3$, which expression may be used to confirm the solution?

   A. $-\dfrac{1}{3}(+21) - 10$ C. $\dfrac{1}{3}(+21) - 10$

   B. $-\dfrac{1}{3}(-7) - 10$ D. $\dfrac{1}{3}(-21) - 10$

4. Which expression is not a correct interpretation of the expression $-\dfrac{3}{5}p$?

   A. $3\left(-\dfrac{1}{5}p\right)$ B. $-3\left(\dfrac{1}{5}p\right)$ C. $\dfrac{3}{5}(-p)$ D. $\dfrac{-3}{5}(-p)$

5. The Deli-Mart sells 3 cartons of chili for $1.79 total. The total cost, C, of buying N cartons of this same chili can be found by which of the following procedures?

   A. Multiplying N by $1.79   C. Dividing N by $1.79

   B. Dividing N by the cost of   D. Multiplying N by the cost of
        one carton   one carton

6. Carrie has half as many movie passes as Jan. Anna has 5 fewer passes than Jan. Together, the three students have a total of 20 movie passes. Which equation can be used to find how many movie passes Jan (J) has?

   A. $J + 2J + (J - 5) = 20$ C. $\dfrac{1}{2}J + (J + 5) + J = 20$

   B. $\dfrac{1}{2}J + J + (J - 5) = 20$ D. $2J + (J + 5) + J = 20$

Section 1: Practice Test (Continued)

7. Two positive integers have a sum of 73. The lesser number is an even number, and the difference between the two integers is 9. What is the even number?

   A. 32   B. 49   C. 26   D. 73

8. Some vacationers were exiting a tour bus, so Josh and his friends decided to count them in various ways. Each looked for something different. Here are the results: 21 people wore jeans; 18 wore sandals; 14 wore hats; 7, sandals and hat; 11, jeans and sandals; 8, hat and jeans; and 5, hat, jeans, and sandals. Five people did not wear a hat, jeans, or sandals. How many people did Josh and his friends count leaving the bus?

   A. 58   B. 37   C. 53   D. 21

9. A package of three Brand B batteries costs $5.85, and a package of three Brand C batteries costs $4.69. Which proportion can be used to determine the percent, N, of the cost of the Brand B batteries that will be saved if the Brand C batteries are purchased?

   A. $\dfrac{(5.85 - 4.69)}{4.69} = \dfrac{N}{100}$ C. $\dfrac{(5.85 - 4.69)}{5.85} = \dfrac{N}{100}$

   B. $\dfrac{4.69}{5.85} = \dfrac{N}{100}$ D. $\dfrac{5.85}{4.69} = \dfrac{N}{100}$

10. A box contains 18 colored cubes. There are 6 blue cubes, 5 red cubes, and 3 yellow cubes. The rest of the cubes are green. The ratio of green cubes to total cubes is equivalent to which probability for drawing out a green cube at random?

    A. $\dfrac{1}{3}$ B. $\dfrac{5}{18}$ C. $\dfrac{1}{6}$ D. $\dfrac{2}{9}$

11. Which equation describes the line that passes through the point (1, –5) and is parallel to the line represented by the equation $-3x + y = -4$?

    A. $y = 3x - 8$ B. $y = \dfrac{1}{3}x - 4$ C. $y = 3x + 1$ D. $y = -\dfrac{1}{3}x + 5$

90

Section 1: Practice Test (Continued)

12. Which pair of equations represents the perpendicular lines shown on the graph? (1 grid segment = 1 unit)

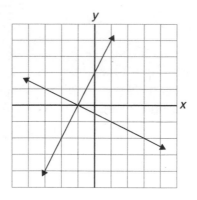

   A. $y = 2x + 2$ and $y = -2x + 2$

   B. $y = -0.5x - 1$ and $y = 2x - 1$

   C. $y = 2x + 2$ and $y = -0.5x - 0.5$

   D. $y = 2x + 2$ and $y = -2x - 1$

13. At the bakery, Carol bought 3 pieces of fudge and 8 chocolate chip cookies, for a total of $4.35. Her friend Juan bought 2 pieces of fudge and 10 chocolate chip cookies for a total of $3.60. Which system of equations could be used to determine the cost, f, of 1 piece of fudge, and the cost, c, of 1 chocolate chip cookie?

   A. $f + c = 23$
   $5f + 18c = \$7.95$

   C. $3f + 2f = \$3.60$
   $8c + 10c = \$4.35$

   B. $3f + 8c = \$4.35$
   $2f + 10c = \$3.60$

   D. $3f + 8c = \$3.60$
   $2f + 10c = \$4.35$

14. What is the x-coordinate of the solution to the system of linear equations $3x + 4y = -8$ and $-2x - 2y = 6$?

   A. +1   B. +4   C. –1   D. –4

Section 1: Algebraic Thinking and Applications:
Answer Key for Practice Test

The objective being tested is shown in brackets beside the answer.

1. C [1]	8. B [4]
2. A [1]	9. C [5]
3. C [2]	10. D [5]
4. D [2]	11. A [6]
5. D [3]	12. C [6]
6. B [3]	13. B [7]
7. A [4]	14. D [7]

Graphs, Statistics, and Probability

Objective 1: Find the Probability of a Compound Event (Independent or Dependent)

A *compound* event occurs when more than one characteristic is being used to describe a set of outcomes. The event may be described with the connectors *and*, *or*, or *not*, using a list of qualities found in the same sample space (for example, "red *and* striped"). Sometimes the situation involves more than one action, such as turning a spinner and rolling a die simultaneously, so that an outcome consists of two or more actions. In any case, students need to be able to identify the outcomes in the sample space. Once that is done, they should be able to find the outcomes that satisfy a particular event description. The following activities provide experience with sample spaces that allow compound events. Special formulas will not be emphasized.

Activity 1
Manipulative Stage

Materials

Bags of colored square tiles (1 bag per pair of students; 4 tiles per bag: red, blue, yellow, green)
Worksheet 2–1a
Regular paper and pencil

Procedure

1.   Give each pair of students a bag of 4 colored tiles (1 red, 1 blue, 1 yellow, and 1 green) and two copies of Worksheet 2–1a.

2.   Have students draw 2 tiles out of the bag without looking, drawing out 1 tile at a time and <u>not replacing</u> the first tile into the bag after it is drawn. They should record the colors of the pair after each draw. For example, a red tile may be drawn first, followed by a blue tile. The pair of tiles should be recorded in the order drawn: (red, blue). After the pair is recorded, the 2 tiles should be returned to the bag and another drawing made. The list of pairs drawn will form Sample Space #1 to be used with Worksheet 2–1a.

3.   Students should continue drawing until they no longer draw out a new pair. No repeats should be recorded in the list for the sample space. Because the order of the draw is considered, (red, blue) and (blue, red) do not represent the same pair.

4.   When a pair of students thinks they have a complete sample space, confirm that they have 12 pairs in their list. Then have them find the probabilities on Worksheet 2–1a that apply to Sample Space #1.

5. Have students repeat the above process, but this time the first tile of the drawing should be <u>replaced</u> into the bag before the second tile is drawn. This allows the pairs—(red, red), (blue, blue), (yellow, yellow), and (green, green)—to be counted. The new list of pairs found will represent Sample Space #2 on Worksheet 2–1a.

6. When students think they have a complete Sample Space #2, confirm that their list has 16 pairs. Then have them find the probabilities on Worksheet 2–1a that apply to Sample Space #2.

7. After all students have completed the worksheet, have them compare the probabilities for the same event description but from different sample spaces. When the probabilities differ, discuss the reason for the difference (the <u>replacement</u> of the first tile before drawing the second tile changes the choices for the second draw, thereby changing what the final pair might be). Have students write a statement at the bottom of Worksheet 2–1a about why these probabilities differ. When the first tile is replaced, the drawing of the second tile is *independent* of the drawing of the first tile. If the first tile is <u>not replaced</u>, the drawing of the second tile is *dependent* on the drawing of the first tile.

As an example of a probability, consider Exercise 1 on Worksheet 2–1a: "P(1st red or 2nd blue) = _____." The notation for the event means that the first tile will be red OR the second tile will be blue in the outcomes (pairs) being sought.

This exercise applies to Sample Space #1, where the first tile was not replaced before the second tile was drawn out of the bag. Have students look at their list of pairs for Sample Space #1. They should find all pairs that show the <u>first tile to be red</u>: (red, blue), (red, green), and (red, yellow).

Since the connector OR is used, the outcomes (pairs, here) that satisfy each separate description should be combined together without any repeats. Therefore, students also need to find all pairs that show the <u>second tile to be blue,</u> but they should not include any pairs already counted in the set where the first tile is red. So (red, blue) will not be counted in this second set. New pairs to include will be (green, blue) and (yellow, blue).

Combining the pairs from the two sets, there will be 3 + 2, or 5, pairs from Sample Space #1 that satisfy the event: first tile red or second tile blue. Since there are 12 pairs in the sample space, the probability for this event will be $\frac{5}{12}$; that is, there will be 5 ways out of 12 ways that a drawn pair might have red for the first tile or blue for the second tile. Students should record $\frac{5}{12}$ in the blank for Exercise 1 on Worksheet 2–1a.

Answer Key for Worksheet 2–1a

1. $\frac{5}{12}$

2. $\frac{6}{12}$ or $\frac{1}{2}$

3. $\frac{1}{12}$

4. $\frac{2}{12}$ or $\frac{1}{6}$

5. $\frac{0}{12}$ or 0

6. $\frac{9}{12}$ or $\frac{3}{4}$

7. $\frac{7}{16}$

8. $\frac{8}{16}$ or $\frac{1}{2}$

9. $\frac{1}{16}$

10. $\frac{2}{16}$ or $\frac{1}{8}$

11. $\frac{1}{16}$

12. $\frac{12}{16}$ or $\frac{3}{4}$

Worksheet 2–1a

Finding Probabilities Using
AND, OR, and NOT

Name _____

Date _____

Use 4 colored tiles to build Sample Spaces #1 and #2. Find the required probabilities for each sample space, using fractions. Reduce the fractions when possible.

For Sample Space #1 (drawing without replacement):

1. P(1st red or 2nd blue) = _____

2. P(1st blue or yellow) = _____

3. P(1st green and 2nd red) = _____

4. P(one is red and one is yellow) = _____

5. P(both are blue) = _____

6. P(2nd not yellow) = _____

For Sample Space #2 (drawing with replacement):

7. P(1st red or 2nd blue) = _____

8. P(1st blue or yellow) = _____

9. P(1st green and 2nd red) = _____

10. P(one is red and one is yellow) = _____

11. P(both are blue) = _____

12. P(2nd not yellow) = _____

Explain in your own words why probabilities for the same event seem to differ for Sample Space #1 and Sample Space #2.

Activity 2
Pictorial Stage

Materials
    Cards Pattern 2–1a (1 per pair of students)
    Scissors (1 pair per student)
    Worksheet 2–1b
    Regular pencils

Procedure
    1. Give each pair of students a copy of the Cards Pattern 2–1a and two pairs of scissors. Also give each student a copy of Worksheet 2–1b.

    2. Students should cut apart the cards on the pattern sheet, then sort them according to the characteristics described on Worksheet 2–1b. Each card is labeled with a letter to help students communicate about the cards easily.

    3. For each event stated in an exercise on Worksheet 2–1b, students should find which cards satisfy the event, then determine the probability that this event will occur when one card is randomly drawn from the set. A fraction comparing the number of cards for the event to the 12 cards total in the set should be written in the blank provided on Worksheet 2–1b. Fractions may be reduced when possible.

    4. After all student pairs have completed the worksheet, have several students share their results with the entire class.

    5. Exercise 6 on Worksheet 2–1b is discussed here as an example.

Exercise 6 on Worksheet 2–1b asks students to find P(striped OR shaded) and P(not striped AND not shaded), using the card set.

Students must first sort their set of cards according to the two characteristics in the event: "striped OR shaded." They should form one pile of cards that contains stripes, along with any additional cards that are shaded but not striped. If a card has stripes or if it is shaded, it will go in this pile. There will be 7 cards in this pile (cards A, B, C, F, G, H, and K), so P(striped OR shaded) will equal $\frac{7}{12}$. Students should record $\frac{7}{12}$ in the first blank for Exercise 6 on Worksheet 2–1b.

The remaining cards will form another pile where each card does NOT belong to the "striped OR shaded" group. That is, they are the *complement* of the first group of cards. Have students confirm that each card in this second group will also satisfy the second event listed in Exercise 6; that is, each card will simultaneously not have stripes AND not be shaded. There are 5 cards (cards D, E, I, J, and L) in this second group, so P(not stripes AND not shaded) will equal $\frac{5}{12}$. Students should record $\frac{5}{12}$ in the second blank for Exercise 6 on Worksheet 2–1b.

The two disjoint card groups used to find the two probabilities for Exercise 6 demonstrate that one group is the complement of the other. Together they form the entire card set. Thus, the two events that those cards satisfy are complements of each other. The results of this exercise also indicate that NOT (striped OR shaded) is equivalent to (not striped) AND (not shaded). Exercises 4, 5, and 7 show similar results.

Answer Key for Worksheet 2–1b

1. $\frac{2}{12}$ or $\frac{1}{6}$ (card L is considered plain, no dots); $\frac{10}{12}$ or $\frac{5}{6}$

2. $\frac{5}{12}$; $\frac{7}{12}$

3. $\frac{7}{12}$; $\frac{5}{12}$

4. $\frac{1}{12}$; $\frac{11}{12}$

5. $\frac{2}{12}$ or $\frac{1}{6}$; $\frac{10}{12}$ or $\frac{5}{6}$

6. $\frac{7}{12}$; $\frac{5}{12}$

7. $\frac{5}{12}$; $\frac{7}{12}$

Cards Pattern 2–1a

Cut cards apart.

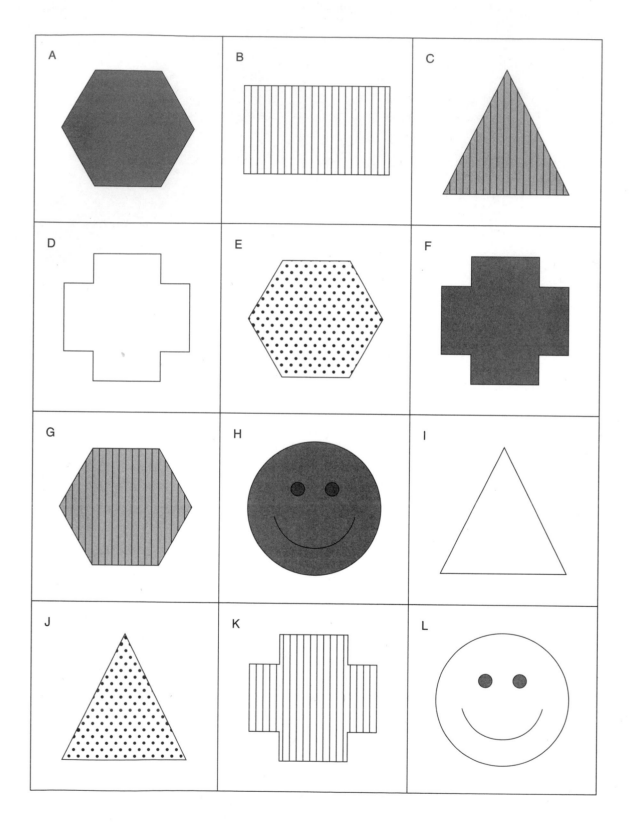

Worksheet 2–1b

Compound Events with
AND, OR, and NOT

Name _____

Date _____

Assume one card is to be drawn randomly from the given set of cards. Find the cards that satisfy each event's descriptors in order to find the probability for that event to occur when one card is drawn. Record the probability as a fraction in the blank provided.

1. P(dotted) = _____

    P(not dotted) = _____

2. P(shaded) = _____

    P(not shaded) = _____

3. P(more than 3 sides) = _____

    P(not more than 3 sides) = _____

4. P(plain AND 3 sides) = _____

    P(not plain OR not 3 sides) = _____

5. P(striped AND shaded) = _____

    P(not striped OR not shaded) = _____

6. P(striped OR shaded) = _____

    P(not striped AND not shaded) = _____

7. P(dotted OR plain) = _____

    P(not dotted AND not plain) = _____

Activity 3
Independent Practice

Materials
Worksheet 2–1c
Regular pencil

Procedure
Give each student a copy of Worksheet 2–1c to complete. Encourage students to identify a sample space before finding probabilities based on that sample space. Remind students to reduce fractions to lowest terms when possible. When all have finished, have various students share their reasoning and answers with the entire class.

Answer Key for Worksheet 2–1c
1. C

2. A

3. B

4. D

5. B

Possible Testing Errors That May Occur for This Objective
* When OR is used in an event, students count the outcomes for each characteristic listed, then add the two amounts together without deleting the repeated outcomes. This results in a probability that is too high.

* When the word NOT is included in the event description, students ignore it and select an outcome that HAS the stated characteristic. For example, if the event requires shapes that are NOT rectangles, students will count only the *rectangles* to find the probability.

* When an event describes outcomes that satisfy two or more characteristics, students will choose outcomes with only one of the required characteristics. For example, if "red AND square" is required, students will select a red shape that is not a square or select a square that is not red.

Worksheet 2–1c   Name _____

Probabilities of Compound Events   Date _____

Complete the following exercises.

1. The faces of a cube are labeled 1 through 6. A spinner has 4 equal sectors, each sector labeled with a color: red, purple, blue, or yellow. If the spinner and the cube are used together in a game, what is the probability that a player will spin the color blue and then roll a 3 or 4 during a turn at play?

   A. $\frac{1}{2}$ B. $\frac{1}{4}$ C. $\frac{1}{12}$ D. $\frac{1}{24}$

2. At a pep rally, 1 senior, 1 junior, and 2 sophomores are seated randomly together in a row. What is the probability that the 2 sophomores are seated next to each other?

   A. $\frac{1}{2}$ B. $\frac{1}{3}$ C. $\frac{1}{4}$ D. $\frac{1}{12}$

3. The Venn diagram shows how many of the 300 students at Wells Middle School have a scooter only, a skateboard only, or both a scooter and a skateboard. Use the information in the diagram to find the probability that 1 student chosen randomly will not have a scooter or a skateboard.

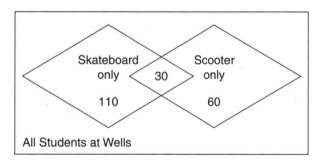

   A. $\frac{1}{30}$ B. $\frac{1}{3}$ C. $\frac{2}{3}$ D. $\frac{6}{11}$

4. A box contains 12 colored disks. There are 3 red disks, 7 yellow disks, and 2 blue disks. If 1 disk is randomly drawn from the box, what is the probability that the disk will be blue or yellow?

   A. $\frac{1}{12}$ B. $\frac{5}{12}$ C. $\frac{2}{9}$ D. $\frac{3}{4}$

5. If two coins are tossed together without order, find P(two heads tossed).

   A. 0   B. $\frac{1}{3}$ C. $\frac{2}{3}$ D. Not here

Objective 2: Interpret the Actions Represented by a Linear or a Quadratic Graph or a Scatter Plot

Linear functions involve constant rates of change, whereas nonlinear functions do not. Students need experience recognizing the graphs and the tables of values for both types of functions. The activities for this objective provide these needed experiences.

Activity 1
Manipulative Stage

Materials

1-inch square tiles (commercial or teacher-made; 100 tiles per pair of students)
Worksheet 2–2a
Red pencil and regular pencil

Procedure

1. Give each pair of students two copies of Worksheet 2–2a, a red pencil, and a packet of 100 inch-square tiles. The tile color is not important.

2. For each exercise on Worksheet 2–2a, students will build different rows of tiles, varying the row length according to the directions given in the exercise.

3. For each exercise, students will plot points on the grid to represent their data found, using ordered pairs of the type: (number of the row, total tiles in the row). For each grid, the vertical axis will need to be labeled "Total Tiles" and marked off with an appropriate scale. The horizontal axis is already numbered for the number of the row built.

4. Students will use a red pencil to connect, in order, the 5 points plotted on each grid. The 5 plotted points should not be connected to the origin of the grid, however, since there is no ordered pair included for that point.

5. After all exercises are completed, discuss the appearance of each red path drawn. If there is a *constant* change in the total amount of tiles occurring from row to row, the red path will be straight. This is a characteristic of a *linear function*. If the red path is not straight but appears to curve upward smoothly, the points belong to a *quadratic function*.

6. Discuss Exercise 1 on Worksheet 2–2a with the entire class before allowing students to work the other exercises on their own.

Consider Exercise 1 on Worksheet 2–2a: "Row 1: 4 tiles. For each new row, increase previous tiles by 3."

Have students build a row of 4 tiles for row 1. Then below that row they should build another row with 4 + 3, or 7 tiles; this is row 2. For row 3, have them build a row of 7 + 3, or 10 tiles. Row 4 will have 10 + 3, or 13 tiles, and row 5 will have 13 + 3, or 16 tiles. Here is the final arrangement of the tiles:

Below Exercise 1, have students list in a column to the left of the grid the ordered pairs that represent the rows and their amounts of tiles: (1, 4), (2, 7), (3, 10), (4, 13), and (5, 16). Then points should be plotted on the grid to represent the ordered pairs. The vertical axis should be numbered with multiples of 2 to accommodate the range of values from 4 to 16 and should be labeled "Total Tiles." The points should then be connected in red pencil, forming a straight path. This indicates that the points belong to a set of points called a *linear function*. Do not connect the points to the origin of the grid. Here is the completed grid:

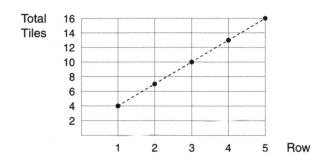

Answer Key for Worksheet 2–2a
The completed graphs are not shown.

1. linear: (1, 4), (2, 7), (3, 10), (4, 13), (5, 16)

2. quadratic: (1, 2), (2, 5), (3, 10), (4, 17), (5, 26)

3. linear: (1, 0), (2, 4), (3, 8), (4, 12), (5, 16)

104

Worksheet 2–2a   Name _____

Building Functions with   Date _____
Square Tiles

Build with square tiles to make 5 different rows as directed in each exercise. Plot points on each grid for ordered pairs found, and connect the points with red pencil. Identify the path type found.

1. Row 1: 4 tiles. For each new row, increase previous tiles by 3.

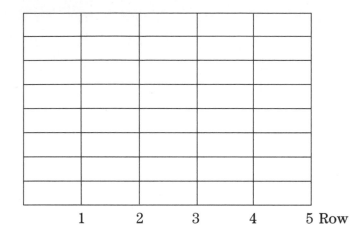

      1   2   3   4   5 Row

2. Row 1: 2 tiles. For each new row, square row # and add 1 tile.

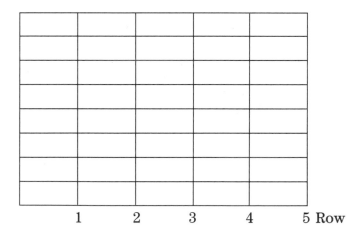

      1   2   3   4   5 Row

Name _____ ____

Date _____

3. Row 1: 0 tiles. For each new row, increase previous tiles by 4.

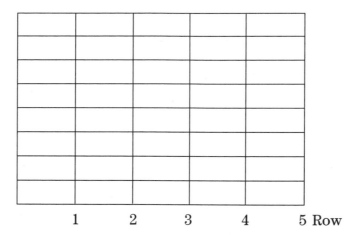

Activity 2
Pictorial Stage

Materials
    Worksheet 2–2b
    Red pencil and regular pencil
    5-millimeter or -centimeter grid paper
    Ruler (inch or centimeter)

Procedure
    1. Give each student a copy of Worksheet 2–2b, a ruler, two sheets of grid paper, and a red pencil.
    2. For each exercise, have students find the ordered pairs needed, and record them in a table. They should then plot points for the ordered pairs on their grid paper. Guide them to properly label and mark the two axes of each grid.
    3. Have students use a ruler to draw a path in red pencil to connect adjacent pairs of plotted points for each exercise. Do not connect to the origin unless that point is included in the list of ordered pairs for the exercise.
    4. Discuss the idea that some of the resulting graphs of points will form straight paths while others will not. The graphs that are <u>straight</u> represent *linear functions*, which are special sets of ordered pairs. The other graphs will be *nonlinear functions*, including *quadratic* functions.
    5. Have students identify how the first numbers change and how the second numbers change within the table of ordered pairs for each exercise. As the first numbers (abscissa) increase by the same amount each time, the second number (ordinate) will also change by a <u>constant</u> amount if the ordered pairs belong to a *linear function*. If the second number is found by squaring the first number or multiplying previous first numbers in some way so that the change in the second number is not constant each time but increases continually, then the ordered pairs belong to a *quadratic function*.
    6. Discuss Exercise 1 on Worksheet 2–2b with the class before allowing students to work on their own.

    Here is Exercise 1 to consider: "Audrey needs to buy ears of corn to sell at the school concession stand. The Farmers' Market has the following price table. Will Audrey save on the cost per ear of corn by buying larger quantities?"

Number of ears	10	20	30	40
Total cost	$3	$6	$9	$12

    Have students prepare a grid with "Number of Ears" as the horizontal axis and "Total Cost" as the vertical axis. The horizontal axis should be numbered from 0 to 40, and the vertical axis should be numbered from $0 to $12. Points should be plotted on the grid to represent the ordered pairs from the table: (10, $3), (20, $6), (30, $9), and (40, $12). The points should then be connected in red pencil, using a ruler to join each pair of adjacent points. The final red path should be straight.

Ask students to look at the numbers in each row of the table and notice how those numbers change from one column to the next. In the top row, the numbers increase by 10 each time. In the bottom row, the amounts increase by $3 each time. Now ask students to look at the graph of the four points and notice how the horizontal distance of each point changes to that of the next point to the right: a <u>constant</u> change of 10 occurs horizontally. Similarly, the vertical distance from one point to the next will change by 3 units each time: there is a <u>constant</u> change of 3 vertically. These constant changes produce the <u>straight</u> graph.

These constant changes in both directions on the graph, as well as on the table, indicate that every 10 ears of corn will cost $3, no matter how many ears Audrey buys. Students should now write below Exercise 1 a response similar to the following: "Each price in the table is based on every 10 ears of corn costing $3, so Audrey will not save by buying larger quantities of corn." Here is the completed graph:

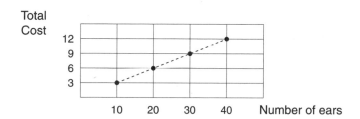

Answer Key for Worksheet 2–2b

1. (10, $3), (20, $6), (30, $9), (40, $12)

    Each price in the table is based on every 10 ears of corn costing $3, so Audrey will not save by buying larger quantities of corn.

2. (1, 5), (2, 8), (3, 12), (4, 14), (5, 20)

    The ordered pairs certainly form a function, but do not represent a linear function (not straight path) or a quadratic function (not continually upward path). Their graph is simply called a *scatter plot*.

3. (2000, $5), (2001, $10), (2002, $15), (2003, $20), (2004, $25)

    Each year the price increases by $5, so in 4 more years, the price will increase by $4 \times $5, or $20, making the new price $25 + $20, or $45 in 2008. The ordered pairs form a linear function.

4. (1, $25), (2, $35), (3, $55), (4, $85)

    The ordered pairs represent a quadratic function because their graph is a continually increasing curve. The path of the points is not straight, so the ordered pairs do not form a linear function. The value of C is increasing, but the change in C is not constant.

Worksheet 2–2b   Name _____

Graphing Linear Functions and   Date _____
Nonlinear Functions

For each exercise, prepare a table of values when needed. Plot points on grid paper for all ordered pairs in the table, and connect the points with red pencil. Label the axes of each graph appropriately. Answer the questions, and justify your answers.

1. Audrey needs to buy ears of corn to sell at the school concession stand. The Farmers' Market has the following price table. Will Audrey save on the cost per ear of corn by buying larger quantities?

Number of ears	10	20	30	40
Total cost	$3	$6	$9	$12

2. Plot the given ordered pairs on a grid, and connect the points to form a path. Do the ordered pairs represent a *linear function* or a *quadratic function*? Explain your answer.

X	1	2	3	4	5
Y	5	8	12	14	20

3. Plot the following ordered pairs on a grid: (2000, $5), (2001, $10), (2002, $15), (2003, $20), (2004, $25). If the price per year continues to increase at a constant rate, predict what the price might be in 2008. Explain your reasoning.

4. The cost, C, for repairing and replastering a room wall is found by the formula $C = \$5y(y - 1) + \$25$, where y is the wall length in feet (wall height is constant). Prepare a table of values for C, using $y = 1, 2, 3,$ and 4, and plot the ordered pairs (y, C) on a grid. Do the ordered pairs represent a *linear function* or a *quadratic function*? Explain your answer.

Activity 3
Independent Practice

Materials

Worksheet 2–2c
Regular pencil

Procedure

Give each student a copy of Worksheet 2–2c to complete. Remind students that a set of ordered pairs, whose graph is a straight path, will be called a *linear function*. A special feature of a linear function is the *constant* change in the dependent value (ordinate) as the independent value (abscissa) changes by some constant, for example, by 1 each time. This constant change may be negative, thereby causing a <u>decrease</u> in the dependent values rather than an increase. Often the known change allows us to predict the dependent values for larger independent values not provided in an initial table of values. Some quadratic and other nonlinear functions are also included on the worksheet. Using a simplistic definition, quadratic functions will have continually increasing or decreasing changes, but not constant changes, in the dependent values. After students have finished the worksheet, have various students share their results with the entire class.

Answer Key for Worksheet 2–2c

1. B

2. C

3. B

4. A

5. D

6. Missing pairs: (5, 150), (6, 210)

Possible Testing Errors That May Occur for This Objective

- Students will plot the ordered pairs incorrectly, using the first number as the vertical distance and the second number as the horizontal distance on the grid.

- When looking for a pattern in a table of values, students will find the difference between the first two numbers in a row (or column) and assume that all other adjacent pairs in that row (or column) have the same difference. This would be incorrect reasoning in cases of nonlinear functions.

- When the constant of change is known and students need to complete a table based on that change, they will use incorrect facts when computing the missing entries for the table.

110

Solving Word Problems About
Linear and Nonlinear Functions

Name _____

Date _____

Solve each exercise provided.

1. Which store's price table is based on a constant unit price for CDs?

A

Number of CDs	2	4	6	8
Total cost	$10	$15	$18	$20

B

Number of CDs	2	4	6	8
Total cost	$10	$20	$30	$40

C

Number of CDs	2	4	6	8
Total cost	$5	$8	$12	$17

D

Number of CDs	2	4	6	8
Total cost	$5	$10	$15	$18

2. The graph of the line representing $y = 3x + 1$ is drawn on the coordinate grid to the right below. Which table contains only ordered pairs for points on this line? (grid segment = 1 unit)

A

x	−2	−1	+1	+2
y	−5	−2	0	+3

B

x	−1	0	+2	+3
y	−2	+1	+3	−1

C

x	−2	−1	0	+1
y	−5	−2	+1	+4

D

x	−2	−1	0	+2
y	0	−2	+1	+4

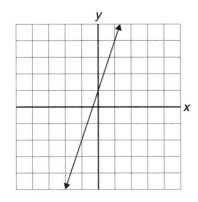

Worksheet 2–2c Continued

Name _____ _____

Date _____

3. A new baseball card was worth $4 in the year 2000. The table shows its value each year for several years after its issue. Based on the table's information, what is a reasonable prediction of the card's value in 2006?

Year	2000	2001	2002	2003
Value of card	$4.00	$4.40	$4.85	$5.35

A. Between $8 and $9

C. Between $6 and $7

B. Between $7 and $8

D. Between $5 and $6

4. Which set of ordered pairs represents a quadratic function?

A. (2, 9), (3, 14), (4, 21), (5, 30)

C. (2, 5), (4, 10), (6, 15), (8, 20)

B. (3, 8), (4, 8), (5, 10), (6, 14)

D. (3, 4), (4, 3), (5, 2), (6, 1)

5. Which set of ordered pairs for (week #, average weekly temperature) does not reflect a constant change in temperature?

A. (1, 80), (2, 84), (3, 88), (4, 92)

C. (1, 98), (2, 95), (3, 92), (4, 89)

B. (1, 55), (2, 56), (3, 57), (4, 58)

D. (1, 75), (2, 84), (3, 79), (4, 81)

6. Complete the table so that its ordered pairs represent a quadratic function.

Number of cookies	1	2	3	4	5	
Total cost in cents	10	30	60	100		

Objective 3: Find the Ordered Pairs for the *x*- and *y*-Intercepts of a Given Linear Equation in Two Variables Either Algebraically or Graphically

Intercepts in real-world situations typically represent the *initial conditions* for the situation, for example, before the action begins or when the time is 0 minutes and the distance is 0 feet. Students need to be able to apply these initial values in order to solve a given problem. Learning how to find ordered pairs for the intercepts by substituting 0 for a variable in an equation or by locating an intercept on an axis of a graph is essential.

Activity 1
Manipulative Stage

Materials

Geoboards with rubber bands (1 board per two students)
Rulers
Worksheet 2–3a
Regular pencils

Procedure

1. Give each pair of students two copies of Worksheet 2–3a, a geoboard with 4 or 5 rubber bands, and a ruler. Discuss the correct way to hook a rubber band on the geoboard. For example, a finger should be placed on top of a peg holding one end of the rubber band while the other end of the rubber band is stretched and looped over another selected peg. This prevents any "flying missiles" in the classroom. The lower left corner of the geoboard is assumed to be the origin.

2. For each exercise on Worksheet 2–3a, students should connect the two pegs for the two given points with a rubber band on the geoboard. The ruler should be aligned with the two pegs and positioned to cross one or both of the axes, whichever is possible.

3. Have students identify the ordered pairs for the intersection points on the vertical and the horizontal axes of the geoboard. These ordered pairs should be recorded below the exercise on Worksheet 2–3a. Since only the first quadrant is used on the geoboard, both intercepts may not be found for some exercises. Write "N.A." (not applicable) in the blank for the intercept not found. Discuss the idea that the vertical intercept is also named with the letter *b*, and just the value of the ordinate of the ordered pair is used, for example, *b* = +3. The equation for *b* should also be recorded below the exercise on the worksheet.

4. Discuss Exercise 1 on Worksheet 2–3a before having students work the other exercises with their partners.

Consider Exercise 1 on Worksheet 2–3a:

(2, 2) and (4, 3)

x-intercept: _____

y-intercept: _____

or $b =$ _____

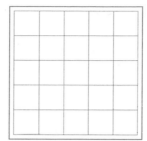

Students should plot the two ordered pairs on the frame shown in the exercise. Then they should locate and connect the corresponding pegs on the geoboard with a rubber band. Remind students that the lower left corner of the geoboard and of the frame is the origin. The ruler should be aligned with the two pegs to show where the intercepts will be. In Exercise 1, the ruler will not cross the x-axis of the first quadrant, so "N.A." should be recorded in the blank for the x-intercept below the exercise. The ruler will cross the y-axis at (0, 1), so students should record (0, 1) in the blank for the y-intercept and record +1 in the blank for the value of b. Here is how the geoboard and ruler should appear:

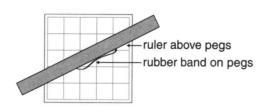

ruler above pegs

rubber band on pegs

Answer Key for Worksheet 2–3a

1. x: N.A.; y: (0, 1); $b = 1$

2. x: (3, 0); y: (0, 3); $b = 3$

3. x: (1, 0); y: N.A.; no b value

4. x: (2, 0); y: (0, 4); $b = 4$

5. x: (0, 0); y: (0, 0); $b = 0$

114

Worksheet 2–3a

Name _____

Using Geoboards to Find Intercepts
of Linear Functions

Date _____

For each exercise, mark the two given points on the frame shown on the worksheet.
Place a rubber band on the geoboard to locate the same two points. Use a ruler on the
geoboard to find any x-intercept or y-intercept that belongs to the same linear function
as the given points. Mark any intercept on the worksheet frame, and record its ordered
pair below the exercise. Also use the b-format to record the y-intercept.

1. (2, 2) and (4, 3)

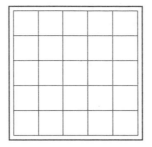

x-intercept: _____

y-intercept: _____

b = _____

2. (1, 2) and (2, 1)

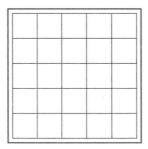

x-intercept: _____

y-intercept: _____

b = _____

Worksheet 2–3a Continued

Name _____

Date _____

3. (3, 2) and (4, 3)

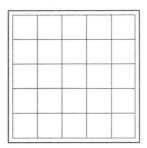

       x-intercept: _____

       y-intercept: _____

             b = _____

4. (1, 2) and (2, 0)

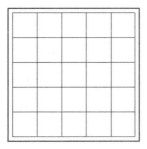

       x-intercept: _____

       y-intercept: _____

              b = _____

5. (2, 2) and (4, 4)

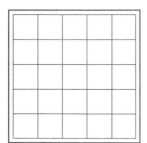

       x-intercept: _____

       y-intercept: _____

              b = _____

Activity 2
Pictorial Stage

Materials

Worksheet 2–3b
Rulers
Regular pencils and paper

Procedure

1.   Give each pair of students two copies of Worksheet 2–3b and a ruler.

2.   For each exercise on Worksheet 2–3b, have students plot two or more points on the grid that satisfy the linear equation, then use the ruler to draw the line that represents the equation.

3.   Students should extend the line to the vertical and the horizontal axes, if necessary, and then circle the points that are the intercepts. They should test the ordered pairs identified as the intercepts in order to be sure that the pairs are solutions to the given linear equation. The correct ordered pairs should then be recorded in the appropriate places below the exercise on the worksheet.

4.   Discuss Exercise 1 with the entire class before having students work with partners to complete the other exercises.

Consider Exercise 1 on Worksheet 2–3b: "$3y - 2x = -6$."

Have students find at least two ordered pairs that will satisfy the linear equation. For example, they might find $(-3, -4)$ and $(1.5, -1)$. Each ordered pair should be tested by substitution in the original equation as follows: $3(-4) - 2(-3) = -6$ and $3(-1) - 2(1.5) = -6$. Once the points have been verified, students should use the ruler to draw a line through the two points and, if necessary, extend the line so that it crosses both axes. Each intercept point should be circled. Here is a sample graph of the extended line:

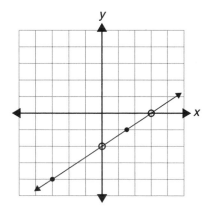

Have students identify the circled intercepts and confirm them as solutions to the original equation. The x-intercept will be $(3, 0)$, and the y-intercept will be $(0, -2)$. Using substitution again, students should write the following: $3(0) - 2(3) = -6$ and $3(-2) - 2(0) = -6$. Since equality holds in each equation, the intercept pairs belong to the line. Students should record the intercept pairs in their proper places below Exercise 1. Remind students that the single letter b is another name for the y-intercept, so $b = -2$ should also be recorded below Exercise 1.

Because the computation is easy, it is possible that some students have already been trained to use $x = 0$ and $y = 0$ to find ordered pairs for a given linear equation. These values produce the two intercepts immediately. If students use this approach, ask them to find one or two additional points as well. This will reinforce the idea that there are other points forming the line besides the two intercepts being requested.

Answer Key for Worksheet 2–3b
The completed graphs are not shown.

1. x-intercept: $(3, -0)$; y-intercept: $(0, -2)$; $b = -2$

2. x-intercept: $(-2, 0)$; y-intercept: $(0, -1)$; $b = -1$

3. x-intercept: $(4, 0)$; y-intercept: $(0, 2)$; $b = 2$

4. x-intercept: $(0, 0)$; y-intercept: $(0, 0)$; $b = 0$

Worksheet 2–3b   Name _____

Using Graphs to Find Intercepts   Date _____
of Linear Functions

For each exercise, graph the given linear equation on the grid. Extend the line so that it crosses the x-axis and the y-axis, if appropriate. Identify the ordered pairs for the two intercepts, and verify the pairs as solutions, then record the pairs below the exercise. Record the value for b as well.

1. $3y - 2x = -6$

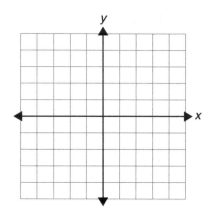

x-intercept: _____

y-intercept: _____

b = _____

2. $x + 2y = -2$

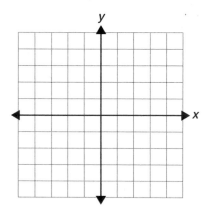

x-intercept: _____

y-intercept: _____

b = _____

Worksheet 2–3b Continued

Name _____ ___

Date _____

3. $4y + 2x = 8$

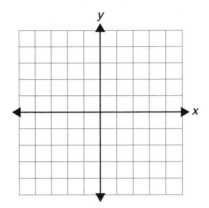

x-intercept: _____

y-intercept: _____

$b =$ _____

4. $-3x + y = 0$

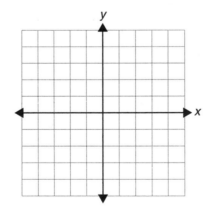

x-intercept: _____

y-intercept: _____

$b =$ _____

Activity 3
Independent Practice

Materials

Worksheet 2–3c
Grid paper
Regular pencils and paper

Procedure

Give each student a copy of Worksheet 2–3c and a sheet of grid paper. Remind students that graphing or substitution may be used to help them find the intercepts of a linear equation. When all have finished the worksheet, ask various students to share their results with the entire class.

Answer Key for Worksheet 2–3c

1. C

2. B

3. D

4. A

5. B

Possible Testing Errors That May Occur for This Objective

- Students may correctly locate an intercept point on a graph and identify its ordered pair, but name it by the wrong axis. For example, the ordered pair (3, 0) on the x-axis is incorrectly called the y-intercept.

- When given an equation to graph, students will find and graph incorrect ordered pairs for the equation, thus producing the wrong intercepts.

- When using substitution to find an intercept, students will apply the wrong ordered pair for the requested intercept. For example, if the y-intercept is needed for $2x + 5y = 7$, students will substitute $y = 0$ in the equation and solve for x, instead of using $x = 0$ and solving for y.

Worksheet 2–3c

Finding Intercepts of Linear
Functions

Name _____

Date _____

Solve each exercise provided. Be ready to share your reasoning and answers with the entire class.

1. Which coordinate points represent the x- and the y-intercepts of the graph shown here?

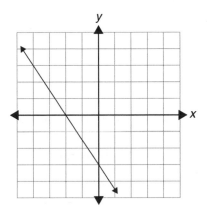

    A. $(0, -2)$ and $(0, -3)$

    B. $(-2, 0)$ and $(-3, 0)$

    C. $(0, -3)$ and $(-2, 0)$

    D. $(3, 0)$ and $(0, 2)$

2. What is the y-intercept of the line that represents $3y - x = -12$?

    A. $b = -12$ B. $b = -4$ C. $b = +3$ D. $b = +4$

3. Find the x-intercept for the equation $4y - 3x = 24$.

    A. $(8, 0)$ B. $(0, 6)$ C. $(6, 0)$ D. $(-8, 0)$

Worksheet 2–3c Continued

Name ______________________

Date ______________________

4. A plumber charges for repair work according to the formula $C = \$45 + T(\$55)$, where C is the total cost for a repair and T is the time in hours needed to make the repair. If T is the independent variable, what does \$45 represent in the graph of this formula?

   A. vertical axis intercept
   B. origin
   C. horizontal axis intercept
   D. slope

5. A store offers 500 bikes on sale. Twenty-five bikes are sold per day, and the last bike is sold on the twentieth day of the sale. If the data pairs (day of sale, # bikes left) were graphed, which ordered pair would represent the horizontal intercept on the graph?

   A. (1, 25)
   B. (20, 0)
   C. (0, 500)
   D. (1, 475)

Objective 4: Find the Slopes of One or Two Lines on a Grid and from Given Equations

Slope is an important concept for students to understand. It represents the rate of change that occurs in a dynamic situation, such as speed, interest accrued per unit of time, or unit cost of an item. Slope is also the constant involved in direct variation problems. Students need experience with finding slope as it occurs in applications, as well as in general algebraic and graphical situations. The activities for this objective will assume that students have already mastered the methods for finding the x- and y-intercepts of a graph or a linear equation.

Activity 1
Manipulative Stage

Materials

Geoboards with rubber bands (1 board per two students)
Strips of lightweight tagboard (red and blue)
Worksheet 2–4a
Colored pencils (red and blue)
Regular pencils

Procedure

1.   Give each pair of students two copies of Worksheet 2–4a, a geoboard with 4 or 5 rubber bands, 1 blue and 1 red pencil, and 1 blue and 1 red strip of tagboard (or lightweight cardstock). The strips should be approximately 0.75 inch by 10 inches in size. Discuss the correct way to hook a rubber band on the geoboard. For example, a finger should be placed on top of a peg holding one end of the rubber band, while the other end of the rubber band is stretched and looped over another selected peg. This prevents any "flying missiles" in the classroom. The lower left corner of the geoboard is assumed to be the origin.

2.   For Exercise 1 on Worksheet 2–4a, students will be given a vertical change and a horizontal change and asked to form the two sides of a right triangle on the geoboard. They will then show the hypotenuse of the triangle with a rubber band, and record the ordered pairs of its end points and its slope on the worksheet.

3.   For the remaining exercises on Worksheet 2–4a, students should connect the two pegs for the two given points with a rubber band on the geoboard. The tagboard strips should be placed to form the vertical (blue) and the horizontal (red) sides of a triangle having the rubber band as the hypotenuse. Students will determine the vertical and the horizontal distances between the two pegs as outlined by the tagboard strips, and record the *V/H* ratio as the slope of the hypotenuse below the exercise on the worksheet.

4.   For each exercise on Worksheet 2–4a, on the given frame students should draw a copy of the triangle built on the geoboard. The hypotenuse and its two end points should be drawn in regular pencil. The vertical side should be drawn in blue pencil and the horizontal side in red pencil. Remind students that the lower left corner of the frame is the origin.

5.   Discuss Exercise 1 on Worksheet 2–4a before having students work the other exercises with their partners.

Consider Exercise 1 on Worksheet 2–4a:

Vertical change = –3 units
Horizontal change = +2 units

Slope = _____
Possible set of end points:

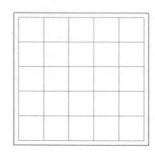

Guide students to arrange the red and the blue tagboard strips beside pegs on the geoboard to form two sides of a right triangle that have the given lengths: vertical, 3 units, and horizontal, 2 units. These lengths are described as *changes*. The blue strip should be placed vertically and the red strip should be placed horizontally to outline a blue-red path. Because the vertical change is negative, students should start at the top end of the blue strip and count down three units on the geoboard to intersect the red strip. Because the horizontal change is positive, students should then turn in the positive, horizontal direction and move two geoboard units along the red strip to the end of the strip. This completes their blue-red path. A possible initial positioning of the blue and the red strips might be as follows:

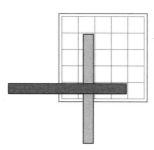

Students should slide the strips together across the geoboard until they identify two pegs to serve as end points of the hypotenuse of the triangle. A rubber band should be used to connect the two pegs found. Here are two possible positions for the triangle on the geoboard, along with the ordered pairs for the end points of the hypotenuse:

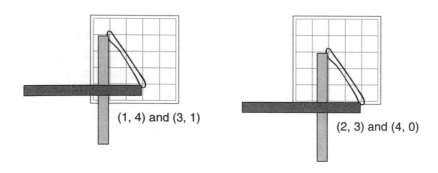

(1, 4) and (3, 1)   (2, 3) and (4, 0)

Have students record the ordered pairs of the two pegs of the hypotenuse, as well as the slope of the hypotenuse, below Exercise 1 on Worksheet 2–4a. One possible recording might be the following: "Slope = $\frac{-3}{+2}$ = $-\frac{3}{2}$ and end points are (1, 4) and (3, 1)." Several sets of ordered pairs will be possible, so encourage students to find and record more than one set. Additional sets might be (2, 3) with (4, 0), (2, 4) with (4, 1), and (0, 3) with (2, 0).

Students should now plot their first set of two ordered pairs and copy their geoboard triangle on the frame shown in Exercise 1. The vertical side of the triangle should be drawn in blue pencil and the horizontal side in red pencil. The hypotenuse should be drawn in regular pencil to connect the two points plotted. Here is how the completed frame should appear:

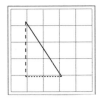

Answer Key for Worksheet 2–4a

1. $m = \frac{-3}{+2} = -\frac{3}{2}$; {(1, 4), (3, 1)} [other possible pairs: {(2, 3), (4, 0)}, {(2, 4), (4, 1)}, and so forth]

2. $V = +4$; $H = +2$; $m = \frac{+4}{+2} = +2$

3. $V = -2$; $H = +2$; $m = \frac{-2}{+2} = -1$

4. $V = +1$; $H = +4$; $m = \frac{+1}{+4} = +\frac{1}{4}$

5. $V = -2$; $H = +3$; $m = \frac{-2}{+3} = -\frac{2}{3}$

Worksheet 2–4a

Using Geoboards to Find Slopes of
Linear Paths

Name _____

Date _____

For each exercise, mark the selected two points on the frame shown on the worksheet. Show vertical and horizontal changes with colored strips on the geoboard, and use a rubber band to connect the two points. On the frame, copy the geoboard triangle; draw the vertical change in blue pencil and the horizontal change in red pencil. Record the data needed for each exercise.

1. Vertical change = –3 units

    Horizontal change = +2 units

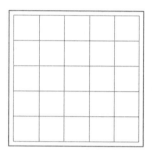

    Slope = _____

    Possible set of two end points:

2. (0, 0) and (2, 4)

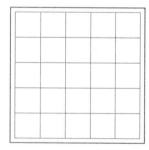

    Vertical change = _____

    Horizontal change = _____

    Slope = _____

Worksheet 2–4a Continued

Name _____

Date _____

3. (2, 3) and (4, 1)

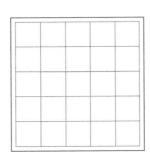

Vertical change = _____

Horizontal change = _____

Slope = _____

4. (0, 2) and (4, 3)

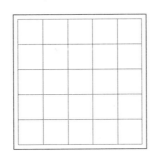

Vertical change = _____

Horizontal change = _____

Slope = _____

5. (1, 4) and (4, 2)

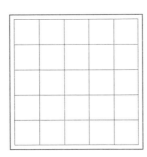

Vertical change = _____

Horizontal change = _____

Slope = _____

Activity 2
Pictorial Stage

Materials

    Worksheet 2–4b
    Rulers
    Red and blue pencils
    Regular pencils and paper

Procedure

    1. Give each pair of students two copies of Worksheet 2–4b, a red and a blue pencil, and a ruler.

    2. For each exercise on Worksheet 2–4b, have students plot two points on the grid that satisfy the given linear equation, and use the ruler and regular pencil to draw the line that represents the equation.

    3. Have students draw a right triangle on the grid, using the segment between the two plotted points as the *hypotenuse*. The vertical side of the triangle should be drawn in blue pencil and the horizontal side drawn in red pencil. Two different triangles will be possible; only one needs to be drawn on the grid.

    4. Students should determine the lengths of the two sides of the triangle by moving continuously along the blue-red path that connects the two points. Remind students that a downward direction on the blue segment is negative and a leftward direction on the red segment is also negative. The directed values should be used to find the *V/H* ratio or slope of the hypotenuse. This information should be recorded below the exercise on Worksheet 2–4b.

    5. After all triangles are drawn and measured, ask students to solve the equation in each exercise for y in terms of x. Have them compare the computed *V/H* ratio or slope to the coefficient of the x-variable in the new equation. The two values should be equivalent. The new equation will be in the $y = mx + b$ format.

    6. Discuss Exercise 1 with the entire class before having students work with partners to complete the other exercises.

Consider Exercise 1 on Worksheet 2–4b:

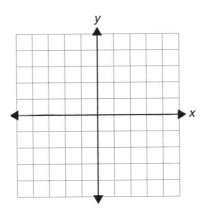

$4y + 3x = +8$

Points: _____

Vertical change = _____

Horizontal change = _____

Slope = _____

$y =$ _____

Have students find two ordered pairs that will satisfy the linear equation. For example, they might find (4, –1) and (–4, 5). Each ordered pair should be tested by substitution in the original equation as follows: $4(-1) + 3(4) = 8$ and $4(5) + 3(-4) = 8$. Once the points have been verified, students should use the ruler to draw a line through the two points. Here is a sample graph of the line:

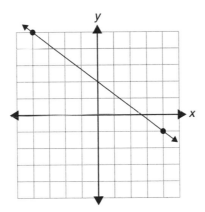

Because the computation is easy, it is possible that some students have already been trained to use $x = 0$ and $y = 0$ to find ordered pairs for a given linear equation. These values produce the two ordered pairs (0, 2) and $(\frac{8}{3}, 0)$ for this equation. If students use this approach, ask them to find one or two additional points as well. This will reinforce the idea that there are other points forming the line besides the two intercepts. Only two ordered pairs should finally be selected, however, to be recorded below Exercise 1 on Worksheet 2–4b. We shall use (4, –1) and (–4, 5) for convenience in this discussion.

Have students draw a triangle on the grid, using the segment connecting the two points as the hypotenuse. Draw the vertical side in blue pencil and the horizontal side in red pencil. Here is one possible way to draw the triangle:

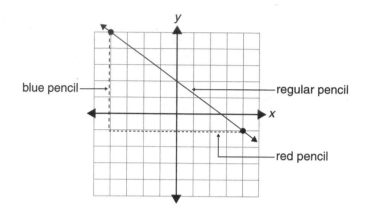

To move along the blue-red path, or the triangle's sides, from (–4, 5) to (4, –1), students must go downward 6 units, which is –6 vertically, then move in a rightward direction 8 units, which is +8 horizontally. If they choose to move from (4, –1) to (–4, 5) instead, they would have –8 and +6 for the side lengths of the triangle. Have students record –6 and +8 below Exercise 1, then compute and record the *V/H* ratio, $\frac{-6}{+8} = \frac{-3}{+4} = -\frac{3}{4}$, for the slope.

Now have students solve the original equation for *y* in terms of *x*. They should obtain the equation $y = -\frac{3}{4}x + 2$ after simplification, and record the equation below Exercise 1. After all exercises are completed, students will be able to observe that the slope and the coefficient of the *x* in this last type of equation are equivalent. A statement regarding this observation should be written as a response to the question at the end of Worksheet 2–4b.

Answer Key for Worksheet 2–4b

Completed graphs are not shown; suggested ordered pairs, their possible *V* and *H* values, and resulting *V/H* ratios are provided.

1. (4, –1) and (–4, 5); *V* = –6, *H* = +8; slope = $\frac{-6}{+8} = \frac{-3}{+4} = -\frac{3}{4}$; $y = -\frac{3}{4}x + 2$

2. (2, –4) and (–2, –2); *V* = +2, *H* = –4; slope = $\frac{+2}{-4} = \frac{+1}{-2} = -\frac{1}{2}$; $y = -\frac{1}{2}x - 3$

3. (0, –2) and (3, 0); *V* = +2, *H* = +3; slope = $\frac{+2}{+3} = +\frac{2}{3}$; $y = +\frac{2}{3}x - 2$

4. (1, 2) and (–2, –4); *V* = –6, *H* = –3; slope = $\frac{-6}{-3} = \frac{-2}{-1} = +2$; $y = +2x + 0$

5. The coefficient of *x* is equal to the slope of the line.

Worksheet 2–4b

Using Graphs to Find Slopes of
Linear Functions

Name _____

Date _____

For each exercise, graph on the grid two solution points for the given linear equation. Draw a triangle that has the segment connecting the two points as the hypotenuse. Draw the vertical side in blue pencil and the horizontal side in red pencil. Compute the slope of the hypotenuse. Solve the equation for y in terms of x.

1. $4y + 3x = +8$

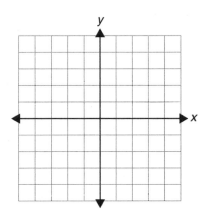

Points: _____

Vertical change = _____

Horizontal change = _____

Slope = _____

y = _____

132

Name _____

Date _____

2. $x + 2y = -6$

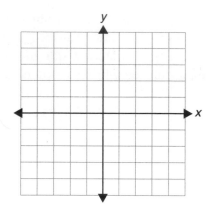

Points: _____

Vertical change = _____

Horizontal change = _____

Slope = _____

$y =$ _____

3. $3y - 2x = -6$

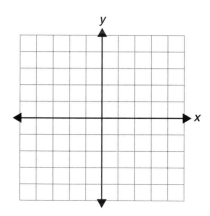

Points: _____

Vertical change = _____

Horizontal change = _____

Slope = _____

$y =$ _____

Worksheet 2–4b Continued

Name _____

Date _____

4. $-2x + y = 0$

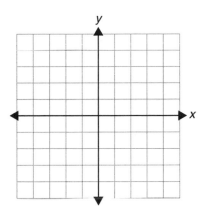

Points: _____

Vertical change = _____

Horizontal change = _____

Slope = _____

$y =$ _____

5. When an equation is written in the $y = mx + b$ format, what does it tell you about the slope of the line that represents the equation?

Activity 3
Independent Practice

Materials

> Worksheet 2–4c
> Grid paper
> Regular pencils and paper

Procedure

Give each student a copy of Worksheet 2–4c and a sheet of grid paper. Remind students that graphing of the $y = mx + b$ format may be used to find the slope of the line representing a linear equation. When all have finished the worksheet, ask various students to share their results with the entire class.

Answer Key for Worksheet 2–4c

1. B

2. D

3. C

4. B

5. A

6. D

Possible Testing Errors That May Occur for This Objective

- When finding the slope of a line from its graph, students reverse the vertical and horizontal values in the slope ratio. For example, if the vertical distance is –5 and the horizontal distance is +2, they will use the ratio $\frac{+2}{-5}$ to find the slope.

- After changing a linear equation to the $y = mx + b$ format, students will incorrectly use the value of b, rather than the value of m, for the slope.

- When finding the vertical or the horizontal change between two ordered pairs or points on a graph, students fail to allow for the direction of the change. For example, if moving from (–1, 3) to (2, –2), students will find the absolute distances of 5 vertically and 3 horizontally and the slope ratio of +5 to +3, instead of using the directed distances of –5 and +3 to find the ratio of –5 to +3.

Worksheet 2–4c   Name _____

Finding Slopes of Lines   Date _____

Solve each exercise provided. Be ready to share your reasoning and answers with the entire class.

1. What will happen to the slope of line p if the line is shifted so that the y-intercept remains the same and the x-intercept increases?

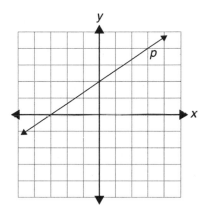

A. The slope will decrease.

B. The slope will increase.

C. The slope will change from positive to negative.

D. The slope will change from negative to positive.

2. What is the slope of the line that represents $3y - x = -12$?

A. -12 B. -4 C. $+3$ D. $+\frac{1}{3}$

Worksheet 2–4c Continued

Name _____

Date _____

3. What is the rate of change of this graph?

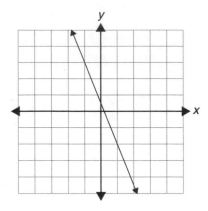

A. –3.0

B. +2.3

C. –2.5

D. +0.5

4. The graph of a line is shown on the grid. If the slope of this line is multiplied by –1 and the y-intercept increases by 3 units, which linear equation represents the new line showing these changes?

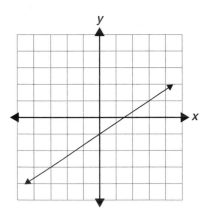

A. $y = \frac{2}{3}x - 1$

B. $y = -\frac{2}{3}x + 2$

C. $y = -\frac{3}{2}x + 2$

D. $y = \frac{3}{2}x - 1$

Worksheet 2–4c Continued

Name _____

Date _____

5. The table shows the number of payments, p, and the remaining balance, b, after each payment on a loan for a used car. Which function can be used to describe the relationship between b and p?

Number of Payments, p	Loan Balance, b
1	$1900
2	$1650
3	$1400
4	$1150
5	$900

A. $b = 2{,}150 - 250p$

B. $b = 1{,}900 + 250p$

C. $b = 900 + 250p$

D. $b = 1{,}650 - 250p$

6. Given two points, $(4, 5)$ and $(3, r)$, and a slope of 8, find a value for r so that a line will pass through the two points and have the given slope.

A. +8   B. +3   C. 0   D. –3

Objective 5: Match a Graph Without a Given Scale to the Relationship Described by a Given Situation

Students need experience with changes that occur in functions. They need to be able to visualize how a change in the independent variable effects a change in the dependent variable. Before they can recognize and interpret graphs without scales shown, however, they must learn to create their own table of values that will satisfy the general description of the function's behavior. The following activities provide experiences that will help students interpret sketches of graphs or trend paths when scales are not provided.

Activity 1
Manipulative Stage

Materials

Building Mat 2–5a
Worksheet 2–5a
1-inch square tiles (40 tiles per two students)
Colored yarn (1 24-inch length per two students)
Colored pencils (dark colors preferred)
Regular pencils

Procedure

1. Give each pair of students two copies of Worksheet 2–5a, one copy of Building Mat 2–5a, a set of 40 square tiles, a colored pencil, and one piece of colored yarn.

2. For each exercise on Worksheet 2–5a, students should build columns of tiles on Building Math 2–5a, which correspond to the description of the situation. Different sizes of columns may satisfy the same description. The horizontal scale of the building mat may need to be extended to accommodate one or two more columns of tiles.

3. After the columns of tiles are built, students should place the yarn piece along the center points of the top edges of the columns. This will form a *trend path* to help students visualize how the vertical distances vary as the horizontal distance increases. The yarn piece should begin on the vertical axis in a position that indicates the initial conditions for the situation being described, for example, when time equals 0 minutes. At the end of the time period covered, the yarn piece should not be dropped down to the horizontal axis unless required by the situation.

4. Students should draw a copy of this trend path with colored pencil on the grid provided on Worksheet 2–5a. If they have used different column sizes to satisfy the same description, discuss the idea that the trend paths will still show increases, decreases, or remain constant within the same horizontal intervals. In general, the trend paths for the same exercise will have similar appearances. Have students record a phrase, for example, *increase–level–decrease*, below the exercise on Worksheet 2–5a to describe the trend path across the grid from left to right.

5. Discuss Exercise 1 on Worksheet 2–5a with the entire class. Then have partners work Exercise 2 together.

Consider Exercise 1 on Worksheet 2–5a: "Initially a car is traveling at 60 mph (1 mile per minute) toward its destination, which is 5 miles away. For the second through the fourth minutes of travel, the car waits at a railroad crossing. At 7 minutes, the car reaches its destination, again traveling at approximately 60 mph."

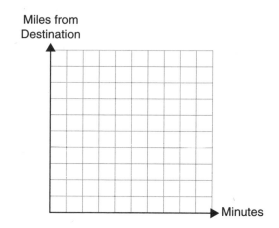

Discuss the situation with the class to help students understand the actions implied. Ask students how far the car is from its destination at the beginning, which is at 0 minutes. Since it is 5 miles from the destination, have students build a column of 5 tiles along the unmarked vertical axis of Building Mat 2–5a. Since the car is moving at 1 mile per minute, after 1 minute of travel, it is 1 mile closer, or 4 miles away from its destination. Have students build a column of 4 tiles above the first mark on the horizontal axis.

After 2 minutes of travel, the car reaches a railroad track and has to stop. It is now 3 miles from its destination, but for the following 3 and 4 minutes of travel time, the car is motionless and does not change its distance from the destination. So the columns at the second, third, and fourth marks on the building mat's horizontal axis should contain 3 tiles each. Here is a sample of the building mat after 4 minutes (axes are labeled temporarily):

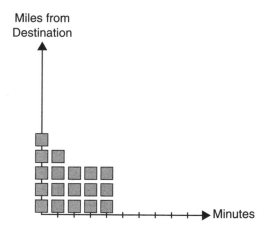

After leaving the railroad crossing and quickly increasing its speed to 60 mph again, the car continues to travel until it reaches its destination at 7 minutes. Its final distance from the destination is now 0 miles. No tiles will form a column at the seventh mark on the horizontal axis. Now the yarn piece should be placed along the top edges of the tile columns, where it eventually slopes down to the horizontal axis at the seventh mark. Here is the final appearance of the tiles and the yarn on Building Mat 2–5a for Exercise 1 (axes are labeled temporarily):

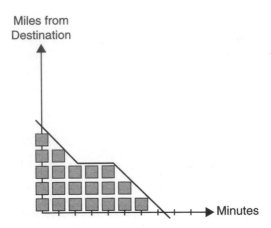

After students have completed the tile graph on the building mat, have them label the scales of the grid for Exercise 1 on Worksheet 2–5a and draw a copy of the *trend path* (shown by the yarn) in colored pencil on the grid. The completed grid should appear as follows:

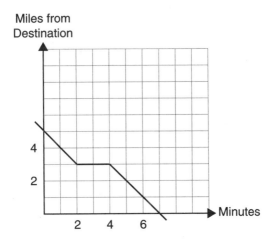

After students have drawn the trend path on the grid of Exercise 1, discuss the idea that the vertical distance begins with 5 miles at 0 minutes, then decreases to 3 miles at 2 minutes, staying level or constant to 4 minutes. Then the vertical distance decreases gradually down to 0 miles at 7 minutes. The *trend pattern*, therefore, is *decrease–level–decrease* or *decrease–constant–decrease*. Have students record this description of the trend below Exercise 1 on Worksheet 2–5a.

Notice that for Exercise 2 on Worksheet 2–5a at 3 minutes after the worker begins, the box contains only 1 metal pin, but at 6 minutes, he has found all 6 metal pins that belong in the box. This indicates that for 4 minutes, 5 minutes, and 6 minutes of time, he has to locate and find 5 metal pins in all. Thus, students should decide how many pins will be found for each of these three times, as long as the total found equals 5 pins. For example, they might choose to have 1 pin, 3 pins, then 1 more pin found for 4, 5, then 6 minutes, respectively. This means that the column of tiles at 4 minutes will contain 2 tiles; at 5 minutes, the column will have 5 tiles; and at 6 minutes, the column will have 6 tiles.

Other combinations are possible. Another possibility is provided in the Answer Key for Worksheet 2–5a. Encourage students to decide for themselves which combination to use. The final trend path will look the same and have the same description phrase, regardless of the combination selected.

Answer Key for Worksheet 2–5a

1. [The final grid and trend description are provided in text.]

2. increase–decrease–increase–level

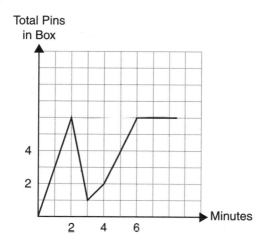

Building Mat 2–5a

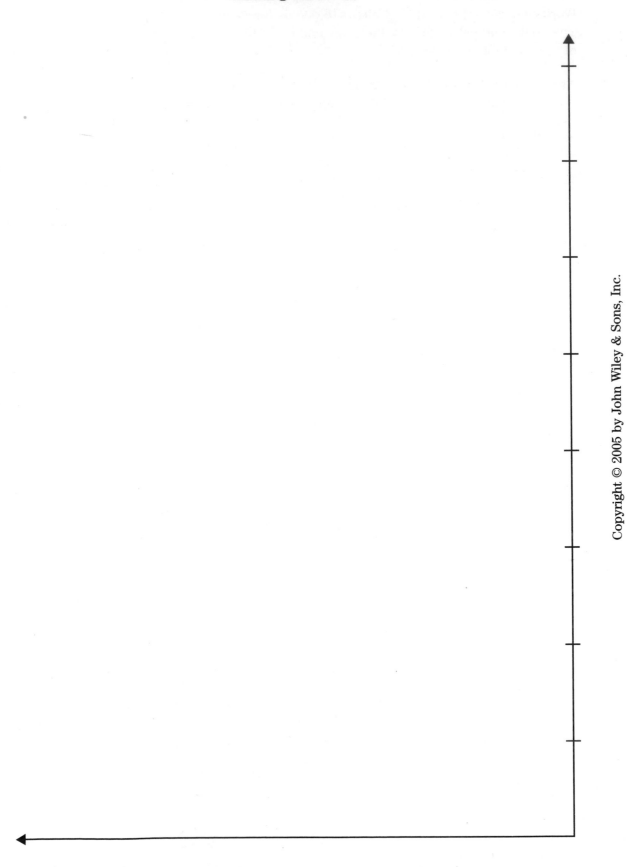

Worksheet 2–5a

Building Graphs to Find Trends

Name _____

Date _____

For each exercise, use tiles on Building Mat 2–5a to build a graph that satisfies the description of the situation. Place a yarn piece along the top edges of the tile columns to show a trend path. Draw a picture of the trend path on the grid provided and describe the trend.

1. Initially a car is traveling at 60 mph (1 mile per minute) toward its destination, which is 5 miles away. For the second through the fourth minutes of travel, the car waits at a railroad crossing. At 7 minutes, the car reaches its destination, again traveling at approximately 60 mph.

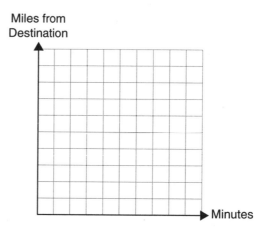

2. A worker is removing the metal pins from used equipment so they can be recycled. He removes 3 pins per minute and puts the pins in a box. At 3 minutes after he begins to work, the box is knocked over and the pins spill out, leaving only 1 pin in the box. From 4 to 6 minutes, the worker finds and picks up the missing pins in random amounts until all pins are back in the box. From 7 to 8 minutes, he takes a short break, not putting any pins into the box.

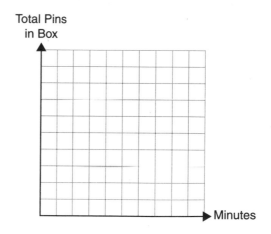

Activity 2
Pictorial Stage

Materials
 Worksheet 2–5b
 Colored pencils (dark colors preferred)
 Regular pencils

Procedure
 1. Give each pair of students two copies of Worksheet 2–5b and a colored pencil.
 2. For each exercise on Worksheet 2–5b, students will create a right column of values in the given table, which satisfies the description of the situation. Several sets of numbers are possible for each table. Students should choose the set they prefer, but they must be able to justify their choice.
 3. The students will plot the table of values on the grid provided and draw the trend path with colored pencil. Below the exercise on the worksheet, they will record a phrase that describes the trend path.
 4. When all students have finished the exercises, have various students share their different tables of values for the same exercise. Discuss the idea that the trend paths will look quite similar, even though different sets of numbers were used.
 5. Discuss Exercise 1 with the entire class. Then allow partners to work Exercise 2 together.

 Consider Exercise 1 on Worksheet 2–5b: "A car is moving initially at 30 mph. During an 8-minute time period, the car gradually slows to 15 mph to enter a school zone. It takes 4 minutes for the car to drive through the school zone. Then the car quickly speeds up to 35 mph by the eighth minute."
 Ask students to identify the initial and the final conditions for the moving car. At 0 minutes, the car is moving at 30 mph, and at 8 minutes, it will be moving 35 mph. One or 2 minutes should be allowed for the car to slow down gradually to 15 mph, so students should select some speeds that are decreasing. For example, at 1 minute, the car might be moving at 25 mph, and at 2 minutes, it might be moving at 20 mph. Then at 3 minutes, it enters the school zone at 15 mph. Since it takes 4 minutes to drive through the school zone, we might use the time interval from 3 minutes to 6 minutes for the 15 mph speed. At 7 minutes, the car speeds up quickly, for example, to 25 mph, then finally to 35 mph by the eighth minute.
 Once students decide how they want to represent the speed changes across the 8-minute period, have them complete the table and plot the ordered pairs on the grid provided below Exercise 1. The finished table and its corresponding graph might appear as follows:

Time in Minutes	Speed of Car
0	30 mph
1	25 mph
2	20 mph
3	15 mph
4	15 mph
5	15 mph
6	15 mph
7	25 mph
8	35 mph

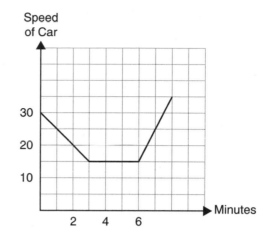

After students have drawn the graph for Exercise 1, have them describe the trend path from left to right across the grid. In the example used here, they should notice that the vertical distances decrease gradually from 0 minutes to 3 minutes, then level off from 3 minutes to 6 minutes. From 6 minutes to 8 minutes, the vertical distances increase somewhat rapidly. Students should record the phrase *decrease gradually–level–increase rapidly* below the table in Exercise 1.

Some students might use 4 minutes to 7 minutes for the school zone interval. Then they would have a slower decrease from 30 mph to 15 mph (0 minutes to 4 minutes) and a faster increase from 15 mph to 35 mph (7 minutes to 8 minutes). The trend path would still look the same and be described with the same phrase. Discuss these different possibilities with the students.

Answer Key for Worksheet 2–5b

1. [One possible table and its corresponding graph and phrase are provided above.]

2. A possible table and graph with phrase for trend path (other tables and graphs are possible): faster decrease–slower decrease

Time in Minutes	Temperature (°C)
0	86°
1	83°
2	80°
3	77°
4	74°
5	71°
6	70°
7	69°
8	68°
9	67°
10	66°

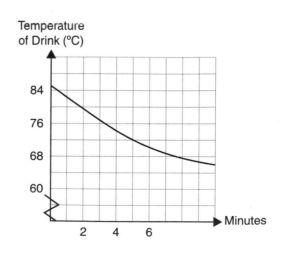

146

Worksheet 2–5b   Name _____

Plotting Data to Find Trends   Date _____

For each exercise, complete the table with a set of numbers that satisfies the description
of the situation. Different sets of numbers may be possible. Plot the table's ordered pairs
on the grid. Draw the trend path of the points on the grid, and describe the trend below
the exercise.

1. A car is moving initially at 30 mph. During an 8-minute time period, the car
   gradually slows to 15 mph to enter a school zone. It takes 4 minutes for the car
   to drive through the school zone. Then the car quickly speeds up to 35 mph by
   the eighth minute.

Time in Minutes	Speed of Car
0	30 mph
1	
2	
3	
4	
5	
6	
7	
8	

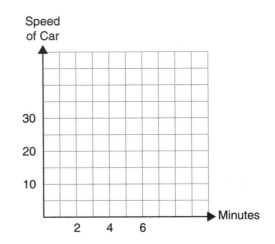

2. A freshly poured cup of hot chocolate has an initial temperature of 86°C. Left sitting
   on the table, the drink gradually cools over a time period of 10 minutes to 66°C. The
   drink cools twice as fast in the first 5 minutes as it does in the last 5 minutes.

Time in Minutes	Temperature (°C)
0	86°
1	
2	
3	
4	
5	
6	
7	
8	
9	
10	

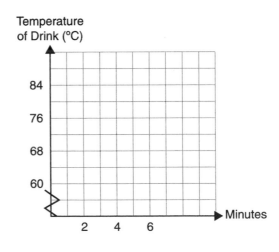

Activity 3

Independent Practice

Materials
>   Worksheet 2–5c
>   Regular pencils

Procedure
Give each student a copy of Worksheet 2–5c to complete independently. After all students are finished, have various students share their reasoning and their answers with the entire class.

Answer Key for Worksheet 2–5c

1.

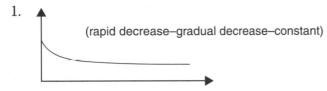

(rapid decrease–gradual decrease–constant)

2. C

3. A

4. D

5. Graphs will vary, but they should reflect any slowing or stopping at a traffic light, slowing while in a school zone, increasing the speed, moving at a constant speed along a main street, and so forth.

Possible Testing Errors That May Occur for This Objective

* Students often confuse the variables involved in a situation with the physical setting. For example, if the situation compares a biker's speed to the time traveled and states that the biker is moving up and down a hill, students will select a graph that contains a "peak" in order to represent the hill. A more appropriate graph would have a *decrease–increase* trend pattern, indicating that the speed decreases as the biker moves uphill and then increases as the biker moves downhill.

* Students ignore the condition that the dependent variable remains constant over a certain time interval. They do not select a graph that includes a level portion with a zero slope.

* An incorrect graph is often selected because it begins at the origin. Students ignore the nonzero initial condition of a situation. For example, if a taxi fare includes an initial fee of $5 plus a fee based on mileage, students will ignore the $5 fee and begin with $0 at 0 miles for the graph.

148

Worksheet 2–5c

Matching Graphs to Their
Relationships

Name _____

Date _____

Complete each exercise. Be ready to share your reasoning and your answers with the entire class.

1. Draw a graph that shows the trend path of temperature changing over time as a hot cup of coffee cools from 180°F to room temperature. Cooling is more rapid at first, then slows down.

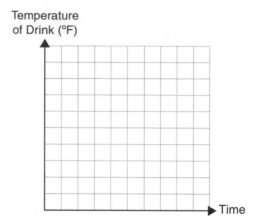

Temperature of Drink (°F)

Time

2. Jill jogs at a steady speed up a hill in the city park. Then she runs down the hill, and her speed increases. Which graph best describes the relationship between Jill's speed and time?

A.

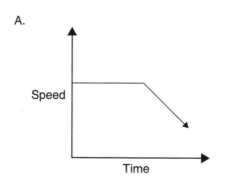

Speed

Time

C.

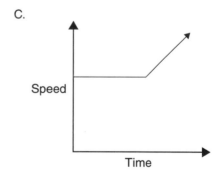

Speed

Time

B.

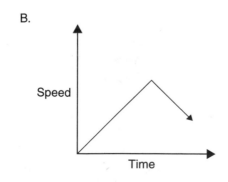

Speed

Time

D.

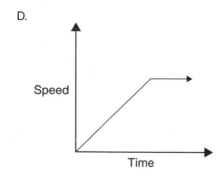

Speed

Time

Worksheet 2–5c Continued

Name _____

Date _____

3. Which of the following relationships between temperature and time is best represented by the graph below?

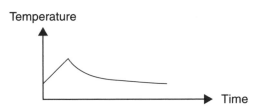

A. Temperature of canned soup that is poured into a bowl, heated in a microwave oven, removed, and then allowed to cool

B. Temperature of a container of hot tea after putting several ice cubes in it

C. Temperature inside a closed car after the air conditioner is turned on

D. Oven temperature while a pie is baking

4. A research study found that people sleep fewer hours as they age until, as adults, their sleeping time becomes constant. After the age of 70, however, their amount of sleeping time increases slightly. Which graph best represents the results of this research study?

A.
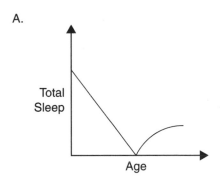

C.
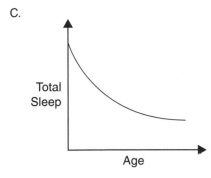

B.
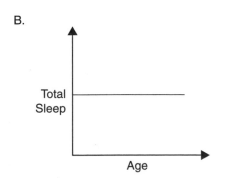

D.
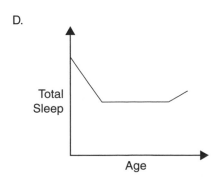

Worksheet 2–5c Continued

Name _____

Date _____

5. Draw a graph without scales that shows the relationship between your speed and time as you travel from home to school each day.

Objective 6: Apply Linear Inequalities to Solve Real-World Problems; Match a Linear Inequality in Two Variables to Its Graph

Inequalities in two variables are difficult for students to comprehend. Students need experience in visually tracking how the change in one variable produces change in the other variable. They need to explore the many solutions possible as a result of working with an inequality. Real-world applications often lead to such multiple solutions, which must satisfy the conditions of the given situation. The following activities will help students begin to visualize how two variables can interact to yield more than one solution. It is assumed that students have already mastered the process for solving a linear equation for one variable in terms of another variable. Encourage students to read each inequality from left to right; for example, in $A + 3 < B$, students should say "A plus 3 is less than B," and not "B is greater than A plus 3." This will help them correctly interpret the inequality.

Activity 1

Manipulative Stage

Materials

Building Mat 2–6a
Paper "equals" markers (1 per pair of students)
Sets of algebra tiles (described in step 1 of Procedure)
Worksheet 2–6a
Regular pencils and paper

Procedure

1. Give each pair of students one copy of Building Mat 2–6a, one paper "equals" marker, a set of algebra tiles, and two copies of Worksheet 2–6a. For the "equals" markers, draw a bold equals sign on each of several 2-inch by 3-inch cards (use cardstock or tagboard). The set of tiles should contain 30 unit tiles and have 8 variable tiles in each of two different sizes (for example, 0.75 inch by 3 inches and 0.75 inch by 3.25 inches). A different color should be used for each variable length. Consider the shorter variable tile as variable A and the longer tile as variable B for notation purposes. Each tile—both unit and variable—should have a large X marked on one side to represent its inverse form.

2. For each exercise on Worksheet 2–6a, have students build the given inequality with tiles on Building Mat 2–6a. If equality is also involved, they should place an "equals" marker near the top edge of the building mat. Students should solve the inequality for the required variable (the first variable shown in brackets for the exercise), using the tiles.

3. If students think they do not have enough variable tiles to solve certain inequalities, remind them that subtracting or *taking* a tile *away* from the mat is equivalent to *adding* the inverse of that tile *to* the mat. Encourage students to isolate the desired variable on the side of the building mat that will yield the plain variable tile (A or B) and not the inverse variable tile ($-A$ or $-B$). This approach avoids having to take the inverse of each side of the mat and "flip the sign," a procedure that many students have difficulty understanding.

4. Using the value stated in the exercise (the second variable shown in brackets for the exercise), students should substitute unit tiles for the variable now in the independent position on the building mat. This yields a *boundary value* and a specific *solution interval* for the variable in the dependent position when the other variable has the fixed

value. Students should select a value from the solution interval that is at least 4 units away from the boundary value of the solution interval.

5. Have students follow your instructions to record their results in word sentences below the exercise on Worksheet 2–6a.

6. When all students are finished with the worksheet, have several students explain how they solved different inequalities with the tiles.

7. Discuss Exercise 1 with the entire class before allowing partners to work the other exercises on Worksheet 2–6a.

Consider Exercise 1 on Worksheet 2–6a: "$B - 3 \leq -2B + 6A$ $\left[B; \ A = -2 \right]$."

Have partners position Building Mat 2–6a to show "less" in the lower left corner of the mat from their viewpoint. Partners should be sitting beside each other so that they can view the building mat from the same angle. Since the left side may also *equal* the right side of the inequality in this exercise, the "equals" marker should be placed at the top edge of the mat. Have students place 1 long variable B tile and 3 negative unit tiles on the left side of the building mat, and place 2 inverse variable B tiles and 6 variable A tiles on the right side of the mat. The initial arrangement of tiles on the building mat should appear as follows:

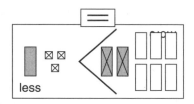

Since the variable B is shown first in the brackets, students should solve the inequality for B in terms of the variable A. In order to isolate one or more of the plain variable B tiles (and not *inverse* variable B tiles) on one side of the mat, students might decide to group the tiles on the left side of the mat. To do this, students should place 2 variable B tiles on each side of the mat; 3 positive unit tiles should also be placed on each side. Then 0-pairs should be formed and removed from the mat, leaving 3 variable B tiles on the left side, and 6 variable A tiles and 3 positive unit tiles on the right side. The mat and tiles for these steps are shown here:

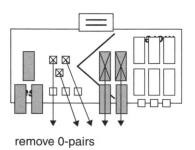

remove 0-pairs

Since 3 variable B tiles still remain on the mat, students should separate them into 3 rows of 1 variable B tile each. The variable tiles may be turned horizontally if mat space is limited. The tiles on the right side must also be separated into 3 equal rows where each row contains 2 variable A tiles and 1 positive unit tile. To solve for the variable B tile, students should remove 2 complete rows of tiles from each side of the mat, thereby leaving a single variable B tile on the left side, and 2 variable A tiles and 1 positive unit tile on the right. The mat will appear as follows:

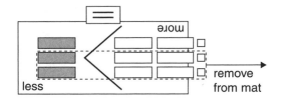

Have students record the following sentence below Exercise 1 on Worksheet 2–6a: $B < 2A + 1$ or $B = 2A + 1$. Since $A = -2$ is shown in the brackets of the exercise, ask students to replace each variable A tile on the current building mat with 2 negative unit tiles, then remove any 0-pairs that form. The variable B tile will remain on the left side of the mat, and 3 negative unit tiles will remain on the right side. This indicates that a *solution interval* for B will contain all real numbers less than –3 or equal to –3 when A equals –2. Ask students to name a possible value for B that is in the solution interval, but is at least 4 units away from the *boundary value*, –3. Students should name several different numbers for B that are less than or equal to –7. Have students record their substitution results below their first sentence for Exercise 1. As an example, if –12 were chosen as the value for B, students might write: "If $A = -2$, then $B < -3$ or $B = -3$. B can equal –12."

Answer Key for Worksheet 2–6a

The final inequality in two variables and the specific inequality for each exercise are provided in symbols below. Student answers should represent these in *word sentences*. The value selected from the specific solution interval will vary with each student.

1. $B < 2A + 1$ or $B = 2A + 1$. If $A = -2$, then $B < -3$ or $B = -3$.

2. $A > -4 + B$. If $B = +3$, then $A > -1$.

3. $-B - 8 < A$. If $B = -1$, then $-7 < A$.

4. $B > -2A - 1$ or $B = -2A - 1$. If $A = 0$, then $B > -1$ or $B = -1$.

5. $+6 + 3B > A$ or $+6 + 3B = A$. If $B = +4$, then $+18 > A$ or $+18 = A$.

6. $-6 + 3A < B$. If $A = +3$, then $+3 < B$.

Building Mat 2–6a

less

more

Worksheet 2–6a   Name _____

Solving Inequalities with Tiles   Date _____

For each exercise, use tiles on Building Mat 2–6a to represent the inequality. Solve for the variable shown first in the brackets. Substitute the value shown in the brackets for its stated variable in the final inequality on the mat to find a specific *solution interval*. Identify a number in that solution interval that is at least 4 units away from the *boundary value* of the solution interval. Below the exercise write sentences to record your results.

1. $B - 3 \le -2B + 6A \quad [B; \; A = -2]$

2. $2A - 2B + 3 > -5 \quad [A; \; B = +3]$

3. $-B - 5 < 3 + A \quad [A; \; B = -1]$

4. $2B + 3 \ge -4A + 1 \quad [B; \; A = 0]$

5. $-2A + 3B \ge -A - 6 \quad [A; \; B = +4]$

6. $-6 - 2B + 4A < A - B \quad [B; \; A = +3]$

Activity 2
Pictorial Stage

Materials

    Worksheet 2–6b

    Colored pencils (2 different dark colors)

    Rulers

    Regular pencils and paper

Procedure

1. Give each pair of students two copies of Worksheet 2–6b, a ruler, and two colored pencils (two different colors).

2. For each exercise on Worksheet 2–6b, have students draw a diagram on regular paper to solve the inequality for the first variable shown in the brackets in terms of the second variable in the brackets. The labels on the axes of the grid below the exercise will identify the *independent* variable and the *dependent* variable of the inequality.

3. When students have isolated the selected variable, have them record the steps they used in symbols on their regular paper. In the new inequality, they should then substitute the value given for the second variable in the brackets to find the *boundary value* for the selected variable. For example, they might obtain $B > -4$, where -4 is the boundary value for B, the isolated variable.

4. The value for the second variable in the brackets should be recorded in the correct column of the table below the exercise. Students should then record the boundary value of the isolated variable in the title row and the first entry row of that variable's column, and choose four other real numbers (including two decimal numbers) that will be solutions for the isolated variable or satisfy the new inequality. If the boundary value is a solution to the inequality, have students write "bd value closed" beside that value in the table. If the boundary value is not included as a solution, have students write "bd value open" beside that value.

5. A line should be drawn in color #1 on the grid below the exercise to represent the equation of the variable and its value given in the brackets, for example, $M = -1$. Then the ordered pairs recorded in the table should be plotted in color #2 on top of that line. If the boundary value is not a solution, students should draw an open or blank dot in color #2 for its point; however, a solid dot should be drawn in color #2 if the boundary value is a solution. Since infinitely many real numbers are possible as solutions, students should draw a half-line in color #2 so that it passes through the points already plotted and represents other potential points.

6. After all exercises on Worksheet 2–6b have been completed, ask students to repeat the process with each exercise, using two other values for the second variable in the brackets. They may need to make new tables if they cannot compute mentally to locate the new points and their respective half-lines directly on the grid. The new points and half-lines should also be drawn in color #2.

7. Then have students use a ruler to draw a dashed line in regular pencil through all the boundary value points found on each grid. For each exercise, ask students to notice where the color #2 half-lines are located with respect to the dashed line connecting the boundary value points. All half-lines should be on the same side of the boundary value line. Discuss the idea that more half-lines are possible and that if all were drawn, the entire half-plane determined by the boundary value line would be covered. This leads to the idea

that an inequality in two variables generally has all the points forming a half-plane as its solution set. Also discuss the idea that the equation that parallels the inequality for the isolated variable has for its solutions all the boundary values found for the inequality. For example, the line for $B = 3M + 2$ would contain the boundary value points for the inequality $B < 3M + 2$. Guide students to record similar ideas on the back of Worksheet 2–6b.

    8.   Discuss Exercise 1 on Worksheet 2–6b with the entire class before allowing students to work the other exercises on their own.

Consider Exercise 1 on Worksheet 2–6b: "$\frac{1}{2}B + 3 \geq M + 1$ $\left[B; M = -1\right]$." Ask students to draw a diagram on regular paper to solve for B in terms of M. We will use M as the *dependent variable* in this exercise. The grid for Exercise 1 shows M on the vertical axis. The initial diagram should appear as follows:

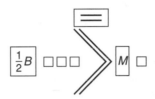

    To solve the inequality for B, students should draw three negative units on both sides of the initial diagram and form 0-pairs of units. Since only half of the variable B is present at first and a solution requires a whole variable B, a horizontal bar should be drawn below the initial diagram to start a new diagram. Two of the half-variable $\left(\frac{1}{2}B\right)$ should be drawn on the left side to form a whole variable B. This requires that two groups of the variable M and –2 be drawn on the right side of the new diagram. The final inequality will be $B \geq 2M - 4$. The completed diagram should appear as shown:

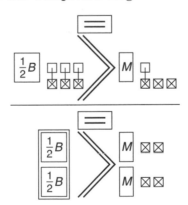

    Have students now record in algebraic notation below the diagram the steps used to solve for B. The following steps might be recorded:

$$\frac{1}{2}B + 3 \geq M + 1$$

$$\underline{+(-3)\qquad +(-3)}$$

$$\frac{1}{2}B \geq M + (-2)$$

$$2\left(\frac{1}{2}B\right) \geq 2M + 2(-2)$$

$$B \geq 2M - 4$$

Ask students to graph the solution interval for B when $M = -1$. Using the table and grid below Exercise 1 on Worksheet 2–6b, students should record the value –1 in each row under M in the right column of the table since M is the dependent variable in this exercise. Using the substitution $B \geq 2(-1) - 4$, the heading for the left column should be "$B \geq -6$." The first entry in the left column should be –6; to the left of –6, students should write "bd value closed" to show that –6 is the boundary value (in this case, the *minimum* value) for the solution interval of B and that –6 itself is also a solution value for B when $M = -1$.

On the adjacent grid, have students draw a horizontal dashed line in color #1 to show $M = -1$. A "closed" or shaded dot should be marked at $(-6, -1)$ in color #2 on the dashed line to show the included boundary point for B's solution interval when $M = -1$. Ask students to suggest four more real numbers, including two decimal numbers, which might be solutions for $B \geq -6$. For discussion, we will use –5, –2.5, +1, and +4.75 for the four numbers. Since all four are greater than –6, the numbers should be recorded in the left column of the table in increasing order under the first entry, –6. Points for these four numbers or their ordered pairs should be located and marked in color #2 on the dashed line. Since these four numbers, as well as all real numbers greater than or equal to –6, are solutions for B when $M = -1$, students should now draw an arrow in color #2 that passes from the boundary point to the right through the other four points. The arrow or *half-line* represents the solution interval for B when $M = -1$. The completed table and graph are shown here.

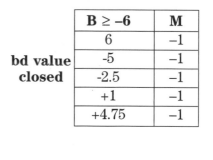

	B ≥ –6	M
	6	–1
bd value	-5	–1
closed	-2.5	–1
	+1	–1
	+4.75	–1

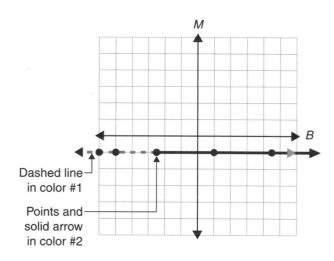

Dashed line in color #1

Points and solid arrow in color #2

Below the completed table on Worksheet 2–6b, have students record the following sentence: "If $B \geq 2M - 4$, then $B \geq -6$ when $M = -1$."

After students have completed all exercises on Worksheet 2–6b, have them select two more values for the second variable given in each exercise and plot several points for each to locate additional half-lines for the inequality. For Exercise 1, they might consider $M = 0$ and $M = +3$. Then they would draw the half-lines for $B \geq 2(0) - 4$ or $B \geq -4$, and for $B \geq 2(+3) - 4$ or $B \geq +2$. These sample half-lines added in color #2 to the graph of Exercise 1, along with a dashed line in regular pencil connecting the boundary value points of the half-lines, would appear as follows (additional plotted points are not shown):

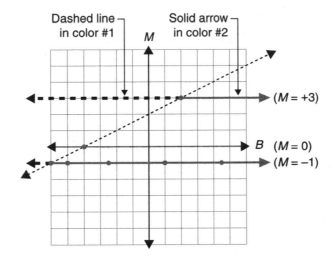

Guide students to notice that all the half-lines for Exercise 1 are on the same side of the dashed line drawn in regular pencil, which contains the boundary value points. In this example, all boundary points are *closed*, but in other exercises, the points might be *open*. Students should realize that the dashed line in regular pencil represents solutions to the equation $B = 2M - 4$. Have students record the additional statement below Exercise 1 on Worksheet 2–6b: $B = 2M - 4$ (boundary). Note that this equation is *not* in slope-intercept form since B is the *independent* variable in Exercise 1. For other exercises, the slope-intercept form will apply. Similar discussions should be conducted for the other exercises as well.

Answer Key for Worksheet 2–6b

The final inequalities, the specific solution intervals based on the given values, and the boundary value equations are provided; no initial graphs or additional graphs are shown.

1. [The inequalities and graphs are shown in the text.]

2. $N < 2 + W$; $N < +5$ when $W = +3$; $N = 2 + W$ (boundary); boundary value points open

3. $A < 3R - 6$; $A < 0$ when $R = +2$; $A = 3R - 6$ (boundary); boundary value points open

4. $-2 - m \leq d$; $-3 \leq d$ when $m = +1$; $-2 - m = d$ (boundary); boundary value points closed

160

Worksheet 2–6b   Name _____

Solving Inequalities with Graphs   Date _____

For each exercise, draw a diagram on regular paper to represent the inequality, and solve for the variable shown first in the brackets. Record your steps in symbols. Then substitute the value of the variable shown second in the brackets into the final inequality to find a specific *solution interval*. Follow the teacher's directions to complete the table and grid for the exercise.

1. $\frac{1}{2}B + 3 \geq M + 1$ $\left[B; M = -1\right]$

B	M

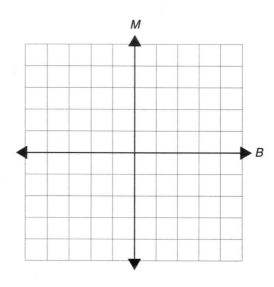

2. $3N - W < +6 + 2W$ $\left[N; W = +3\right]$

W	N

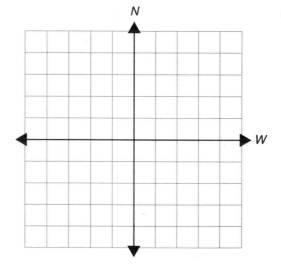

Worksheet 2–6b Continued

Name _____

Date _____

3. $\frac{1}{3}A + 1 < R - 1$ $\left[A;\ R = +2\right]$

A	R

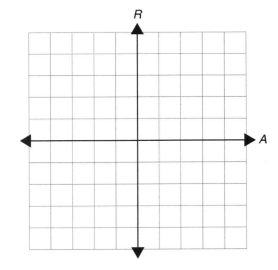

4. $-d + (-4) \le d + 2m$ $\left[d;\ m = +1\right]$

m	d

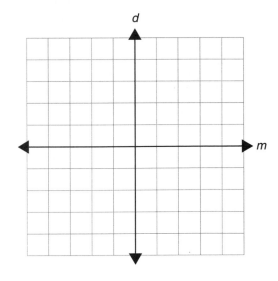

Activity 3
Independent Practice

Materials
Worksheet 2–6c
Regular pencils and paper

Procedure
Give a copy of Worksheet 2–6c to each student to complete. When all have finished, have various students share their reasoning and results for the different exercises.

Answer Key for Worksheet 2–6c
1. B

2. C

3. A

4. D

5. C

Possible Testing Errors That May Occur for This Objective

- Students select a solid line for the boundary of the solution set of an inequality when the line should be dashed or represent an open set of points. For example, when the inequality involves <, students assume it is an ≤ relationship.

- Students shade the region or half-plane on the wrong side of the boundary line of the inequality. For example, they fail to recognize that the y-values of the solutions should be greater than, not less than, the y-values of the boundary line.

- When graphing the line for the boundary values of the inequality, students use the wrong slope or y-intercept to locate the line on the grid.

Worksheet 2–6c   Name _____

Solving Inequalities   Date _____

Solve each exercise provided. Be ready to discuss your reasoning and your solutions with the rest of the class.

1. Rita makes designer bracelets. Her overhead costs are $100 per week, and she pays an additional $3 per bracelet in material costs. If Rita sells each bracelet for $8, how many bracelets must she sell each week in order to *break even*, that is, have her income equal her costs for that week?

   A. 13   B. 20   C. 34   D. 50

2. Which point on the grid satisfies the conditions $x \geq -2$ and $y < +3$?

   A. *E*   C. *G*

   B. *F*   D. *H*

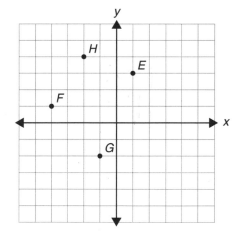

Worksheet 2–6c Continued

Name _____

Date _____

3. When the inequality $x + 3y \leq -12$ is graphed on a grid, which quadrant will not contain any of its solution points?

   A. Quadrant I

   C. Quadrant III

   B. Quadrant II

   D. Quadrant IV

4. Which inequality best describes the graph shown below?

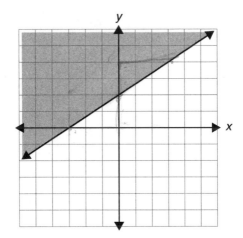

   A. $y \leq -\frac{3}{2}x + 2$

   B. $y > +\frac{2}{3}x + 2$

   C. $y \geq +\frac{3}{2}x - 3$

   D. $y \geq +\frac{2}{3}x + 2$

Worksheet 2–6c Continued

Name _____

Date _____

5. Which graph best represents all the pairs of numbers (x, y) such that $x + y < -5$?

A.

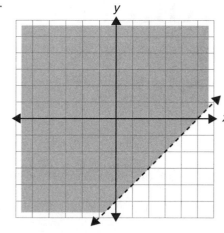

C.

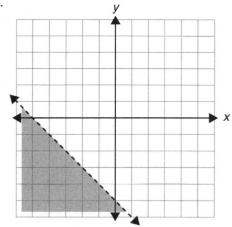

B.

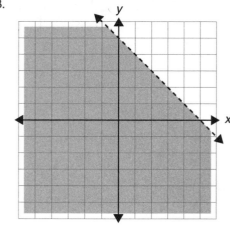

D.

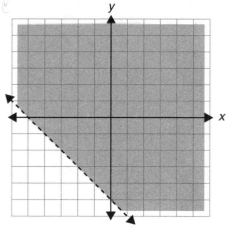

GRAPHS, STATISTICS, AND PROBABILITY: PRACTICE TEST ANSWER SHEET

Directions: Use the answer sheet to darken the letter of the choice that best answers each question.

1. ◯ ◯ ◯ ◯   7. ◯ ◯ ◯ ◯
   A B C D   A B C D

2. ◯ ◯ ◯ ◯   8. ◯ ◯ ◯ ◯
   A B C D   A B C D

3. ◯ ◯ ◯ ◯   9. ◯ ◯ ◯ ◯
   A B C D   A B C D

4. ◯ ◯ ◯ ◯   10. ◯ ◯ ◯ ◯
   A B C D   A B C D

5. ◯ ◯ ◯ ◯   11. ◯ ◯ ◯ ◯
   A B C D   A B C D

6. ◯ ◯ ◯ ◯   12. ◯ ◯ ◯ ◯
   A B C D   A B C D

Section 2: Graphs, Statistics, and Probability: Practice Test

1. The faces of a cube are labeled 1 through 6. A spinner has 4 equal sectors, each sector labeled with a color: red, green, blue, or yellow. If the spinner and the cube are used together in a game, what is the probability that a player will spin the color red and then roll a 2 or 5 during a turn at play?

   A. $\frac{1}{24}$
   B. $\frac{1}{12}$
   C. $\frac{1}{4}$
   D. $\frac{1}{2}$

2. At a band concert, 2 seniors, 1 junior, and 1 sophomore are seated randomly together in a row. What is the probability that the 2 seniors are seated next to each other?

   A. $\frac{1}{2}$
   B. $\frac{1}{3}$
   C. $\frac{1}{4}$
   D. $\frac{1}{12}$

3. A new baseball card was worth $3 in the year 2000. The table shows its value each year for several years after its issue. Based on the table's information, what is a reasonable prediction of the card's value in 2006?

Year	2000	2001	2002	2003
Value of card	$3.00	$3.30	$3.65	$4.05

   A. Between $8 and $9

   C. Between $6 and $7

   B. Between $7 and $8

   D. Between $5 and $6

4. Complete the table so that its ordered pairs represent a quadratic function.

Number of Cookies	1	2	3	4	5
Total Cost in Cents	6	18	36	60	

   A. 180
   B. 120
   C. 90
   D. 72

5. A plumber charges for repair work according to the formula: $C = T(\$55) + \$60$, where C is the total cost for a repair and T is the time in hours needed to make the repair. If T is the independent variable, what does $60 represent in the graph of this formula?

   A. Vertical axis intercept

   C. Horizontal axis intercept

   B. Origin

   D. Slope

Section 2 Practice Test (Continued)

6. Which coordinate points represent the x- and the y-intercepts of the graph shown here?

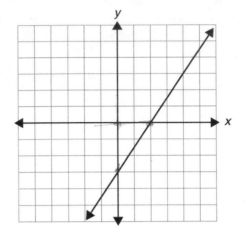

A. (0, 2) and (0, –3)

B. (2, 0) and (–3, 0)

C. (0, 2) and (–3, 0)

D. (2, 0) and (0, –3)

7. Given two points, (4, –5) and (3, r), and a slope of –3, find a value for r so that a line will pass through the two points and have the given slope.

A. –3   B. –2   C. 0   D. +2

8. What is the rate of change of this graph?

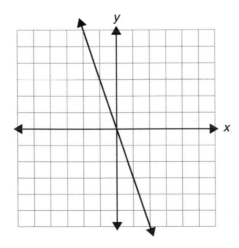

A. –2.5   C. –3.0

B. +2.3   D. +0.5

Section 2 Practice Test (Continued)

9. Which of the following relationships between temperature and time is best represented by the graph below?

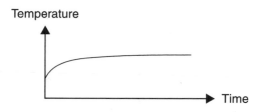

A. Temperature of canned soup that is poured into a bowl, heated in a microwave oven, removed, and then allowed to cool

B. Temperature of a container of hot tea after putting several ice cubes in it

C. Temperature inside a closed car after the air conditioner is turned on

D. Oven temperature when the oven is first turned on, then while a pie is baking

10. Jill jogs at a steady speed up a hill in the city park. Reaching level ground, she is tired, and her speed decreases. Which graph best describes the relationship between Jill's speed and time?

A.

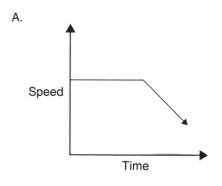

C.

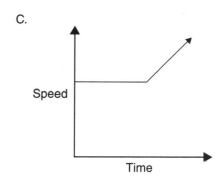

B.

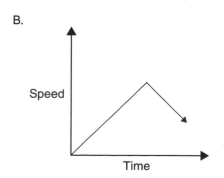

D.

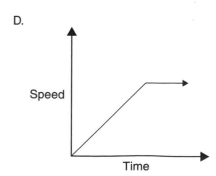

170

Section 2 Practice Test (Continued)

11. Which point on the grid satisfies the conditions $x \leq -3$ and $y \geq +1$?

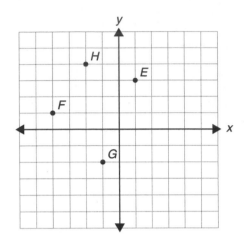

   A. E B. F C. G D. H

12. Which graph best represents all the pairs of numbers (x, y) such that $x + y < +5$?

A.

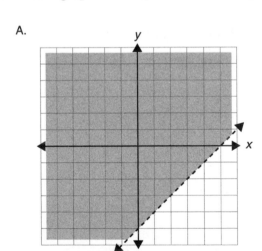

C.

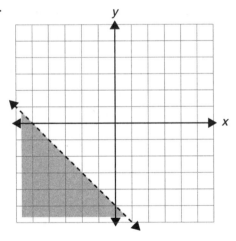

B.

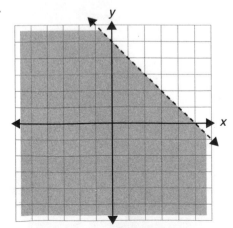

D.

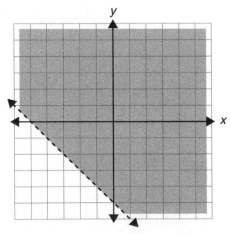

Section 2: Graphs, Statistics, and Probability:
Answer Key for Practice Test

The objective being tested is shown in brackets beside the answer.

1. B [1]   7. B [4]

2. A [1]   8. C [4]

3. D [2]   9. D [5]

4. C [2] [uses $3n(n + 1)$]   10. A [5]

5. A [3]   11. B [6]

6. D [3]   12. B [6]

LINEAR AND QUADRATIC FUNCTIONS AND THEIR PROPERTIES

Objective 1: Find Solutions to Linear Functions of the General Form $y = ax + b$

Students need experience in finding solutions to linear functions. One strategy is to use substitution of given values in a linear equation involving two variables. Practice should include fractional coefficients of variables, so a review of Objective 2 in Section 1 might be helpful. Recognition of the notation $f(x)$ as the dependent variable when x is the independent variable is also important, so the following activities focus on the substitution method and functional notation.

Activity 1
Manipulative Stage

Materials

   Sets of algebra tiles (1 set per pair of students)
   Building Mat 3–1a
   Worksheet 3–1a
   Extra construction paper (use a color that matches the variable A tiles in the sets)
   Scissors
   Regular pencils

Procedure

1.   Give each pair of students a set of algebra tiles, a copy of Building Mat 3–1a, scissors, one sheet of construction paper, and two copies of Worksheet 3–1a. The initial set of tiles should contain 30 unit tiles and have 8 variable tiles in a shorter length and 1 variable tile in a longer length (for example, 0.75 inch by 3 inches and 0.75 inch by 3.25 inches). A different color should be used for each type of tile: the unit tile and the two variable tile lengths. Consider the shorter variable tile as variable A and the longer tile as variable B for notation purposes. Each tile—both unit and variable—should have a large X marked on one side to represent its inverse form.

2. Students will also need some fractional variable *A* tiles. To make such tiles, have students cut out 6 rectangular strips from their sheet of construction paper. The paper strips should be the same size and color as the variable *A* tiles. Show students how to fold the paper strips, mark the creases, and label the parts with fractional names. Two strips should be folded and labeled for halves, yielding 4 half-variables total. Two more strips should be folded and labeled for thirds, and another 2 strips for fourths. Use the ratio format for labeling the fractional parts, for example, $\frac{1}{2}$, $\frac{1}{3}$, and $\frac{1}{4}$. On one side of each fractional part made, have students mark a thin, large X to represent the *inverse* of the fractional part. Be sure that the X does not show through on the other side of the paper. Additional paper strips may be cut out as needed.

3. For each exercise on Worksheet 3–1a, have students place tiles on Building Mat 3–1a to represent the equation. If an equation includes *f(A)*, remind students that this is notation for the dependent variable, so they should use the variable *B* tile to represent *f(A)*. Also, if the distributive property is involved, students should build the required groups on the mat before making any substitutions. For example, for 3(*A* + 2), students should build *A* + 2 three times, which yields 3*A* and +6 in tiles on the building mat. Students need much experience with this particular property.

4. Have students substitute unit tiles for each variable tile on the building mat according to the values of the given ordered pair: *(A, B)* or *(A, f(A))*. If the total value of the left side of the mat equals the total value of the right side of the mat, then the ordered pair represents a *solution* of the equation. If the total values do not equal each other, the ordered pair is *not* a solution.

5. Have students write a number sentence below the exercise on Worksheet 3–1a to show the substitution. They should also record a statement about whether the ordered pair is a solution for the given equation.

6. Discuss Exercise 1 on Worksheet 3–1a with the class before allowing students to work with a partner.

Consider Exercise 1: "$B = -\frac{1}{2}A + 3$; test *(A, B)* = (+4, − 5)."
Have students place tiles on Building Mat 3–1a to represent the given equation. The initial appearance of the mat is shown here. In the illustration, the shaded variable tile represents the inverse of half of variable *A*, and the plain variable tile represents variable *B*.

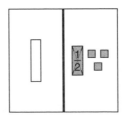

The ordered pair to be tested is *(A, B)* = (+4, –5). Have students replace the variable *B* tile on the left side of the mat with 5 negative unit tiles. Since the variable tile on the right side of the mat represents the inverse of half of variable *A*, students should replace the tile with the *opposite* of half of +4, or –2. Then 0-pairs of unit tiles should be formed and removed from the right side of the mat, leaving a total value of +1 on the right side. The value of –5 on the left clearly does not equal the remaining value of +1 on the right, so (+4, –5) is *not* a solution for the given equation. The final mat should have the following appearance:

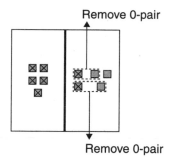

Remove 0-pair

Remove 0-pair

Students should record the substitution step and the conclusion below Exercise 1 on the worksheet as follows: $(-5) = -\frac{1}{2}(+4) + 3 = -2 + 3 \otimes$ shows $-5 \neq +1$. So (+4, –5) is *not* a solution for the equation.

Answer Key for Worksheet 3–1a

Here are possible statements to record below the exercises.

1. $(-5) = -\frac{1}{2}(+4) + 3 = -2 + 3 \otimes$ shows $-5 \neq +1$. So (+4, –5) is *not* a solution for the equation.

2. $(-9) = 3(-2) + 3(-1) = (-6) + (-3)$ shows $-9 = -9$. So (–2, –9) is a solution for the equation.

3. $(+11) = +\frac{2}{3}(+9) + 5 = (+6) + 5$ shows $+11 = +11$. So (+9, +11) is a solution for the equation.

4. $(+2) = (-2)(-3) + (-2)(+4) = (+6) + (-8) \otimes$ shows $+2 \neq -2$. So (–3, +2) is *not* a solution for the equation.

5. $(-9) = 3(-1) - 4 + 2(-1)$ shows $-9 = -9$. So (–1, –9) is a solution for the equation.

Building Mat 3–1a

Worksheet 3–1a   Name _____

Finding Solutions Through   Date _____
Substitution

For each exercise, place tiles on Building Mat 3–1a to represent the equation. Based on the given ordered pair, substitute unit tiles for each variable on the building mat. Write a number sentence below the exercise to show the substitution, and state whether the given ordered pair *(A, B)* or *(A, f(A))* is a solution of the equation.

1. $B = -\frac{1}{2}A + 3$; test *(A, B)* = (+4, –5).

2. $B = 3(A - 1)$; test *(A, B)* = (–2, –9).

3. $f(A) = +\frac{2}{3}A + 5$; test *(A, f(A))* = (+9, +11).

4. $f(A) = -2(A + 4)$; test *(A, f(A))* = (–3, +2).

5. $B = 3A - 4 + 2A$; test *(A, B)* = (–1, –9).

Activity 2
Pictorial Stage

Materials
>   Worksheet 3–1b
>   Red pencils
>   Regular pencils and regular paper

Procedure

  1.   Give each pair of students two copies of Worksheet 3–1b and two red pencils. Students are to draw diagrams of various linear equations. Small squares should be drawn for positive and negative units. Long rectangular bars should be drawn for variables and labeled with the <u>letters</u> of the different variables in order to identify the bars. The length of a variable bar will not matter in a diagram, since different <u>lengths</u> are difficult for students to draw or recognize visually. A large X should be drawn on a shape in order to represent an inverse form.

  2.   For Exercises 2 and 4 on Worksheet 3–1b, students are required to draw a diagram of the given equation on regular paper and to test a single possible solution pair provided in a word problem. They will draw unit squares in red pencil on or above each variable bar according to the given ordered pair to show that the total values found on both sides of the diagram are equivalent.

  3.   For Exercises 1 and 3 on the worksheet, in addition to drawing a diagram of the given equation, students are required to use two given table entries for the independent variable to find the corresponding dependent variable's value. Two diagrams for the same equation will be needed. One partner should draw unit squares in red pencil on one diagram for the first table entry shown, and the other partner should draw red unit squares for the second table entry on the other copy of the same diagram.

  4.   On Worksheet 3–1b, students should record number sentences below each exercise that show the substitutions of the given ordered pair or of the table entries for the independent variable. A statement about an ordered pair being a solution or not should also be recorded below the exercise.

  5.   Discuss Exercise 1 on Worksheet 3–1b with the entire class before allowing partners to work the other exercises.

  Consider Exercise 1 on Worksheet 3–1b: "What is the value of $f(x)$ in $f(x) = -\frac{1}{2}x - 5$ when $x = -6$ or $x = +2$?"

  Since there are two values of x to be substituted, partners will need two copies of their diagram for the given equation. Remind students that $f(x)$ is simply another name for the dependent variable. Here is a possible diagram, which shows labeled rectangles for the variables:

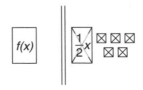

Since both $x = -6$ and $x = +2$ need to be substituted to find values for $f(x)$, students should first find the opposite of half of –6, which is +3, and draw three positive unit squares in red pencil on or above the bar for $-\frac{1}{2}x$ on the right side of the diagram. Then positive and negative unit squares should be connected with regular pencil to form 0-pairs. The total value remaining on the right side equals the value of $f(x)$, which will be –2. Here is a possible completed diagram for $x = -6$:

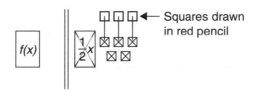

Similarly, on the second diagram, students should find the opposite of half of +2, which is –1, and draw one negative unit square on or above the bar for $-\frac{1}{2}x$ on the right side of the diagram. Since no 0-pairs can be formed, the total value on the right side will be –6, which equals $f(x)$ on the left side of the diagram.

Have students complete the table below Exercise 1, writing –2 as the first entry for $f(x)$ and –6 as the second entry for $f(x)$. Below the exercise they should record the substitutions they used for the two values of x as follows: $f(x) = -\frac{1}{2}(-6) - 5 = -2$ and $f(x) = -\frac{1}{2}(+2) - 5 = -6$. Also have students record the following conclusion: (–6, –2) and (+2, –6) are solutions of the given equation.

Answer Key for Worksheet 3–1b
Only substitutions and solution statements are shown; possible diagrams are not provided except for Exercise 1.

1. $f(x) = -\frac{1}{2}(-6) - 5 = -2$ and $f(x) = -\frac{1}{2}(+2) - 5 = -6$. (–6, –2) and (+2, –6) are solutions of the given equation.

2. $18 = 2(6) + 2(2) = 12 + 4 \otimes$ shows $18 \neq 16$. (6, 18) is *not* a solution of the given equation. [$2(c + 2)$ is drawn as two variables and two groups of +2.]

3. $p = 3(+2) + 2 = +8$ and $p = 3(+3) + 2 = +11$. (2, 8) and (3, 11) are solutions of the given equation.

4. $7 = 2(3) + 1$ shows $7 = 7$. (3, 7) is a solution of the given equation.

180

Worksheet 3–1b
Finding Solutions Through
Substitution

Name _____

Date _____

For each exercise, draw a diagram of the given equation on regular paper. To substitute an ordered pair or a given table value in the equation, draw unit squares in red pencil on each appropriate variable in the diagram. Below the exercise on the worksheet, record the number sentence used for each substitution. State whether the ordered pair is a solution, and, if applicable, complete the blanks in the given table.

1. What is the value of $f(x)$ in $f(x) = -\frac{1}{2}x - 5$ when $x = -6$ or $x = +2$?

x	f(x)
-6	
+2	

2. A candy company sells lemon tarts in a box. The empty box weighs 4 ounces, and each piece of candy weighs 2 ounces. The equation for the total weight in ounces, w, of a box of candies in terms of c, the number of candies in the box, is $w = 2(c + 2)$. If 6 candies are in a box, will the total weight of the packed box be 18 ounces?

3. Use $p = 3n + 2$ to find the missing values in the table:

n	2	3
p		

4. George installed three bird feeders in his backyard. Later he saw 7 birds at the feeders. Does the equation $B = 2F + 1$ represent a possible relationship between the number of feeders, F, and the number of birds, B, seen at the feeders?

Activity 3
Independent Practice

Materials
> Worksheet 3–1c
> Regular pencils

Procedure
Give each student a copy of Worksheet 3–1c to complete. When all are finished, have various students share their answers and their reasoning with the entire class.

Answer Key for Worksheet 3–1c
1. B
2. C
3. A
4. B
5. D
6. C

Possible Testing Errors That May Occur for This Objective
- When substituting a value for a variable in an equation, students make computational errors.
- Students reverse the values being substituted. For example, if $x = 5$ and $y = -2$, they will replace x with -2 and y with 5, which leads them to the wrong conclusion about a possible solution.
- When selecting an equation that must be satisfied by several ordered pairs, students find an equation that is satisfied by only one of the ordered pairs. They do not test all of the pairs in the same equation.

182

Finding Solutions of Linear
Equations   Date _____

Solve each exercise. Be ready to share your reasoning and your answers with other students in the class.

1. The total cost, C, of a wedding can be represented by the equation $C = 50N + 800$, where N is the number of people attending the wedding. If a wedding cost \$7,050, how many people attended the wedding?

   A. 96   B. 125   C. 141   D. 183

2. If a point lies on a line, its ordered pair is a solution of the equation that describes the line. Which equation represents the line that passes through the two points (–3, 3) and (5, –1)?

   A. $y = -\frac{1}{2}x + \frac{7}{2}$ B. $y = -\frac{3}{2}x + \frac{13}{2}$ C. $y = -\frac{1}{2}x + \frac{3}{2}$ D. $y = -2x - 3$

3. The algebraic form of a linear function is $D = \frac{1}{5}L$, where D is the total distance in miles and L is the number of laps. Which of the following choices identifies the same linear function?

   A. For every 5 laps around the track, an athlete runs a total of 1 mile.

   B. For every lap around the track, an athlete runs one-tenth of a mile.

   C.

L	0	1	2
D	0	$\frac{1}{5}$	$\frac{1}{2}$

   D.

L	$\frac{1}{2}$	1	4
D	$\frac{1}{10}$	$\frac{1}{2}$	1

Worksheet 3–1c Continued

Name _____

Date _____

4. Sally borrowed money to buy a used car. The equation $f(p) = 2560 - 225p$ shows the remaining loan balance, $f(p)$, after p payments have been made. What is Sally's loan balance after she makes 5 payments?

   A. $1,125   B. $1,435   C. $2,335   D. $2,560

5. José wants to find the total cost, c, for gasoline and repairs for his car in the last three months. The total cost included $200 for repairs. Gasoline cost $1.83 per gallon. Which of the following equations can be used to determine the total cost if José knows the number of gallons of gas, g, he bought in the last three months?

   A. $1.83g - 200 = c$ C. $1.83 - 200g = c$

   B. $1.83 + 200g = c$ D. $1.83g + 200 = c$

6. The table represents solutions of the function $f(x) = 2(x - 3) - 8$. There is an error in the table. Which ordered pair is not a solution for the function?

x	5	10	15	20
f(x)	-4	6	18	26

   A. (5, –4)   B. (10, 6)   C. (15, 18)   D. (20, 26)

Objective 2: Find Specific Solutions for a Given Quadratic Function in Order to Solve a Problem

Students need experience in finding solutions to quadratic functions. One strategy is to use substitution of given values in a quadratic equation involving two variables. Practice should include applications of the distributive property. Recognition of the notation $f(x)$ as the dependent variable when x is the independent variable is also important, so the following activities focus on the substitution method and functional notation.

Activity 1

Manipulative Stage

Materials

Sets of algebra tiles (1 set per pair of students)
Building Mat 3–2a
Worksheet 3–2a
Regular pencils

Procedure

1.   Give each pair of students a set of algebra tiles, a copy of Building Mat 3–2a, and two copies of Worksheet 3–2a. The initial set of tiles should contain 30 unit tiles and have 8 linear variable tiles in a shorter length and 1 linear variable tile in a longer length (for example, 0.75 inch by 3 inches and 0.75 inch by 3.25 inches). The set should also contain 4 quadratic variable tiles, whose side lengths equal the length of the shorter linear variable tile (for example, 3 inches by 3 inches). A different color should be used for each type of tile, that is, for the unit tile and the two linear variable tile lengths; however, the quadratic variable tile should be the same color as the shorter linear variable tile. Consider the shorter linear variable tile as variable A and the longer linear tile as variable B for notation purposes. The large square or quadratic variable tile will represent A^2, because it measures A by A in size. Each tile—both unit and variable—should have a large X marked on one side to represent its inverse form.

2.   For each exercise on Worksheet 3–2a, have students place tiles on Building Mat 3–2a to represent the equation. If an equation includes $f(A)$, remind students that this is notation for the dependent variable, so they should use the variable B tile to represent $f(A)$. Also, if the distributive property is involved, students should build the required groups on the mat before making any substitutions. For example, for $3(A^2+A+2)$, students should build (A^2+A+2) three times, which yields $3A^2$, $3A$, and $+6$ in tiles on the building mat. Students need much experience with this particular property.

3.   Have students substitute unit tiles for each variable tile on the building mat according to the values of the given ordered pair: (A, B) or $(A, f(A))$. If the total value of the left side of the mat equals the total value of the right side of the mat, then the ordered pair represents a *solution* of the equation. If the total values do not equal each other, the ordered pair is *not* a solution.

4.   Have students write a number sentence below the exercise on Worksheet 3–2a to show the substitution. They should also record a statement about whether the ordered pair is a solution for the given equation.

5.   Discuss Exercise 1 with the class before allowing students to work with a partner.

Consider Exercise 1 on Worksheet 3–2a: "$B = -3(A^2 - A - 1)$; test $(A, B) = (-2, -5)$."

Have students place tiles on Building Mat 3–2a to represent the given equation. One variable B tile should be placed on the left side of the mat. Since the distributive property is involved, the inverse of 3 groups of A^2, the inverse of 3 groups of $-A$, and the inverse of 3 groups of -1 need to be represented on the right side of the building mat. So 3 of $-A^2$, 3 of A, and 3 of $+1$ need to be placed on the right side. The initial appearance of the mat is shown here. In the illustration, the shaded variable tiles represent the variable A and the inverse of variable A-squared, and the unshaded variable tile represents variable B.

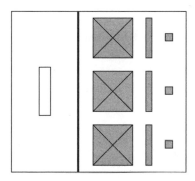

The ordered pair to be tested is *(A, B) = (–2, –5)*. Have students replace the variable B tile on the left side of the mat with its given value of 5 negative unit tiles. Since A-squared has a value of $(-2)(-2)$ or $+4$, on the right side of the mat, each tile for the inverse of variable A-squared should be replaced with the *opposite* of $+4$, or 4 negative unit tiles. Each variable A tile should be replaced with its given value, or two negative unit tiles. Then 0-pairs of unit tiles should be formed and removed from the right side of the mat, leaving a total value of –15 on the right side. The value of –5 on the left clearly does not equal the remaining value of –15 on the right, so (–2, –5) is *not* a solution for the given equation. The final mat should have the following appearance:

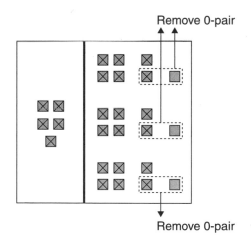

Students should record the substitution step and the conclusion below Exercise 1 on the worksheet. Here is one possible recording to use: $-5 = -3(-2)^2 - 3(+2) - 3(-1) = -12 - 6 + 3 \otimes$ shows $-5 \neq -15$. So (–2, –5) is *not* a solution for the equation.

Answer Key for Worksheet 3–2a

Here are possible statements to record below the exercises. When appropriate, the distributive property was applied before substitutions were made.

1. $-5 = -3(-2)^2 - 3(+2) - 3(-1) = -12 - 6 + 3 \otimes$ shows $-5 \neq -15$. So $(-2, -5)$ is *not* a solution for the equation.

2. $+4 = (+3)^2 - 5 = +9 - 5$ shows $+4 = +4$. So $(+3, +4)$ is a solution for the equation.

3. $-3 = -5 - 3(+2) + 2(+2)^2 = -5 - 6 + 8$ shows $-3 = -3$. So $(+2, -3)$ is a solution for the equation.

4. $+6 = -(+2)^2 + 2(+2) + 6 = -4 + 4 + 6$ shows $+6 = +6$. So $(+2, +6)$ is a solution for the equation.

5. $+5 = 2(1) - 4(-1)^2 + 2(-1) = 2 - 4 - 2 \otimes$ shows $+5 \neq -4$. So $(-1, +5)$ is *not* a solution for the equation.

Building Mat 3–2a

188

Worksheet 3–2a   Name _____

Finding Solutions Through   Date _____
Substitution

For each exercise, place tiles on Building Mat 3–2a to represent the equation. Based on
the given ordered pair, substitute unit tiles for each variable on the building mat. Write a
number sentence below the exercise to show the substitution, and state whether the
given ordered pair *(A, B)* or *(A, f(A))* is a solution of the equation.

1. $B = -3(A^2 - A - 1)$; test *(A, B)* = (–2, –5).

2. $B = A^2 - 5$; test *(A, B)* = (+3, +4).

3. $B = -5 - 3A + 2A^2$; test *(A, B)* = (+2, –3).

4. $f(A) = -A^2 + 2A + 6$; test *(A, f(A))* = (+2, +6).

5. $f(A) = 2(1 - 2A^2 + A)$; test *(A, f(A))* = (–1, +5).

Activity 2
Pictorial Stage

Materials

> Worksheet 3–2b
> Red pencils
> Regular pencils and regular paper

Procedure

1. Give each pair of students two copies of Worksheet 3–2b and two red pencils. Students are to draw diagrams of various quadratic equations. Small squares should be drawn for positive and negative units. Long rectangular bars should be drawn for variables and labeled with the <u>letters</u> of the different variables in order to identify the bars. The length of a variable bar will not matter in a diagram, since different <u>lengths</u> are difficult for students to draw or recognize visually. Large squares should be drawn and labeled for any quadratic variables. A large X should be drawn on a shape in order to represent an inverse form.

2. For each exercise on Worksheet 3–2b, students are required to draw a diagram of the given equation on regular paper and to test a single possible solution pair or substitute a specific value given for one of the variables in order to find the other variable's value. They will draw unit squares in red pencil on or above each variable bar according to the given ordered pair or specific value to see if the total values found on both sides of the diagram are equivalent. A trial-and-error strategy applied to products of integers will be useful for Exercises 1 and 4, particularly if students have not yet mastered the standard factoring method or the quadratic formula for solving quadratic equations.

3. For Exercise 3 on the worksheet, in addition to drawing a diagram of the given equation, students are required to use two given table entries for the independent variable to find the corresponding dependent variable's value. Two diagrams for the same equation will be needed. One partner should draw unit squares in red pencil on one diagram for the first table entry shown, and the other partner should draw red unit squares for the second table entry on the other copy of the same diagram.

4. On Worksheet 3–2b, students should record number sentences below each exercise that show the substitution of the given ordered pair or of the specific entries for a certain variable. A statement about an ordered pair being a solution or not should also be recorded below the exercise, if appropriate.

5. Discuss Exercise 1 on Worksheet 3–2b with the entire class before allowing partners to work the other exercises.

Consider Exercise 1 on Worksheet 3–2b: "What is the value of x in $y = x^2 + 2x - 5$ when $y = 10$? Is more than one value possible for x? Solve by applying number properties."

Have students draw a diagram that represents the equation. A long rectangle labeled as y should be drawn on the left side of the "equals" or separation bar, and 1 large square, 2 long rectangles, and 5 small unit squares should be drawn on the right side. Here is a possible diagram, which shows labeled rectangles for the variables:

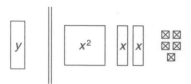

Since y = 10, have students draw 10 small red squares over the rectangle for y on the left side of the diagram. Because we are applying a trial-and-error strategy, instead of the quadratic formula, to solve this exercise, have students isolate the x-variable shapes on the right side by drawing 5 positive units in regular pencil on the right side, then on the left side. Positive and negative unit squares should be connected with regular pencil to form 0-pairs on the right side. The total value remaining on the left side will be 10 + 5, or 15. Here is a possible completed diagram:

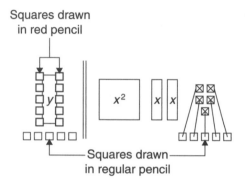

At this point, students may approach the problem in two different ways: (1) guess which value will work for the variable x, so that the value squared plus twice the value will equal 15; or (2) first rearrange the x shapes into a rectangular region in order to estimate what the value of x might be. If the first approach is used, students should start with a small positive value for x since 15 is relatively small. For example, they might try $x = 2$ and then $(2)(2) + 2(2) = 8$, which is less than 15. For $x = 3$, they will have $(3)(3) + 2(3) = 15$. So one value for x will be +3. Students also need to consider negative values for x and test them in a similar way. For example, if $x = -3$, the sum would be $(-3)(-3) + 2(-3) = +3$, which is less than 15. For $x = -5$, they would have $(-5)(-5) + 2(-5) = 15$. So another value for x will be –5.

To use the second approach, have students redraw the large square and the two long rectangles of the x variable so that they form a larger, but partial, rectangular shape. Here are two possible arrangements for the shapes:

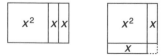

The arrangement on the left has an area of x by $(x + 2)$, and the arrangement on the right has an approximately square area of $(x + 1)$ by $(x + 1)$. Since we are dealing with integers and 15 is not a perfect square, the arrangement on the right does not apply. Looking at the left arrangement, we need to find two consecutive even or two consecutive odd integers whose product equals +15. This leads to x being 3 and $(x + 2)$ being 5, where both are odd integers. Have students also consider any negative integers that might satisfy the same conditions. They should discover that $x = -5$ and $(x + 2) = -3$, where their product is +15 as well. So by the second approach, we find that $x = 3$ or $x = -5$.

Now that possible values have been found for x, have students make new copies of the initial diagram and substitute each value into the original equation by drawing unit squares in red pencil on the appropriate variable shapes in the diagram. Since two different values of x need to be tested, have some students test one value on their diagrams, while other students test the second value. Have students substitute for y, as well as for x, in the new copy of the initial diagram. Remind students that $(-5)(-5)$ is positive, so 25 positive units will need to be drawn for x-squared when $x = -5$. Here is a completed diagram for testing $x = -5$. If students form 0-pairs of positive and negative units on the right side of the diagram, there will be 10 positive units remaining on the right side to balance or equal the 10 positive units drawn on the left side.

Below Exercise 1, have students record the substitutions they used for the two values of x as follows: $10 = (+3)(+3) + 2(+3) - 5 = +9 + 6 - 5$ and $10 = (-5)(-5) + 2(-5) - 5 = +25 - 10 - 5$. Also have students record the following conclusion: "(3, 10) and (–5, 10) are solutions of the given equation."

Answer Key for Worksheet 3–2b
Only substitutions and solution statements are shown. Apply the distributive property before making any substitutions; possible diagrams are not provided except for Exercise 1 shown in the procedure.

1. $10 = (+3)(+3) + 2(+3) - 5 = +9 + 6 - 5$ and $10 = (-5)(-5) + 2(-5) - 5 = +25 - 10 - 5$. (3, 10) and (–5, 10) are solutions of the given equation.

2. $0 = 2(-2)^2 + (-2) - 6 = 8 - 2 - 6$. (–2, 0) is a solution of the given equation.

3. $p = -3(+2)^2 + 2 = -10$ and $p = -3(+3)^2 + 2 = -25$. (2, –10) and (3, –25) are solutions of the given equation.

4. $0 = (3)^2 + (3) - 12 = 9 + 3 - 12$ and $0 = (-4)^2 + (-4) - 12 = 16 - 4 - 12$. The x-intercepts of the graph for the given equation are $x = 3$ and $x = -4$. Also, (3, 0) and (–4, 0) are solutions of the given equation.

5. $y = 2(-1)^2 - 6(-1) + 2 = 2 + 6 + 2 = 10$. So $y = 10$ when $x = -1$. (–1, 10) is a solution of the given equation.

Worksheet 3–2b   Name _____

Finding Solutions Through   Date _____
Substitution

For each exercise, draw a diagram of the given equation on regular paper. To substitute an ordered pair or a given table value in the equation, draw unit squares in red pencil on each appropriate variable in the diagram. Below the exercise on the worksheet, record the number sentence used for each substitution. State whether the ordered pair is a solution or not, and, if applicable, complete the blanks in the given table.

1. What is the value of x in $y = x^2 + 2x - 5$ when $y = 10$? Is more than one value possible for x? Solve by applying number properties.

2. Does the ordered pair (–2, 0) represent a root of the function $f(x) = 2x^2 + x - 6$?

3. Use $p = -3n^2 + 2$ to find the missing values in the table:

n	2	3
p		

4. The x-intercepts of a graph occur where $f(x) = 0$. Find the values of x that are the x-intercepts of the graph of the equation $f(x) = x^2 + x - 12$. Properties of integers will be helpful here.

5. What is the value of y in $y = 2(x^2 - 3x + 1)$ when $x = -1$?

Activity 3
Independent Practice

Materials
Worksheet 3–2c
Regular pencils

Procedure
Give each student a copy of Worksheet 3–2c to complete. When all are finished, have various students share their answers and their reasoning with the entire class.

Answer Key for Worksheet 3–2c
1. D

2. B

3. A

4. C

5. A

6. C

7. D

Possible Testing Errors That May Occur for This Objective
- When substituting a value for a variable in an equation, students make computational errors.

- Students reverse the values being substituted. For example, if $x = 5$ and $y = -2$, they will replace x with -2 and y with 5, which leads them to the wrong conclusion about a possible solution.

- When selecting an equation that must be satisfied by several ordered pairs, students find an equation that is satisfied by only one of the ordered pairs. They do not test all of the pairs in the same equation.

- When a quadratic variable is present, students find a positive value for the variable being squared, but fail to test for another possible value, in particular, a negative value. For example, for $f(x) = x^2 + 3$, when $f(x) = 7$, then x may equal -2, as well as $+2$.

Worksheet 3–2c

Finding Solutions of
Quadratic Equations

Name _____

Date _____

Solve each exercise. Be ready to share your reasoning and your answers with other students in the class.

1. What are the x-intercepts of the graph of the equation $f(x) = x^2 + 4x - 12$?

    A. $x = 3, x = 4$ B. $x = -2, x = 6$ C. $x = -3, x = -4$ D. $x = 2, x = -6$

2. If a point lies on a graph, its ordered pair is a solution of the equation that describes the graph. Which equation represents the parabola that passes through the two points $(0, -7)$ and $(-2, -31)$?

    A. $y = -5x^2 - 2x + 7$ C. $y = 5x^2 + 3x - 7$

    B. $y = -5x^2 + 2x - 7$ D. $y = 5x^2 + 2x - 3$

3. What is the value of w when $t = 3$ in the equation $w = 10t^2 - 8t + 5$?

    A. 71   B. 66   C. 61   D. 50

4. What is the solution set for x in the equation $3(2x - 1)^2 = 48$?

    A. $\left\{ +\dfrac{5}{2}, -\dfrac{5}{2} \right\}$ B. $\left\{ +\dfrac{3}{2}, -\dfrac{5}{2} \right\}$ C. $\left\{ +\dfrac{5}{2}, -\dfrac{3}{2} \right\}$ D. $\left\{ +\dfrac{3}{2}, -\dfrac{3}{2} \right\}$

5. A chemical reaction is represented by the equation $t = 150 - 5d - d^2$, where d is the temperature in degrees Celsius of the reaction and t is the time in seconds needed to complete the reaction. If the reaction takes 100 seconds, what is the temperature of the reaction? If helpful, use a trial-and-error strategy.

    A. 5°C   B. 10°C   C. 15°C   D. 20°C

6. The table represents solutions of the function $f(x) = 2(x - 3)^2 - 8$. There is an error in the table. Which ordered pair is not a solution for the function?

x	−1	0	2	5
$f(x)$	24	10	6	0

    A. $(-1, 24)$ B. $(0, 10)$ C. $(2, 6)$ D. $(5, 0)$

7. Which ordered pair represents one of the roots of the function $f(x) = -20 + 3x + 2x^2$?

    A. $(-10, 0)$ B. $(+3, 0)$ C. $(0, -20)$ D. $(-4, 0)$

Objective 3: Recognize and Apply the General Forms of Linear and Quadratic Parent Functions

Linear and quadratic functions behave in their own unique way. Their graphs have definite appearances that students should be able to recognize. The following activities provide experiences in predicting changes in graphs based on changes in certain parameters in the equations of functions, for example, the constant, which causes a vertical shift. The exercises focus on the algebraic forms $y = ax + b$ and $y = ax^2 + b$.

Activity 1

Manipulative Stage

Materials

> 1-inch square tiles (commercial or teacher-made; 50 tiles per pair of students)
> Building Mat 3–3a
> Worksheet 3–3a
> Red pencil and regular pencil

Procedure

1. Give each pair of students a copy of Building Mat 3–3a, two copies of Worksheet 3–3a, a red pencil, and a packet of 50 1-inch square tiles. The tile color is not important.

2. For each exercise on Worksheet 3–3a, students will substitute the required values of x into the given equation to find the corresponding values of y. The ordered pairs found should be recorded below the exercise on the worksheet, using the format (number of the column, total tiles in the column). Students should then build different columns of tiles on Building Mat 3–3a, varying the column height according to the ordered pair represented. Encourage them to notice the shape or direction of the path created by the top edges of the columns of tiles.

3. For each exercise, students will plot points on the grid to represent their ordered pairs. For each grid, the vertical axis will need to be labeled as "Total Tiles per Column" and marked off with an appropriate scale.

4. Students will use a red pencil to connect, in order, the five points plotted on each grid.

5. After students complete Exercises 1 through 4, discuss the appearance of each red path drawn. Each path should be either straight or curved (as a parabola) and closely resemble the path formed by the top edges of the columns of tiles built for the same exercise. The straight path will have a positive or a negative slope, and it may be very steep or nearly level (horizontal). The curved path will be symmetrical and might have either a high point (maximum) or a low point (minimum); it will also have a narrow curvature (or narrow spread) or a wide curvature. Guide students to compare the changes in the parameters of the equations to the changes in the graphs in order to complete Exercise 5.

6. Discuss Exercise 1 on Worksheet 3–3a with the entire class before allowing students to work the other exercises with their partners.

Consider Exercise 1 on Worksheet 3–3a: "$y = 3x^2$ where $x = -2$ through $+2$."

Have students make substitutions in the given equation for the different values of x. They should obtain the following ordered pairs: (–2, 12), (–1, 3), (0, 0), (1, 3), and (2, 12). These pairs should be recorded below Exercise 1 on the worksheet.

Students should then build columns on Building Mat 3–3a using the 1-inch tiles. There should be no tiles placed at the 0-mark on the mat, because y equals 0 when $x = 0$. Here is the final arrangement of the tiles on the mat:

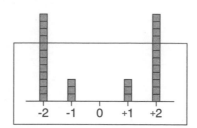

Encourage students to notice that the top edges of the columns seem to form a U-shaped curve, which touches the horizontal bar of the mat at 0. The curve has a vertical line of symmetry at the 0-mark.

Students should plot the five ordered pairs on the grid below Exercise 1 on Worksheet 3–3a. The points should be connected with red pencil. The path formed should be similar to the curve created by the top edges of the columns of tiles on the building mat. The completed grid should appear as shown:

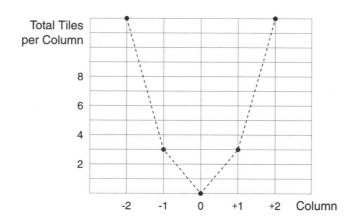

Note: If a negative value were obtained for y, the required number of tiles would be placed *below* the horizontal bar of the building mat to represent the negative amount. For example, in the equation $y = -3x^2 + 5$, when $x = -2$ or $+2$, y would equal –7; 7 tiles would need to be placed below the horizontal bar of the mat to show this negative effect. The *bottom* edges of those negative columns of tiles would then be considered, along with the top edges of any columns above the horizontal bar, when forming a curve. The equations used in this activity do not require any negative values for y.

Answer Key for Worksheet 3–3a

Only ordered pairs are provided for each exercise; no graphs are shown, except for Exercise 1 in the text.

1. (–2, 12), (–1, 3), (0, 0), (1, 3), (2, 12)

2. (–2, 11), (–1, 9), (0, 7), (1, 5), (2, 3)

3. (–2, 4), (–1, 1), (0, 0), (1, 1), (2, 4)

4. (–2, 3), (–1, 5), (0, 7), (1, 9), (2, 11)

5. Possible observations: In Exercises 1 and 3, each equation has a quadratic term. Both curves are U-shaped and have a minimal point at (0, 0), but the curve for Exercise 1, which has a coefficient of +3 on the quadratic term, is narrower or less spread out than the curve for Exercise 3, which has a coefficient of +1 on the quadratic term.

    The equations for Exercises 2 and 4 have a linear term but not a quadratic term. The graphs are both lines, but the line for Exercise 2 has a negative slope (–2) and the line for Exercise 4 has a positive slope (+2). The two lines have the same y-intercept, each passing through (0, 7).

Building Mat 3–3a

Worksheet 3–3a

Building Functions with
Square Tiles

Name _____

Date _____

Build with square tiles to make 5 different columns as directed in each exercise. Plot
points on each grid for ordered pairs found and connect the points with red pencil.

1. $y = 3x^2$ where $x = -2$ through $+2$

Total Tiles
per Column

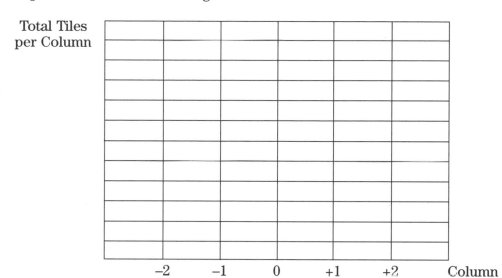

2. $y = -2x + 7$ where $x = -2$ through $+2$

Total Tiles
per Column

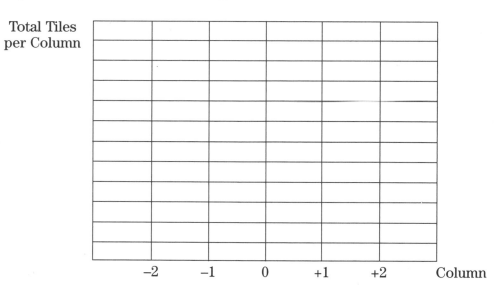

Worksheet 3–3a Continued   Name _____

                                  Date _____

3. $y = x^2$ where $x = -2$ through $+2$

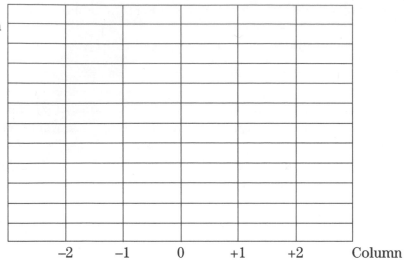

Total Tiles per Column

         −2   −1   0   +1   +2   Column

4. $y = +2x + 7$ where $x = -2$ through $+2$

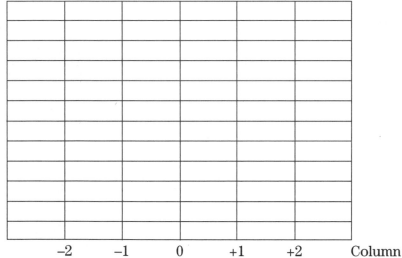

Total Tiles per Column

         −2   −1   0   +1   +2   Column

5. What do you notice about the appearance of each graph when compared to the other graphs? How do the coefficients or constants in the equations compare?

Activity 2
Pictorial Stage

Materials

Worksheet 3–3b
Red and blue pencils
Regular pencils

Procedure

1. Give each pair of students two copies of Worksheet 3–3b with one red pencil and one blue pencil.

2. For each exercise on Worksheet 3–3b, have students find ordered pairs for each equation provided, using x as –3 through +3. Then have them plot the ordered pairs on the grid below the equation.

3. After the two graphs have been drawn for an exercise, guide students to compare each new graph with the graph of the parent function already shown on the same grid. For Exercise 1, graph (a) will be shaped like the quadratic parent function's graph, but will be shifted upward by 2 units; its minimum point will be at (0, 2). Graph (b) will also have a U-shape, but will be flattened more toward the x-axis or have a wider curvature; its minimum point will remain at (0, 0). For Exercise 2, graph (a) will be a line parallel to the linear parent function's graph, but it will be shifted downward 3 units; its y-intercept will be at –3 instead of at 0. Graph (b) will also be a line, but it will be closer to the horizontal position than the parent function's graph; it will still cross the y-axis at (0, 0). Ideas similar to these should be recorded below each exercise beside the appropriate equation.

4. Along with the statements recorded at the bottom of each exercise, have students circle in red the coefficient or constant that differs in equation (a) or (b) from the corresponding element in the parent function. Have them circle in blue the coefficient or constant that is the same as the corresponding element in the parent function. Remind students that the absence of a constant means that the constant equals 0. Guide students to relate these numerical changes to the changes found in graphs (a) or (b) when compared to the graph of the corresponding parent function.

5. Discuss Exercise 1, equation (b), with the entire class before allowing partners to prepare the other graphs on their own.

Consider Exercise 1, equation (b): "Graph $y = +\frac{1}{2}x^2$ on the given grid. How does the graph of equation (b) compare to the graph of the *parent function:* $y = +1x^2 + 0$?
(b) $y = +\frac{1}{2}x^2 + 0$ _____ "

Have students use values of x from –3 through +3 to find ordered pairs that satisfy equation (b). The ordered pairs will be the following: $\left(-3, +\frac{9}{2}\right)$, (–2, +2), $\left(-1, +\frac{1}{2}\right)$, (0, 0), $\left(+1, +\frac{1}{2}\right)$, (+2, +2), and $\left(+3, +\frac{9}{2}\right)$. After these pairs are plotted on the grid below equation (b) and connected with regular pencil, the completed grid will appear as shown:

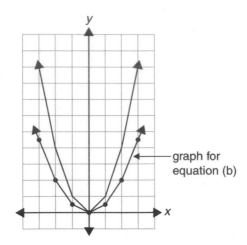

Beside equation (b), $y = +\frac{1}{2}x^2 + 0$, below the completed grid, students should record statements about how the graph of the equation compares to the graph of the quadratic parent function. Possible observations might be as follows:

"Both graphs have a minimum point at (0, 0)."
"Both graphs have a U-shape or form a parabola."
"The graph of equation (b) opens wider or has a wider curvature than the graph of the quadratic parent function."
"Points for equation (b) are closer to the x-axis than are the corresponding points for the parent function."

Using equation (b) beside the recorded statement, have students identify the symbolic likenesses and differences between the parent function and equation (b) in the following manner. The coefficient of the quadratic term in equation (b) is $+\frac{1}{2}$, instead of +1, so students should draw a circle in <u>red</u> pencil around the $+\frac{1}{2}$ in equation (b). Also, since the constant for both equations is 0, students should draw a circle in <u>blue</u> pencil around the 0 in equation (b). Help students connect the following ideas together: the <u>common</u> 0 in the two equations corresponds to their common y-intercept or minimum point at (0, 0); and the coefficient $+\frac{1}{2}$ on the quadratic term in equation (b) being <u>less</u> than the +1 on x^2 in the parent function corresponds to the graph of equation (b) being wider in its curvature or nearer the x-axis than the graph of the parent function.

Answer Key for Worksheet 3–3b
Only comparison statements are provided; no graphs are shown except for Exercise 1, equation (b), in the text.

1. .(a) The graph of equation (a) has the same curvature as the quadratic parent function (common quadratic coefficient of +1), but the graph is vertically shifted 2 units above the parent function and has a y-intercept or minimum point at (0, 2) (constant of +2 instead of 0); blue circle drawn around +1 and red circle drawn around +2 in equation (a).

    (b) [See details in the text.]

2. (a) The graph of equation (a) is parallel to the graph of the linear parent function (common slope of +1), but the graph is vertically shifted 3 units below the parent function (constant of –3 instead of 0); blue circle drawn around +1 and red circle drawn around –3 in equation (a).

(b) The graph of equation (b) is nearer the x-axis than is the graph of the linear parent function (slope of $+\frac{1}{4}$ is <u>less</u> than slope of +1 on the parent function), but both graphs pass through $(0, 0)$ or have the same y-intercept (common constant of 0); blue circle drawn around 0 and red circle drawn around $+\frac{1}{4}$ in equation (b).

204

For each exercise, graph the given equations, using x as –3 through +3. To compare equations, circle the coefficients/constants that differ with red pencil, and circle the ones that are alike with blue pencil.

1. The graph for $y = x^2$, the quadratic *parent function*, is already shown on each grid. Plot a graph on the corresponding grid for the equation provided above the grid.

(a) $y = x^2 + 2$ (b) $y = +\dfrac{1}{2}x^2$

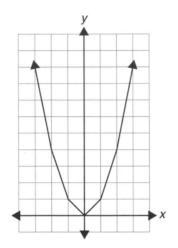 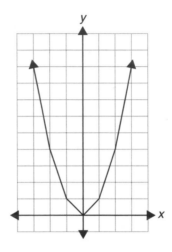

How does the graph of each equation compare to the graph of the *parent function:* $y = +1x^2 + 0$?

(a) $y = +1x^2 + 2$ _____

(b) $y = +\dfrac{1}{2}x^2 + 0$ _____

Worksheet 3–3b Continued

Name _____

Date _____

2. The graph for $y = x$, the linear *parent function*, is already shown on each grid. Plot a graph for the equation provided above each grid.

(a) $y = x - 3$

(b) $y = +\dfrac{1}{4} x$

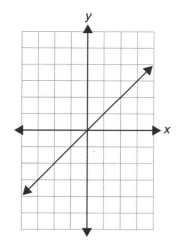

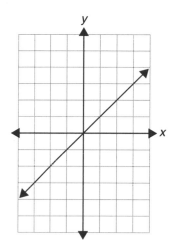

How does the graph of each equation compare to the graph of the *parent function:* $y = +1x + 0$?

(a) $y = +1x - 3$ _____

(b) $y = +\dfrac{1}{4} x + 0$ _____

Independent Practice

Materials
   Worksheet 3–3c
   5-millimeter grid paper
   Regular pencil

Procedure
Give each student a copy of Worksheet 3–3c to complete. Grid paper will be helpful. This activity includes some quadratic coefficients that are negative. When all have finished, ask various students to explain their reasoning and their answers for the exercises.

Answer Key for Worksheet 3–3c
   1. B

   2. A

   3. C

   4. A

   5. D

   6. B

   7. C

   8. D

Possible Testing Errors That May Occur for This Objective
   • Students do not recognize graphs by their types and their corresponding equations, such as linear and quadratic graphs.

   • Students incorrectly think that a change in the constant of a function causes a horizontal shift of the graph rather than a vertical shift.

   • Students ignore the negative sign in $y = -x$ or $y = -x^2$, and do not realize that it causes the graph of the parent function to reflect across the x-axis.

Worksheet 3–3c

Comparing Graphs Using
Parent Functions

Name _____

Date _____

Complete each exercise. Each grid step equals one unit. Be ready to share your reasoning and your answers with the entire class.

1. Which equation is the *parent function* of the graph represented?

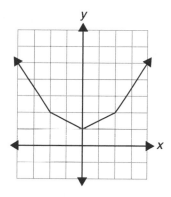

    A. $y = \sqrt{x}$ B. $y = x^2$ C. $y = |x|$ D. $y = x$

2. Which equation will produce the widest parabola when graphed?

    A. $y = 0.3x^2$ B. $y = 4x^2$ C. $y = -5x^2$ D. $y = -0.8x^2$

3. What is the effect on the graph of the equation $y = x - 8$ when the equation is changed to $y = 3x - 8$?

    A. The curve translates or shifts in the positive x direction.

    B. The graph is congruent, but the y-intercept changes.

    C. The slope of the graph increases.

    D. The slope of the graph decreases.

4. What is the effect on the graph of the equation $y = -x^2 + 1$ when the equation is changed to $y = -x^2 + 7$?

    A. The graph is congruent, but the vertex of the graph shifts vertically upward.

    B. The slope of the graph changes.

    C. The graph narrows.

    D. The graph is congruent but is flipped to open upward.

Worksheet 3–3c Continued   Name _____

                                  Date _____

5. Given the function $y = 3.4x - 26.5$, which statement best describes the effect on the graph of the function if the y-intercept is increased by 25.3, but no other changes are made in the parameters of the equation?

   A. The new line has a greater rate of change.

   B. The new line is perpendicular to the original line.

   C. The x-intercept increases.

   D. The new line is parallel to the original, but crosses the y-axis at a higher point.

6. Which shows the functions correctly listed in order from narrowest to widest graph?

   A. $y = -6x^2$, $y = -\dfrac{3}{4}x^2$, $y = +\dfrac{1}{2}x^2$, $y = 2x^2$

   B. $y = -6x^2$, $y = 2x^2$, $y = -\dfrac{3}{4}x^2$, $y = +\dfrac{1}{2}x^2$

   C. $y = 2x^2$, $y = +\dfrac{1}{2}x^2$, $y = -\dfrac{3}{4}x^2$, $y = -6x^2$

   D. $y = +\dfrac{1}{2}x^2$, $y = -\dfrac{3}{4}x^2$, $y = 2x^2$, $y = -6x^2$

7. Which equation describes the new graph when the graph for $y = -3x^2$ is reflected across the x-axis?

   A. $y = x^2$ B. $y = -\dfrac{1}{3}x^2$ C. $y = +3x^2$ D. $y = +\dfrac{1}{3}x^2$

8. Which equation is the *parent function* of the graph represented?

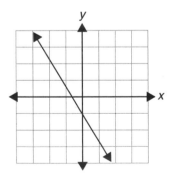

   A. $y = \sqrt{x}$ B. $y = |x|$ C. $y = x^2$ D. $y = x$

Objective 4: Find an Algebraic Expression for the Generalization or Rule Represented by Linear Data Collected or Given in a Table; Extend the Table or Sequence to New Values, Using the Rule or Number Patterns

Students need much practice with finding and extending patterns in linear sequences, particularly as the sequences occur within tables of values. They also need to be able to prepare their own tables by finding a rule that will generate the table. These skills are necessary for further studies in algebra. The following activities provide such practice. Additional practice with building or extending quadratic sequences may be found in Section 3, Objective 5.

Activity 1
Manipulative Stage

Materials

     100 square tiles per 4 students
     Paper and regular pencil

Procedure

    1. Give each group of 4 students a set of 100 square tiles (1-inch paper squares or commercially available square tiles). Have each student prepare a 2-column table. The left column heading should be "Number of Design," and the right column heading should be "Number of Tiles." There should be a minimum of 6 rows of entries in the table.

    2. Have groups build a simple, flat design several times, increasing the tiles according to the same pattern each time to gradually enlarge the design. Students should complete their tables as they build, each time recording which design it is and how many tiles total are in the design.

    3. After the students have built the first three designs based on the same pattern, ask them to predict how the fourth design will look.

    4. Then present a word problem that involves the designs. Students should continue to build their designs, checking and recording the total tiles each time, until they build the design required to answer the question in the problem.

    5. Have students write a sentence below their tables that answers the question in the problem.

    6. Ask several students to describe how they built each design. Then guide them to make a general statement about how to build the sequence of designs, based on the number of the design within the sequence.

    7. Here is a discussion of the first sequence. Then repeat the process, using a new design pattern and a new table.

The first pattern to make is a 4-wing design. The first 3 designs in the sequence are shown below. A possible prediction for the fourth design might be "4 wings with 4 square tiles per wing."

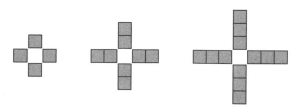

After students have built the first three designs and predicted the fourth design, present the following problem to them: "George wants to cover a tabletop with blue tiles arranged in a 4-wing design. The background will be in white tiles. He plans to use 24 tiles for the design. Which design in your sequence will he be using?"

The students should continue to build their designs, checking and recording the total tiles each time, until they build the sixth design, which will use 24 tiles. Have students write a sentence below their tables that answers the question in the problem—for example, "George will use the sixth design or 24 tiles to make his tabletop."

The final table entries will be the following pairs: (1, 4), (2, 8), (3, 12), (4, 16), (5, 20), (6, 24). The numbers in the right column of the table will increase by 4 each time. The left column numbers will increase by 1 each time. Guide students to notice that the total tiles in the design equal four times the number of the design each time. Students should record this observation in words below their tables. (They will do more writing with algebraic expressions in Activity 2.)

Here are the first three designs for a second pattern to build, making a tower-and-wall design. A possible prediction for the fourth design might be "4 single tiles connecting pairs of towers with five towers total." Here is a word problem to use: "The Chiu family is building a low concrete block fence along one side of their backyard. It will have the tower-and-wall design. Each square tile represents a concrete block. If the fence is to have 6 towers, including a tower on each end, how many blocks will they need to build the fence?" Students will continue to build until they reach the fifth design, which requires 17 tiles. A sentence to record is the following: "The Chius will need 17 concrete blocks for their fence." If building continues, table entries might be the following six pairs: (1, 5), (2, 8), (3, 11), (4, 14), (5, 17), (6, 20). Right column numbers increase by 3 each time, while the left column increases by 1. Several observations are possible for relating the total tiles of a design to the number of the design. For example, the number of the design tells how many single tiles and how many 2-tile towers are needed, plus one extra tower. So design #3 has 3 single tiles, 3 2-tile towers, plus 1 more 2-tile tower. Another approach would be to consider the tower at the left end as connected to the first single tile, forming a 3-tile unit. Then the number of the design would indicate how many 3-tile units are needed, plus one more tower at the right end. Design #3 would have three 3-tile units, plus one 2-tile tower at the right end.

Activity 2
Pictorial Stage

Materials

Worksheet 3–4a

Regular pencils

Procedure

1. Give each student a copy of Worksheet 3–4a. Have students work with partners to draw the sequences on the worksheet. Tables will now be presented in row format.

2. Ask students to extend each sequence to the sixth design. They should complete the table given with each sequence.

3. Students should answer the question given with the fence designs, using the data from the completed table.

4. For each sequence, students should write a numerical expression below each design that relates the total tiles to the number of the design. Then they should generalize these expressions into a rule for the Nth design. The new rule should be recorded below the completed table. The students' numerical expressions will vary, but the same type of expression should be used for all designs within the same sequence in order for a generalization to be formed.

5. Discuss the first sequence on Worksheet 3–4a before allowing students to work independently. Here are the first four designs and the completed table for the first sequence from Worksheet 3–4a. The top row numbers in the table change by 1 each time and the bottom row numbers change by 2 each time. The fifth design will use 11 tiles.

Number of Design	1	2	3	4	5	6
Total Tiles	3	5	7	9	11	13

After the designs and the table are completed, have students write a numerical expression below each design that shows how the total number of tiles is found, using the number of the design. One possible way for this first sequence is to add the top row (which corresponds to the number of the design) to the bottom row (which is one more than the top row each time). The expression for design #1 becomes $(1 + 2)$; for design #2, $(2 + 3)$; and so forth. The rule becomes $N + (N + 1)$ for the total tiles in the Nth design. Have students record the following below the completed table: $T(N) = N + (N + 1)$. Do not simplify the expression to $2N + 1$ at this time.

Another view of this first sequence would be to see each design as two equal rows with one extra tile on the bottom row. Then the numerical expression for design #1 would be $(2 \times 1) + 1$; for design #2, $(2 \times 2) + 1$; for design #3, $(2 \times 3) + 1$; and so forth. The generalization becomes $(2 \times N) + 1$ for the total tiles in the Nth design. Students would record the following below the table: $T(N) = (2 \times N) + 1$.

Answer Key to Worksheet 3–4a
Answers and table entries only are given.

1. Fifth design uses 11 tiles; (1, 3), (2, 5), (3, 7), (4, 9), (5, 11), (6, 13)

2. Eighth design uses 12 tiles; (1, 5), (2, 6), (3, 7), (4, 8), (5, 9), (6, 10)

3. Sixth design uses 18 tiles; (1, 3), (2, 6), (3, 9), (4, 12), (5, 15), (6, 18)

Worksheet 3–4a   Name _____

Using Tables to Solve Problems   Date _____

Draw the next 3 terms or fence designs for each sequence given below. Complete the table for each sequence. Answer each question. Find a rule for generating each sequence.

1. Which fence design will use 11 tiles?

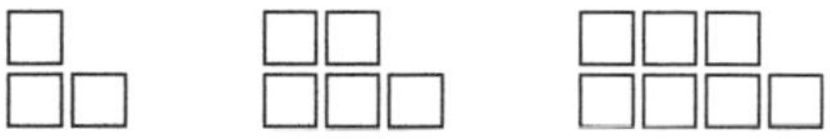

_____   _____   _____

Number of Design	1	2	3			
Total Tiles	3			9		13

2. How many tiles will the eighth fence design use?

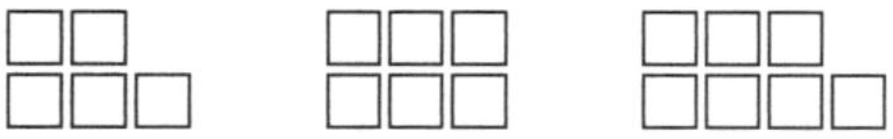

_____   _____   _____

Number of Design	1	2	3			
Total Tiles	5					

Name _____

Date _____

3. Which fence design will use 18 tiles?

_____   _____   _____

Number of Design	1	2	3			
Total Tiles						

Activity 3
Independent Practice

Materials
> Worksheet 3–4b
> Regular pencils

Procedure
Give each student a copy of Worksheet 3–4b. Have students work independently to complete the worksheet. Then discuss their results. Ask various students to explain the numerical patterns found in each table.

Answer Key for Worksheet 3–4b
Possible sentences are given for items 1 and 2.

1. 42 cookies will be in 7 packages.

2. Ms. Gomez can buy 18 bags for $24.

3. B

4. D

5. C

Possible Testing Errors That May Occur for This Objective
- The number given is the next one for the other column (or row) in the table, not the column that is requested. For example, for the pairs of data for [boxes, cookies]—(1, 4), (2, 8), (3, 12)—if the next amount of cookies is requested, students might respond with 4 (which follows 1, 2, 3 boxes), instead of with 16 (which follows 4, 8, 12 cookies).

- The first missing number in a column (or row) is found for the answer, but the test item actually requires the second or third missing number for the answer. Further extension of the sequence is needed.

- One of the numbers actually shown in the table is selected to answer the test question, rather than a number resulting from extending the listed values based on an observed pattern.

Worksheet 3–4b   Name _____

Using Patterns in Tables or   Date _____
Sequences

Apply patterns to complete or extend the tables or sequences provided below and use the information to answer the given questions. For Exercises 1 and 2, write a sentence to describe the answer.

1. If the number of packages and number of cookies continue in the pattern shown, how many cookies will there be in 7 packages?

Number of Packages	1	2	3	4			
Number of Cookies	6	12	18	24			

2. Large bags of chips are on sale at the grocery store this week. The chart shows the cost of the chips, including tax. If the pattern continues, how many bags of chips can Ms. Gomez buy for her party with $24?

Number of bags	Total Cost
3	$4
6	$8
9	$12
12	$16

3. Make your own 2-column table with appropriate headings and record the following data in the table: 4 pens for $2, 8 pens for $4, and 12 pens for $6. If you continue to buy pens at this same rate, which expression can be used to find the total cost in dollars for p pens?

A. $2p$ B. $0.5p$ C. $p - 2$ D. $p + 4$

Worksheet 3–4b Continued

Name _____

Date _____

4. Rectangular tables will be used at a high school drama banquet. The diagram shows the seating arrangements for 1 and 2 tables.

 = one person

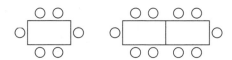

Which expression can be used to determine the number of people who can sit together if y tables are joined to form one long table?

A. $6y$ B. $4(y + 1)$ C. $2(y + 1)$ D. $4y + 2$

5. Which ordered set of numbers is the first five terms of a sequence whose Nth term is generated with the expression $(5N - 3)$?

A. 1, 2, 3, 4, 5   C. 2, 7, 12, 17, 22

B. 3, 8, 13, 18, 23   D. 8, 11, 14, 17, 20

Objective 5: Find an Algebraic Expression for the Generalization or Rule Represented by Quadratic Data Collected or Given in a Table; Extend the Table or Sequence to New Values, Using the Rule or Number Patterns

Students need much practice with finding and extending patterns in quadratic sequences, particularly as the sequences occur within tables of values. They also need to be able to prepare their own tables by finding a rule that will generate the table. These skills are necessary for further studies in algebra. The following activities provide such practice. Additional practice with building or extending linear sequences may be found in Section 3, Objective 4.

Activity 1
Manipulative Stage

Materials

    100 square tiles per 4 students
    Paper and regular pencil

Procedure

1. Give each group of 4 students a set of 100 square tiles (1-inch paper squares or commercially available square tiles). Have each student prepare a 2-column table. The left column heading should be "Number of Shape," and the right column heading should be "Total Tiles in Shape." There should be a minimum of 10 rows of entries in the table.

2. Have groups build a simple, flat design several times, increasing the tiles according to the same pattern each time to gradually enlarge the design or form a new shape. Students should complete their tables as they build, each time recording which shape it is in the sequence and how many tiles total are in the shape.

3. After they have built the first three shapes based on the same pattern, ask them to predict how the fourth shape will look, and then build it. Have some students describe in their own words what each shape looks like. Students should continue to build their shapes, checking and recording the total tiles each time.

4. Ask students to predict how the tenth shape might look and how many tiles in all they will need, based on their previous descriptions. Have them complete their table through the tenth shape with its total tiles. Some students may need to build the other shapes (#5 through #9) to confirm their predictions of the total tiles needed for the tenth shape. They will not have enough tiles to keep all shapes built concurrently; they will need to dismantle earlier shapes in order to build each new, larger shape that follows shape #5. Discuss how the numbers in the "Total Tiles" column change (increase by a different amount each time) as the shape number increases by 1.

5. Guide students to generalize their shape descriptions by asking them to describe how to find the total tiles needed for making the Nth shape. The algebraic expression should follow the language pattern used previously in steps 3 and 4. Have students write the letter N above the "Number of Shape" column of their table and write their algebraic expression above the "Total Tiles" column.

6. Here is a discussion of the first sequence. Then repeat the process, using a new shape pattern and a new table.

For the first sequence, have students build rectangular regions with their tiles, building them in order of size with the smallest one first as shown below:

Have students make a 2-column table to record their work. The left column for "Number of Shape" should show 1, 2, 3, . . . and the right column for "Total Tiles in Shape" should show the totals 2, 6, 12, . . . The number of tiles in each shape represents a *rectangular number*.

Ask several students to tell how the first and second shapes are alike and how they are different. Possible responses are:

"Both shapes are rectangular where each has equal rows of tiles."
"Shape #2 has 1 more row and 1 more tile per row than #1 has, [or #2 has 2 rows instead of 1 row and 3 tiles per row instead of 2 tiles]."

Ask how the second shape differs from the third one. (Responses should be similar to those for #1 and #2. Some students may see shape #2 as <u>adding 1 more</u> tile to the row of #1, then <u>adding 1 more</u> row of 3 tiles; then to get shape #3, 1 more tile may be added to each row in #2 and then another row of 4 tiles added on. This approach is a <u>repetitive additive</u> approach and will result in a <u>finite series</u>, $2 + 4 + 6 + \ldots + 2(N - 1) + 2N$, for the Nth term, which we do not want at this stage since we are focusing on quadratic sequences, that is, sequences whose Nth term is a second-degree polynomial. To avoid the <u>series</u> approach, encourage students to view each new term or shape as a complete arrangement or array of tiles rather than a shape formed by joining new sections to previous sections.) Encourage the following type of details: "The first shape has 1 row of 2 tiles; #2 has 2 rows of 3 tiles each; #3 has 3 rows of 4 tiles each," and so forth.

Ask students to build the fourth shape (it should have 4 rows with 5 tiles per row) to the right of the first three. They should record the total tiles used, 20 tiles, in the fourth row of their table.

Have students predict how the tenth shape might look and how many tiles total will be needed, based on their previous descriptions. (Example: "#10 has 10 rows of 11 tiles each.") Have them complete their table through the tenth shape with its total tiles, 110 tiles. Some students may need to build the other shapes (#5–#9) to confirm their predictions of the total tiles needed for the tenth shape. They will not have enough tiles to keep all shapes built concurrently; they will need to dismantle earlier shapes in order to build each new, larger shape that follows shape #5. Discuss how the numbers in the right column change (increase by a different amount each time) as the shape number increases by 1.

Now ask them to describe how to find the total tiles needed for making the Nth rectangular shape. The algebraic expression should follow the language pattern used previously: "The Nth shape will use N rows of $(N + 1)$ tiles per row, or $N \times (N + 1)$ or $N(N + 1)$ tiles total." Have students write the letter N above the left column of their table and their expression $N(N + 1)$ above the right column. Note: Do not rewrite $N(N + 1)$ as $N^2 + N$ at this stage; physically, the two expressions may have different meanings, and students must be allowed to see the difference. $N(N + 1)$ is N rows of $(N + 1)$ tiles each, whereas $N^2 + N$ implies some amount N has been <u>added</u> to a squared amount.

Now lead the class through the building of other sequences of shapes, following the same procedure and questioning used in steps 1 through 6. Be sure that the sequences are quadratic; that is, each shape's total tiles requires the squaring of the shape's position number in some way. For each sequence, have students record their numbers in a 2-column table. Encourage alternative descriptions of the sequence, but multiplication must be involved. Here are two additional sequences to use, along with descriptions of (1) the type of language needed to describe the shapes and (2) the Nth shape's description and the expression for its total tiles.

Example 2

(1) *Language:* Shape #1 has 1 row of 1 tile; shape #2 has 2 rows of 2 tiles each; shape #3 has 3 rows of 3 tiles each; and so forth. Remember that for consistency of interpretation, *rows* of tiles are always defined as left-to-right or horizontally connected tiles.

(2) Nth *shape:* The Nth shape has N rows of N tiles each; total tiles = $N(N)$ or N^2 tiles. The power form is used here as another name for the monomial; this is not considered *simplification* in this objective since the multiplication does not produce any other terms of a final polynomial. The tile totals form the sequence of *squared* numbers.

Example 3

(1) *Language:* Shape #1 has 1 row of 3 tiles; shape #2 has 2 rows of 4 tiles each; shape #3 has 3 rows of 5 tiles each; and so forth.

(2) Nth *shape:* The Nth shape has N rows of $(N + 2)$ tiles each; total tiles = $N(N + 2)$ tiles. This is another sequence of *rectangular* numbers.

Activity 2
Pictorial Stage

Materials
    Worksheet 3–5a
    Regular pencils

Procedure
    1. Give each student a copy of Worksheet 3–5a. Have students work with partners to draw the sequences on Worksheet 3–5a. Tables will now be presented in row format.

    2. Ask students to extend each sequence to the sixth shape. They should complete the table given with each sequence.

    3. For each sequence, students should write a numerical expression below each shape that relates the total tiles to the number of the shape. Then they should generalize these expressions into a rule for the Nth shape. The new rule should be recorded below the completed table. Numerical expressions will vary among students, but the same type of expression should be used by one student for all shapes within the same sequence in order for a generalization to be formed.

    4. Discuss the first sequence on Worksheet 3–5a before allowing students to work independently.

    Here are the first four shapes and the completed table for the first sequence from Worksheet 3–5a:

Number of Shape	1	2	3	4	5	6
Total Tiles	1	3	8	15	24	35

    Discuss likenesses and differences: "Shape #2 has 1 stack of 2 tiles more than #1 has; shape #3 is taller and wider than #2," and so forth. Have students describe each shape: "#1 has 1 tile; #2 has 1 stack of 2 tiles and 1 more tile; #3 has 2 stacks of 3 tiles each and 1 stack of 2 tiles."

    Ask students to draw the fourth shape according to the changes they have seen. (Shape 4 should have 3 stacks of 4 tiles each and 1 stack of 3 tiles.) Then have them draw the fifth and sixth shapes.

    Below each shape drawn, a numerical expression should be recorded to describe the pattern found in the tiles. For example, below shape #4, students might record the following: "(3)(4) + (1)(3)." Since shape #1 has only 1 tile and does not seem to satisfy the same pattern as the other shapes, have students simply record "(1)" below that shape for the moment.

All students should complete the table for the sequence. The top row will have 1, 2, 3, 4, ... and the bottom row will have 1, 3, 8, 15, ... The top row numbers in the table change by 1 each time, and the bottom row numbers increase by different amounts each time. To answer the question on Worksheet 3–5a, the fifth design will use 24 tiles.

Using the pattern they have found, guide students to predict how the tenth shape will look (#10 should have 9 stacks of 10 tiles each and 1 stack of 9 tiles). Now ask students to describe the Nth shape in the sequence. Following the language used for the earlier shapes, the Nth shape should have $(N - 1)$ stacks of N tiles each and 1 stack of $(N - 1)$ tiles, or $(N - 1)N + (1)(N - 1)$ tiles total. Testing for shape #1, we have $(0)(1) + (1)(0) = 0$ tiles total, which is not correct, even though the rule or formula does work for all the other shapes. In such cases, we say that for $N = 1$, shape #1 will have 1 tile, but for all other N, shape #N will have $(N - 1)N + (1)(N - 1)$ tiles total. Students should record this information as a statement below the completed table. Often in sequences, the first (and sometimes even the second) term must be given specifically, along with a general rule or formula for all other terms of the sequence.

The method previously discussed for the first sequence on Worksheet 3–5a was <u>additive</u> in that each shape was seen as a combination of two different groups of tiles. The shapes may also be viewed in a <u>subtractive</u> sense; that is, a shape may be viewed as part of a larger set of tiles from which some tiles have been removed. In the first sequence, we may view each shape as a squared arrangement where 1 tile has been removed from the upper right corner. In other words, shape #2 has 2 rows of 2 tiles each, less 1 tile; shape #3 has 3 rows of 3 tiles each, less 1 tile; and so forth. Shape #N will have N rows of N tiles each, less 1 tile, or $(N^2 - 1)$ total tiles. Testing shape #1, we have 1 row of 1 tile decreased by 1 tile, or 0 tiles, which is again incorrect. So once again we must state what shape #1 is, then apply the rule to find the total tiles in all other shapes in the sequence. Have students record this alternative statement below the table as well.

Answer Key to Worksheet 3–5a
Answers, table entries, and unsimplified rules only are provided.

1. Fifth design uses 24 tiles; (1, 1), (2, 3), (3, 8), (4, 15), (5, 24), (6, 35).

    Additive rule: For $N = 1$, $T = 1$; for $N > 1$, $T = (N - 1)(N) + (1)(N - 1)$.

    Alternative subtractive rule: For $N = 1$, $T = 1$; for $N > 1$, $T = N^2 - 1$.

2. Eighth design uses 72 tiles; (1, 2), (2, 6), (3, 12), (4, 20), (5, 30), (6, 42).

    Rule: For all N, $T = (N + 1)(N)$.

3. Sixth design uses 58 tiles; (1, 8), (2, 14), (3, 22), (4, 32), (5, 44), (6, 58).

    Additive rule: For all N, $T = (N + 1)(N + 2) + 2$.

    Alternative subtractive rule: For all N, $T = (N + 2)(N + 2) - N$.

Worksheet 3–5a

Finding Rules for
Quadratic Sequences

Name _____

Date _____

Draw the next 3 terms or shapes for each sequence given below. Complete the table for each sequence. Answer each question. Find a rule for generating each sequence.

1. Which shape will use 24 tiles?

Number of Shape	1	2	3			
Total Tiles	1			15		35

2. How many tiles will the eighth shape use?

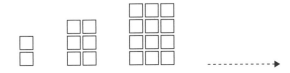

Number of Shape	1	2	3			
Total Tiles	2					

Worksheet 3–5a Continued

Copyright © 2005 by John Wiley & Sons, Inc.

Name _____

Date _____

3. Which shape will use 58 tiles?

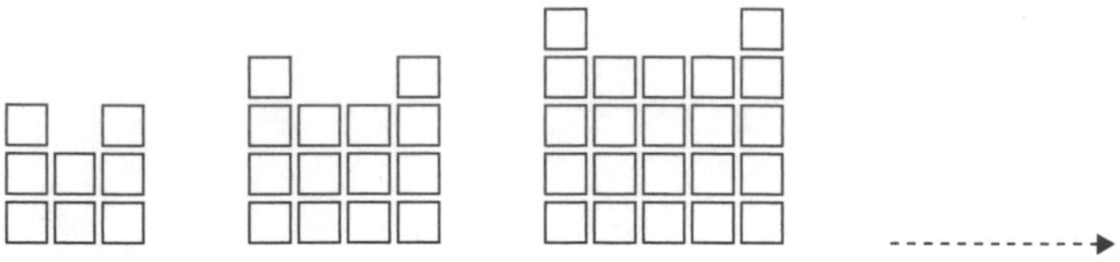

Number of Shape	1	2	3			
Total Tiles		14				

Activity 3

Independent Practice

Materials

> Worksheet 3–5b
>
> Regular pencils

Procedure

Give each student a copy of Worksheet 3–5b. Have students work independently to complete the worksheet, then discuss their results. Ask various students to explain the numerical patterns found in each table.

Answer Key for Worksheet 3–5b

1. 75, 108, and 147

2. D

3. A

4. C

5. B

Possible Testing Errors That May Occur for This Objective

- The number given is the next one for the <u>other</u> column (or row) in the table, not the column that is requested. For example, for the pairs of polygon data for [# sides, # diagonals]: (3, 0), (4, 2), (5, 5), if the next number of diagonals is requested, students might respond with 6 (which follows 3, 4, 5 sides), instead of with 9 (which follows 0, 2, 5 diagonals).

- The first missing number in a column (or row) is found for the answer, but the test item actually requires the second or third missing number for the answer. Further extension of the sequence is needed.

- One of the numbers shown in the table is selected to answer the test question rather than a number resulting from extending the listed values beyond the table based on an observed pattern.

Worksheet 3–5b

Using Patterns in Tables
or Sequences

Name _____

Date _____

Apply patterns to complete or extend the tables or sequences provided below, and use the information to answer the given questions.

1. Find the pattern and complete the table.

X	1	2	3	4	5	6	7
Y	3	12	27	48			

2. The number of sides and number of diagonals for each of several polygons are shown in the table. Based on the number patterns found in the table, which expression best represents the number of diagonals of any convex polygon having N sides?

Polygon	Number of Sides	Number of Diagonals
Triangle	3	0
Quadrilateral	4	2
Pentagon	5	5
Hexagon	6	9
Heptagon	7	14

A. $N - 3$　　　　B. $N(N - 3)$　　　C. $\dfrac{N - 3}{2}$　　　D. $\dfrac{N(N - 3)}{2}$

3. At Louie's Pizza Shop, the number of slices of pepperoni placed on a pizza depends on the size of the pizza. The number, n, of slices used is determined by the equation $n = r^2 + 1$, where r is the radius in inches of the pizza. Pizza sizes are 3, 6, 7, 8, and 10 inches. How many pepperoni slices should be placed on a super-large pizza, which has a radius of 10 inches?

A. 101　　　　　B. 100　　　　　　C. 21　　　　　　D. 10

Worksheet 3–5b Continued   Name _____

                                  Date _____

4. Designs made with small tiles are used to cover tabletops of different sizes. The first three sizes for the designs are shown here:

   If the pattern continues for larger tabletops, which expression can be used to determine the number of small tiles needed to make the Nth design?

   A. $N(N + 2)$ B. $2N + 4$ C. $(N + 2)(N + 2)$ D. $N^2 + 4$

5. Which ordered set of numbers is the first five terms of a sequence, whose Nth term is generated with the expression $(3N^2 - 2)$?

   A. 1, 2, 3, 4, 5   C. 3, 6, 9, 12, 15

   B. 1, 10, 25, 46, 73   D. 3, 12, 27, 48, 75

Objective 6: Identify the Domain, Range, Intercepts, and Other Properties of a Function from a Given Graph, Equation, or Situation

Functions play a major role in real-world applications. In many situations, specific limits are naturally placed on the values of the domain and the range. Students need experience identifying such limits when they exist. In the following activities, students generate ordered pairs of functions and identify elements in both the domain and the range of a function.

Activity 1
Manipulative Stage

Materials

> Packets of 1-inch square tiles (50 tiles per packet)
> Worksheet 3–6a
> Regular pencil

Procedure

1. Give each pair of students a packet of tiles and two copies of Worksheet 3–6a.

2. For each exercise on Worksheet 3–6a, have students build a sequence of tile shapes and complete the table with the required numbers. The shapes will demonstrate a portion of a function in each case, indicating a possible domain and a possible range for the function.

3. Based on the data recorded in the table of an exercise, students should answer the questions provided in the exercise.

4. Discuss Exercise 1 on Worksheet 3–6a with the entire class before allowing partners to work on their own.

Consider Exercise 1 on Worksheet 3–6a: "Build square shapes with the tiles according to the given edge lengths. Find the perimeter of each square shape. Find the missing values for the table. [D = Domain, R = Range]

edge length (D)	1	2	3	4
perimeter (R)				

> Is it reasonable for 0 also to be in the domain of the function?
> If there were enough tiles to build more shapes if necessary,
> (a) would 3.5 be an element of the domain? Explain.
> (b) would 10 be in the range? Explain.
> (c) would 52 be in the range? Explain."

Have students build four square shapes with their tiles, using edge lengths 1 through 4. The shapes should appear as follows:

The perimeters of the squares will be 4, 8, 12, and 16, respectively. Have students record these values in the correct spaces of the table. Remind students that a *function* is simply a set of ordered pairs, where any first member found in the ordered pairs corresponds to a unique second member; that is, a specific first member must be used in only one ordered pair in the set. The ordered pairs may be listed, displayed in a table, or shown as a graph.

Guide students to answer the questions provided in the exercise:

"Can 0 be in the *domain* if other squares are possible? Yes, since 0 as the edge length of a square corresponds to 4×0, or 0 units, as the perimeter. Since 0 is a multiple of 4, it belongs to the *range* of the function."

"Can 3.5 be in the domain? No, because we are limited to whole tiles when building the square shapes. We cannot build a square shape, whose edge length equals 3.5 units."

"Can 10 be in the range? No, because all range members are integers, which are multiples of 4. Ten is not a multiple of 4."

"Can 52 be in the range? Yes, because 52 equals 4×13; that is, 52 is a multiple of 4."

Students should record similar statements below the appropriate questions in Exercise 1.

Note: The sequence of pyramids for Exercise 3 should appear as shown:

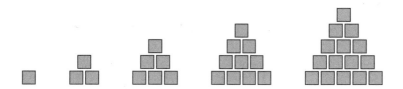

Answer Key for Worksheet 3–6a

1. [See details in the text.]

2. Areas for the table will be 1, 4, 9, and 16, respectively; 0 may be in the domain, because its shape will have an area of 0×0 square units, or 0 square units, as a member of the range; (a) 8 will not be in the range, because 8 is not a perfect square; (b) 36 will be in the range, because 36 is a perfect square.

3. Range entries (total tiles) for the table will be 1, 3, 6, 10, and 15; 0 may be in the domain, because a pyramid with a base size of 0 will contain 0 total tiles as the range member, which supports the numerical pattern found in the range values; (a) 3.9 will not be in the domain since only whole tiles are used to build the pyramids; (b) 7 will not be in the range, because it represents only one more tile than the total tiles found in the pyramid with base size 3; (c) 45 will be in the range, because it equals the total tiles found in the pyramid having base size 9, when the numerical pattern of the range members is extended.

Worksheet 3–6a   Name _____

Building Functions with Tiles   Date _____

For each exercise, build sequences of tile shapes, and record the data in the table. Use the information in the table to answer the given questions.

    For Exercises 1 and 2, build square shapes with the tiles according to the given edge lengths. Find the missing values for each table. [D = Domain, R = Range]

1. Find the perimeter of each square shape.

edge length (D)	1	2	3	4
perimeter (R)				

Is it reasonable for 0 also to be in the domain of the function?

If there were enough tiles to build more shapes if necessary,

(a) would 3.5 be an element of the domain? Explain.

(b) would 10 be in the range? Explain.

(c) would 52 be in the range? Explain.

2. Find the area of each square shape.

edge length (D)	1	2	3	4
area (R)				

Is it reasonable for 0 also to be in the domain of the function?

If there were enough tiles to build more shapes if necessary,

(a) would 8 be an element of the range? Explain.

(b) would 36 be in the range? Explain.

Worksheet 3–6a Continued

Name _____

Date _____

3. Build a sequence of 5 flat pyramid-like shapes, where for each pyramid, the bottom row is the base and each upper row has 1 tile fewer than the previous lower row, ending with one tile on the top row. A pyramid with a bottom row of three tiles has a *base size* of 3. Find the missing values for the table:

base size (D)	1	2	3	4	5
total tiles (R)					

Is it reasonable for 0 also to be in the domain of the function?

If there were enough tiles to build more shapes if necessary,

(a) would 3.9 be an element of the domain? Explain.

(b) would 7 be an element of the range? Explain.

(c) would 45 be in the range? Explain.

Activity 2

Pictorial Stage

Materials

> Worksheet 3–6b
>
> Red pencil and regular pencil

Procedure

> 1. Give each pair of students a red pencil and two copies of Worksheet 3–6b.
>
> 2. For each exercise, students will plot ordered pairs of a function on a grid, using pairs in a list or pairs that satisfy a given equation.
>
> 3. Students will describe the domain and the range of the function in the exercise, as well as answer any other question provided in the exercise.
>
> 4. Discuss Exercise 1 with the entire class before allowing partners to work the other exercises on their own.

Consider Exercise 1 on Worksheet 3–6b: "Plot the ordered pairs: (–3, –2), (–2, –1), (–1, –1), (0, 0), (1, 0), (2, 1), (3, 1), and (4, 2). For this function, describe in words the members of the domain and the range."

The resulting graph will be a scatter plot. The points are not connected. Discuss the idea that the first members of the ordered pairs form the domain and the second members form the range. Have students record sentences below Exercise 1 that describe the domain and the range elements. For example, the domain is the set of integers –3 through +4, and the range is the set of integers –2 through +2. Here is the completed graph:

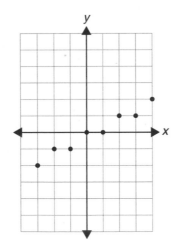

Answer Key for Worksheet 3–6b
The graphs are not shown here.

1. [See details in the text.]

2. (a) The domain is the set of all real numbers from $-\infty$ to $+\infty$.

    (b) The range is the set of all nonnegative real numbers, or all real numbers ≥ 0.

    (c) The graph has a minimum point at (0, 0).

3. Possible entries for the table might be the ordered pairs: (–1, –12), (0, –5), (1, 0), (2, 3), (3, 4), (4, 3), (5, 0), and (6, –5). Other pairs like (2.5, 3.75) might also be used. Students should select the pairs needed to graph a complete parabola on the grid provided.

    (a) The value 4.3 is not in the range, because the maximum value for $f(x)$ in the graph is 4.

    (b) The x-intercepts for the graph of this function are $x = 1$ and $x = 5$.

    (c) (1) The valid values of x shown in the table for the ball problem will be any real numbers from 1 through 5, including 1 and 5. Only these numbers should be circled in red pencil. For any x-values less than 1 or greater than 5, the value of $f(x)$ will be negative, implying that the ball would be <u>below</u> ground level.

    (2) The range for the ball problem is the interval of all real numbers from 0 to 4, or [0, 4]. Ground level is at $f(x) = 0$, and the ball's maximum height is at $f(x) = 4$.

    (3) The value 2.5 is in the domain of the ball problem, because it is in the interval [1, 5]. The value of $f(2.5)$ is 3.75, which is less than the maximum value 4 and therefore in the range of the ball problem.

Worksheet 3–6b   Name _____

Graphing Functions on Grids   Date _____

For each exercise, draw the graph indicated. Use the information from the graph to answer the questions with word sentences. Each grid segment equals 1 unit.

1. Plot the ordered pairs: (–3, –2), (–2, –1), (–1, –1), (0, 0), (1, 0), (2, 1), (3, 1), and (4, 2). For this function, describe in words the members of each set below.

   (a) Domain:

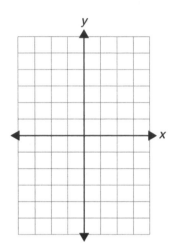

   (b) Range:

2. Graph the quadratic parent function $y = x^2$. Describe in words the following for this function:

   (a) Domain:

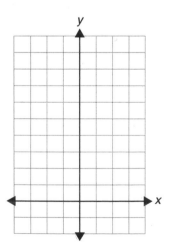

   (b) Range:

   (c) Minimum or maximum point:

Worksheet 3–6b Continued   Name _____

                              Date _____

3. Draw a graph for $f(x) = -(x-3)^2 + 4$. Select six or more values for x, and record their corresponding ordered pairs in the table. Use enough pairs to show the complete shape of a parabola.

x									
$f(x)$									

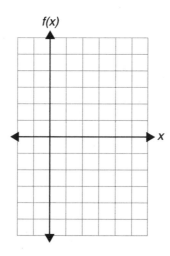

(a) Is 4.3 in the range of this function? Why or why not?

(b) What are the x-intercepts for the graph of this function?

(c) Consider $f(x)$ as the height of a ball in the air when it is thrown from ground level.

   (1) Circle in red the values of x in the table that are valid as domain members for the "thrown ball" situation.

   (2) What is the interval for the range in the situation?

   (3) Is the value 2.5 in the domain of the situation? Why or why not?

Activity 3
Independent Practice

Materials
Worksheet 3–6c
Regular pencil

Procedure
Give each student a copy of Worksheet 3–6c to complete. When all have finished, ask various students to share their reasoning and their answers with the entire class.

Answer Key for Worksheet 3–6c
1. C

2. D (The *range* will be $-4 < y \le +5$.)

3. A

4. B

5. D

6. B

7. A

8. C

Possible Testing Errors That May Occur for This Objective
- Students typically confuse the definitions of the domain and the range.
- Students do not realize that the *roots* of a function and the *x-intercepts* of the function's graph correspond to the same ordered pairs for the function.
- Students are unable to read a graph correctly in order to identify from the grid the proper intervals for the domain and the range of the function.

Worksheet 3–6c   Name _____

Identifying Properties of Functions   Date _____

Complete each exercise provided. Be ready to share your reasoning and your answers with the entire class. On unmarked scales of grids, 1 grid segment equals 1 unit.

1. Which of these equations describes a function in which every real number x corresponds to a nonnegative real number y?

   A. $y = x$ B. $y = -x$ C. $y = x^2$ D. $y = x^3$

2. What is the domain of real numbers for the function shown on the graph?

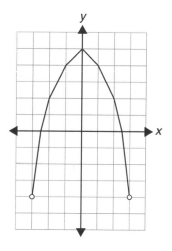

   A. $-4 \leq x \leq +5$

   B. $-4 < x < +5$

   C. $-3 \leq x \leq +3$

   D. $-3 < x < +3$

3. Which equation describes a function, whose roots are $x = -2.5$ and $x = +2.5$?

   A. $y = x^2 - 6.25$ B. $y = x^2 + 6.25$ C. $y = -x^2 - 6.25$ D. $y = 2.5x^2 - 2.5$

4. Which equation describes a parabola that opens downward?

   A. $y = -2x + 5$ B. $y = -3x^2 + 1$ C. $y = x^3 - 2$ D. $y = 0.5x^2 + 3$

238

Name _____

Date _____

Use the graph below to answer Exercises 5–8.

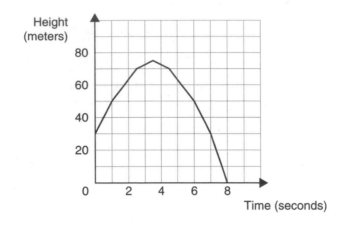

5. The graph shows the height of a baseball from the time it is thrown from the top of a cliff to the time it hits the ground below the cliff. How much time elapses while the ball is 65 meters or more above the ground?

   A. 6 sec.

   B. 5 sec.

   C. 4 sec.

   D. 3 sec.

6. What was the maximum height reached by the baseball?

   A. 80 m   B. 75 m   C. 70 m   D. 65 m

7. From the graph, what conclusion can be made about the movement of the baseball?

   A. At 0 seconds, the baseball was 30 meters above the ground.

   B. The ball was in the air for 6 seconds.

   C. The ball reached its maximum height after 4.5 seconds.

   D. The height of the baseball was 0 meters when it was first released into the air.

8. Apply symmetry to the graph, and extend the given curve to form a complete parabola. Predict where the intercepts on the horizontal axis of the complete parabola would be located.

   A. 8 and 30   B. 0 and 8   C. –1 and 8   D. 0 and 30

Name _____

Date _____

LINEAR AND QUADRATIC FUNCTIONS AND THEIR PROPERTIES: PRACTICE TEST ANSWER SHEET

Directions: Use the answer sheet to darken the letter of the choice that best answers each question.

1. ○ A ○ B ○ C ○ D   7. ○ A ○ B ○ C ○ D

2. ○ A ○ B ○ C ○ D   8. ○ A ○ B ○ C ○ D

3. ○ A ○ B ○ C ○ D   9. ○ A ○ B ○ C ○ D

4. ○ A ○ B ○ C ○ D   10. ○ A ○ B ○ C ○ D

5. ○ A ○ B ○ C ○ D   11. ○ A ○ B ○ C ○ D

6. ○ A ○ B ○ C ○ D   12. ○ A ○ B ○ C ○ D

Section 3: Linear and Quadratic Functions and Their Properties: Practice Test

1. Marian wants to find the total cost, c, for gasoline and repairs for her car in the previous three months. The total cost included $240 for repairs. Gasoline cost $1.89 per gallon. Which of the following equations can be used to determine the total cost if Marian knows the number of gallons of gas, g, she bought in the previous three months?

   A. $1.89g - 240 = c$

   B. $1.89 + 240g = c$

   C. $1.89 - 240g = c$

   D. $1.89g + 240 = c$

2. The table represents solutions of the function $f(x) = 3(x - 2) - 5$. There is an error in the table. Which ordered pair is not a solution for the function?

x	5	10	15	20
$f(x)$	4	18	34	49

   A. (5, 4)   B. (10, 18)   C. (15, 34)   D. (20, 49)

3. What is the solution set for x in the equation $2(3x - 1)^2 = 50$?

   A. $\left\{+2, -\frac{4}{3}\right\}$ B. $\{+2, -2\}$ C. $\left\{+\frac{4}{3}, -2\right\}$ D. $\left\{+\frac{4}{3}, -\frac{4}{3}\right\}$

4. A chemical reaction is represented by the equation $t = 194 - 5c - c^2$, where c is the temperature in degrees Celsius of the reaction and t is the time in seconds needed to complete the reaction. If the reaction takes 110 seconds, what is the temperature of the reaction? If helpful, use a trial-and-error strategy.

   A. 15°C   B. 10°C   C. 7°C   D. 5°C

5. Which equation will produce the widest parabola when graphed?

   A. $y = 0.2x^2$ B. $y = 4x^2$ C. $y = -5x^2$ D. $y = -0.7x^2$

6. What is the effect on the graph of the equation $y = -2x^2 + 7$ when the equation is changed to $y = +2x^2 + 7$?

   A. The graph is congruent, but the vertex of the graph shifts vertically upward.

   B. The slope of the graph changes.

   C. The graph narrows.

   D. The graph is congruent but is flipped to open upward.

Section 3 Practice Test (Continued)

7. Which ordered set of numbers is the first five terms of a sequence, whose *N*th term is generated with the expression $(3N - 2)$?

   A. 1, 2, 3, 4, 5

   B. 1, 4, 7, 10, 13

   C. 2, 5, 8, 11, 14

   D. 3, 5, 7, 9, 11

8. Bags of chips are on sale at the grocery store this week. The chart shows the cost of the chips, including tax. If the pattern continues, how many bags of chips can Sonya buy for her party with $18?

Number of Bags	4	8	12	16
Total Cost	$3	$6	$9	$12

   A. 20   B. 21   C. 24   D. 28

9. Designs made with small tiles are used to cover tabletops of different sizes. The first three sizes for the designs are shown here:

   If the pattern continues for larger tabletops, which expression can be used to determine the number of small tiles needed to make the *N*th design?

   A. $N^2 + 2N$ B. $(N + 1)(N + 2)$ C. $(N + 2)(N + 2)$ D. $N^2 + 4$

10. At Dino's Pizza Shop, the number of slices of pepperoni placed on a pizza depends on the size of the pizza. The number, *n*, of slices used is determined by the equation $n = r^2 + 3$, where *r* is the radius in inches of the pizza. Pizza sizes are 3, 6, 7, 8, and 10 inches. How many pepperoni slices should be placed on a super-large pizza, which has a radius of 10 inches?

    A. 103   B. 100   C. 23   D. 10

242

Section 3 Practice Test (Continued)

11. The graph shows the height of a baseball from the time it is thrown from the top of a cliff to the time it hits the ground below the cliff. How much time elapses while the ball is 50 meters or more above the ground?

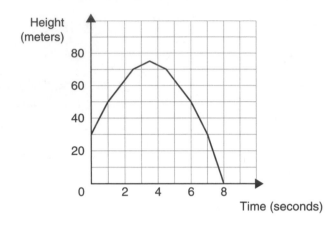

A. 3 sec.   B. 4 sec.   C. 5 sec.   D. 6 sec.

12. What is the range of real numbers for the function shown on the graph?

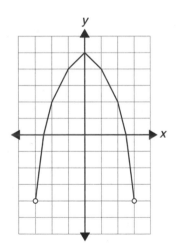

A. $-4 \leq y \leq +5$

B. $-4 < y \leq +5$

C. $-3 \leq y \leq +3$

D. $-3 < y < +3$

Section 3: Linear and Quadratic Functions and Their Properties: Answer Key for Practice Test

The objective being tested is shown in brackets beside the answer.

1. D [1]	7. B [4]
2. B [1]	8. C [4]
3. A [2]	9. B [5]
4. C [2]	10. A [5]
5. A [3]	11. C [6]
6. D [3]	12. B [6]

GEOMETRY AND MEASUREMENT WITH APPLICATIONS

Objective 1: Apply the Circumference and Area of a Circle to Solve a Real-World Problem

Applications of the circle occur in many situations in our daily lives. Students need to view the formulas of a circle as more than just some letters to memorize. The role of pi in both circumference and area is unique to the circle and should be developed carefully. The activities for this objective provide the necessary experience with pi.

Activity 1

Manipulative Stage

Materials

Assorted plastic circular lids (3- to 5-inch diameters; 1 lid per pair of students)
Cotton string (nonstretchable; 1 20-inch piece per pair of students)
Scissors (1 per pair of students)
Centimeter grid paper (on colored paper; 1 sheet per pair of students)
Transparent tape (1 roll per pair of students)
Worksheet 4–1a
Regular pencil and paper

Procedure

1.   Give each pair of students a plastic circular lid, one piece of 20-inch cotton string, scissors, 1 sheet of colored centimeter grid paper, tape, and Worksheet 4–1a. The lesson is more effective if students have different-sized lids instead of all having the same size.

2.   Have students wrap the string around the outer rim of their plastic lid to measure the lid's circumference. Students should mark the string to show where the end point falls or the wrapping stops.

3.   Ask students to predict how many times the diameter length of their lid might be made from the newly marked-off portion of string. Write their predictions on the board.

4.   Have students place the marked-off portion (circumference) of the string across the diameter of the plastic lid, starting with one end of the string touching the edge of the lid. They should slide the string across the lid, matching or counting off each diameter

length until the marked-off portion of string has been used as much as possible. Three diameter lengths should be counted or matched with the string, with a small portion of string left over, regardless of the lid size used.

5.   Compare the final diameter count of "3 and a little more" to the predictions that students made earlier. Have students write on the back of Worksheet 4–1a the following results: "The circumference of a circle equals the length of 3 and a little more of the circle's diameter." Here is an example of the wrapping of a lid and the measuring or counting off of the lid's diameter with the string:

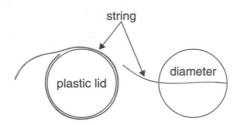

6.   Now have students continue to work with Worksheet 4–1a. For each circle on the worksheet, from the colored centimeter paper have students cut out 4 large squares, whose edges equal the length of the circle's radius. Circle A requires 2-centimeter by 2-centimeter squares and circle B requires 3-centimeter by 3-centimeter squares. Each circle's special squares will be called the circle's *related squares.*

7.   Ask students to predict how many of each circle's *related squares* will be needed to cover the interior of that circle. Write their predictions on the board.

8.   For each circle, each large colored paper square should be cut apart in various ways in order to fit inside the circle, but the squares should not be cut apart into individual square centimeter units. Students should strive to use a minimal number of cuts on each large square. One paper square should be cut apart and *all* its pieces placed inside the circle <u>before</u> another paper square is cut apart. As students place cut paper pieces inside a circle, they should tape down the small pieces to hold them in place. The paper pieces should not overlap each other. Students should also try to cover a circle so that no gaps are left between paper pieces.

9.   After students have finished each circle, have them compare the number of paper squares they actually used to the number they had predicted. The actual covering should use 3 large whole squares plus a small part of a fourth square, regardless of which circle is being covered.

10. Discuss the relationship of the *related square*'s area to the area of its circle. At the bottom of Worksheet 4–1a, have students write a statement about the two areas like the following: "A circle's area equals 3 and a little more of the area of the circle's related square, where the edge length of the related square equals the radius length of the circle." Here is an example of a covered circle (centimeter grid marks are not shown):

Worksheet 4–1a   Name _____

Modeling the Area of a Circle   Date _____

For each circle, from colored centimeter grid paper cut out 4 large squares, whose edge lengths equal the radius length of the circle. Cover the interior of the circle with as many of these *related squares* as needed, completely using one full square before starting the next square.

Circle A [radius = 2 centimeters]

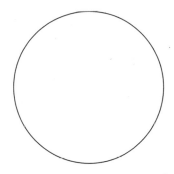

Circle B [radius = 3 centimeters]

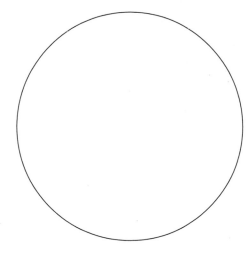

Activity 2
Pictorial Stage

Materials

Worksheet 4–1b
Adding machine tape
Centimeter rulers
Calculators
Red pencil and regular pencil

Procedure

1. Give each pair of students two copies of Worksheet 4–1b, a centimeter ruler, a calculator, a red pencil, and a strip of adding machine tape about 18 inches long.

2. Students are to use the paper strip to form a stand-up "collar" around each circle to find its circumference. They should mark off the paper to show where the wrapping stops. This marked-off distance should be measured with the centimeter ruler in order to find the circumference in centimeters to the nearest tenth.

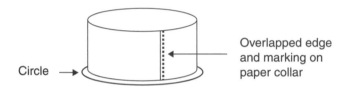

3. The diameter of each circle should be measured by counting the centimeter grid units across the circle *through the center point* of the circle. Ask students to compute how many diameters, d, will equal the circumference, c, of each circle. Have them compute $c \div d$ to the nearest hundredth. The equation should be recorded on Worksheet 4–1b beside the appropriate circle.

4. Since the measurement for the circumference of the same circle will vary slightly among the students, their quotient for $c \div d$ will also vary. Collect all their quotients for the same circle, and have the class compute the mean for these values. The mean of these quotients should be close to 3.14 for each circle. Have students write on the back of Worksheet 4–1b the following statement: "A circumference equals about 3.14 of the diameter's length." Then have them write with abstract symbols: $c \approx 3.14 \times (d)$ or $3.14d$. This is the formula used when computing circumference.

5. Now have students estimate the area of each circle on Worksheet 4–1b by counting the whole or partial unit squares in the interior of the circle. The total unit squares found will vary. Encourage students to mentally combine various parts of unit squares to form a "whole" unit square when estimating. Have each pair of students record their own totals beside the appropriate circles on their copies of Worksheet 4–1b.

6. For each circle, students should find the area of the *related square*, whose edge length equals the radius of the circle. They should find how many times the area of the *related square* may be removed or subtracted completely from the estimated area of the circle. Each time they subtract, have them draw with red pencil a related square overlapping the circle. After this area has been removed a possible three times, have

students compare the remaining portion of the circle's area to the square's area to find what fractional part of another related square will be needed to finish matching the square's area to the circle's total area. The fractional part should be computed to the nearest hundredth.

7.   For each circle, all students should have used 3 areas of the related square plus a decimal portion of another area of the related square to equal their circle's estimated area. On the board, write the different numbers of squares used for each circle and have students compute the mean of these numbers. The mean should be close to 3.14 for each circle on Worksheet 4–1b. On the back of the worksheet, have students write the statement: "The area of a circle equals about 3.14 of the area of the circle's related square."

8.   Now guide students to transform their statement about area to a more abstract formula. Have them write the following sequence of statements below the initial area statement:

Area of circle of radius $r \approx 3.14$ of area of square of edge r
Area of circle of radius $r \approx 3.14 \times (r \times r)$ or $3.14(r^2)$

Discuss the idea that the second statement represents the formula that is often used when computing the area of a circle. Advanced mathematics is needed to find the actual formula, which uses pi, but since pi is an irrational number, we must use an approximation of its value, here 3.14, when computing a circle's area.

As an example of finding area, consider circle A on Worksheet 4–1b. A possible estimate of its area in square centimeters might be 28 square centimeters. Since the circle has a radius of 3 centimeters, its related square will be 3 centimeters by 3 centimeters, which has an area of 9 square centimeters.

The related square's area may be subtracted from the circle's estimated area three times: $28 - 9 = 19$, $19 - 9 = 10$, and $10 - 9 = 1$. Then 3 areas of the related square will "cover" or equal most of the circle's area, leaving 1 square centimeter of the circle still to be matched. Some students may want to divide 28 by 9, instead of subtracting 9 repeatedly; this is acceptable as long as they understand what the remainder means in this situation.

Students should draw with red pencil the three related squares overlapping the circle as shown below. This helps students to visualize that the <u>entire</u> area of a fourth related square will not be needed because the external "corners" of the 3 drawn squares must be moved inside the circle, thereby leaving only a small portion of the circle uncovered.

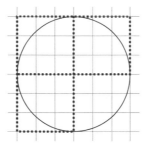

So only 1 square centimeter out of a fourth related square's area is needed to complete the circle's area. This is 1 square centimeter out of 9 square centimeters of area, which equals $\frac{1}{9}$ or about 0.11 of the fourth related square's area. Therefore, 3 + 0.11, or

3.11 of the areas of the related square equal the estimated area of the circle. The students with an estimate of 28 square centimeters for circle A's area should record the following beside their circle A on Worksheet 4–1b: 3.11 of (3 × 3) ≈ 28 square centimeters of area.

For this same circle, other students may have estimates of 27 or 29 square centimeters for the circle's area, so they will have different decimal numbers for their results. For 27, they will have 3.00, and for 29, they will have 3.22. The class mean of all such decimal numbers found by all pairs of students, including any repeats, should be close to 3.14.

Answer Key for Worksheet 4–1b
Possible statements are given for each circle; equations may vary.

Circle A: 18.9 cm ÷ 6 cm = 3.15 diameters in circumference

   3.11 of (3 × 3) ≈ 28 sq cm of area

Circle B: 24.9 cm ÷ 8 cm = 3.11 diameters in circumference

   3.19 of (4 × 4) ≈ 51 sq cm of area

Worksheet 4–1b

Finding the Circumference and
Area of a Circle

Name _____

Date _____

For each circle, use a ruler and a *paper collar* to find the circumference. Find the area by overlaying the circle with *related squares* drawn on the grid and counting their unit squares.

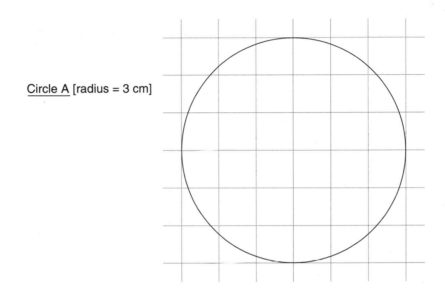

Circle A [radius = 3 cm]

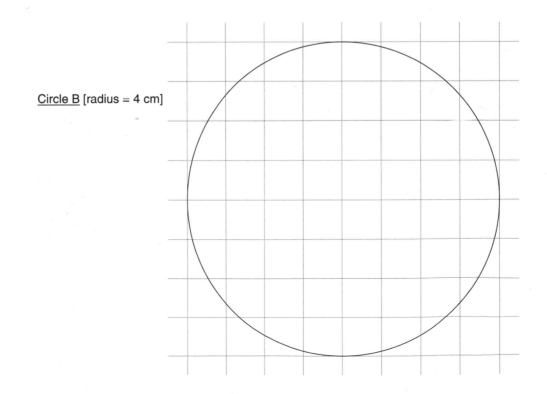

Circle B [radius = 4 cm]

Activity 3
Independent Practice

Materials
Worksheet 4–1c
Regular pencil

Procedure
Give each student a copy of Worksheet 4–1c to complete independently. Encourage students to draw and label diagrams when solving word problems. Also remind them to write the needed formula in words or symbols, including 3.14 instead of pi, before substituting the numbers and performing the computation. When all have completed the worksheet, have various students share their results with the entire class.

Answer Key for Worksheet 4–1c
1. B

2. D

3. C

4. B

5. C

Possible Testing Errors That May Occur for This Objective
- Students confuse the two concepts of area and circumference and apply one when the other is needed.

- A single radius value is used to compute the circumference instead of doubling the radius value or using the diameter value. That is, students use 3.14r, instead of 3.14 (2r) or 3.14d, when finding the circumference.

- The area of a circle is computed by squaring the radius value, but this product is not then multiplied by 3.14 or some other approximation for pi. That is, students use (r)(r) for the area, instead of 3.14 (r)(r).

Worksheet 4–1c   Name _____

Applying the Circumference and   Date _____
Area of a Circle

Solve the exercises provided.

1. A bicycle wheel travels about 75 inches for each full rotation. Find the diameter
    of the wheel to the nearest inch.

    A. 26 in.   B. 24 in.   C. 15 in.   D. 10 in.

2. A circular flower garden has a radius of 5 feet. What total area, to the nearest
    square foot, is needed to determine the amount of fertilizer to purchase?

    A. 16 sq. ft.   B. 25 sq. ft.   C. 63 sq. ft.   D. 79 sq. ft.

3. The figure below shows a circle inside a rectangle.

    Which procedure should be used to find the area of the shaded region?

    A. Find the area of the circle, and then subtract the area of the rectangle from it.

    B. Find the circumference of the circle, and then subtract the perimeter of the
       rectangle from it.

    C. Find the area of the rectangle, and then subtract the area of the circle from it.

    D. Find the perimeter of the rectangle, and then subtract the circumference of
       the circle from it.

Worksheet 4-1c Continued

Name _____

Date _____

4. A 6.0-centimeter square is inscribed in a circle with a radius of approximately 4.2 centimeters. What is the area of the shaded region to the nearest tenth?

A. 17.6 sq cm

C. 36.0 sq cm

B. 19.4 sq cm

D. 55.4 sq cm

5. The White House had a circular garden with a radius of 20 feet. All of the fencing around the garden was removed and used to enclose a new square garden. What was the approximate side length of the square garden?

A. 126 ft.   B. 63 ft.   C. 31 ft.   D. 20 ft.

Objective 2: Apply the Area of Parallelograms and Triangles to Solve Real-World Problems

Students seem to have much experience with the area of a rectangle, but not with the area of a parallelogram and its corresponding triangles. They are efficient in working with the adjacent side lengths of a rectangle but often are unable to identify the perpendicular dimensions of nonrectangular parallelograms. They need more experience in locating these special dimensions. The following activities focus on ways to find the appropriate measures for computing area. Perimeter is considered a prerequisite concept for this objective. Trapezoids are discussed as composite shapes in a later objective.

Activity 1

Manipulative Stage

Materials

      Worksheet 4–2a (patterns for parallelograms)

      Scissors (1 per pair of students)

      Transparent tape (1 roll per pair of students)

      Red and blue markers (1 set per pair of students)

      Regular paper and pencil

Procedure

    1. Give each pair of students a copy of Worksheet 4–2a, scissors, transparent tape, and one red and one blue marker.

    2. Ask students to cut out the two parallelograms drawn on Worksheet 4–2a, and trace around each cutout shape on a plain sheet of paper.

    3. For each cutout parallelogram, ask students to find a *simple* way to rearrange the shape into a rectangle without losing any of the original area. This should be done by cutting the grid shape apart, making the fewest number of cuts possible. To prevent possible confusion, all cuts should be made along grid segments that are perpendicular to one of the longer sides of the parallelogram. One major strategy is to try to rearrange the more obvious triangular sections of the parallelogram. A cut closer toward the center of the shape is also possible.

    4. Once students have converted a grid shape into a rectangle, have them temporarily tape the parts together and mark off a line segment or bar in red along the rectangle's longer side or edge. Have them also mark off another segment in blue along the shorter or adjacent edge.

    5. They should then find the rectangle's area, using the grid units to measure the red and blue segments. Below the traced outline of the parallelogram, students should write the number sentence used to find the area of the rectangle and, hence, the area of the parallelogram.

    6. Now have the students untape and move the parts back into their original positions to re-form the original parallelogram by placing the parts on the shape's outline traced previously. The parts can now be taped down on this tracing of the parallelogram.

    7. Ask students what they notice about the locations of the colored line segments or bars on the re-formed shape. One colored segment should be in a perpendicular direction to the second colored segment. One colored segment should correspond to one edge

of the parallelogram. The other colored segment will be perpendicular to that edge of the parallelogram and extend to the edge of the parallelogram that is opposite to the first edge.

8.   Guide students to understand that each parallelogram and its corresponding rectangle have the same area. One shape has just been rearranged to form the other shape. Conservation of area is not intuitively obvious to some students.

9.   The first parallelogram will be discussed below in detail.

As an example, Shape I from Worksheet 4–2a should be cut out and traced onto a plain sheet of paper. Then the parallelogram should be cut apart to form a rectangle. Following are two possible ways that this first parallelogram might be cut <u>one time</u> and rearranged into a rectangle. Other cuts are possible as well. The arrow indicates how the section to the left of the cut might be moved to the extreme right in order to form a rectangle.

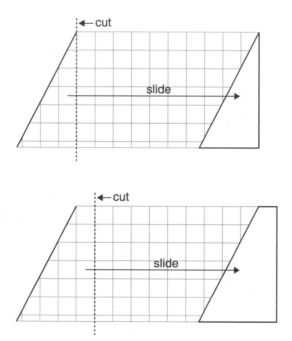

After the rectangle has been formed by either cutting method and the parts taped together, a colored bar (red or blue) should be drawn along each of two adjacent edges of the rectangle, using a different color for each edge. Counting the grid units (approximately centimeter lengths), the two dimensions of the rectangle are found to be about 6.3 units (length of the cutting edge) and 9.7 units (the adjacent edge). The area of the rectangle, and hence the parallelogram, may now be computed to the nearest tenth with the equation or number sentence $6.3 \times 9.7 = 61.11$, or 61.1 square units (or square centimeters). This equation should be recorded below the traced outline of Shape I. The rectangle with its two differently colored edges is shown here.

The two sections of the rectangle should now be rearranged as the original parallelogram and taped onto the traced copy of the parallelogram. Depending on which cutting method was used, the two differently colored bars from the rectangle will appear on the original parallelogram in one of the following ways:

Guide students to observe that the two colored bars are perpendicular to each other in either case. One colored bar is drawn along one of the edges of the parallelogram. The other colored bar is drawn between that edge and its opposite edge. The two colored bars represent the lengths on the original parallelogram that need to be measured directly in order to find the area of the parallelogram.

Answer Key for Worksheet 4–2a

Possible equations are shown below; measures may vary.

Shape I: $6.3 \times 9.7 = 61.11$, or 61.1 square units (or square centimeters)

Shape II: $3.5 \times 8.2 = 28.70$, or 28.7 square units (or square centimeters)

258

Worksheet 4–2a

Name _____

Rearranging Parallelograms
into Rectangles

Date _____

Cut out each parallelogram. Follow the teacher's instructions to change each shape into
a rectangle.

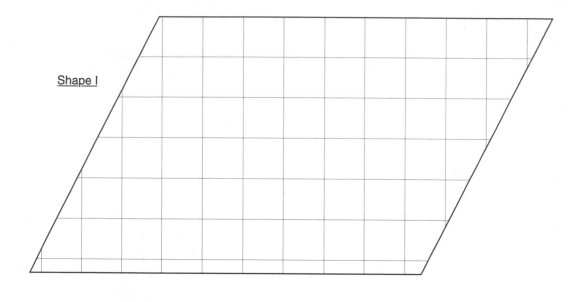

Shape I

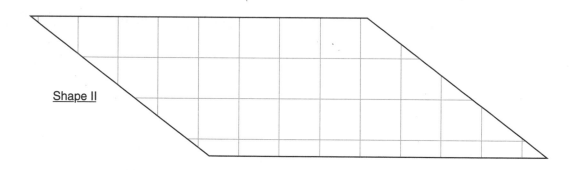

Shape II

Activity 2
Pictorial Stage

Materials

Worksheet 4–2b
Centimeter rulers (1 per pair of students)
Small index cards
Red and blue markers (1 set per pair of students)
Calculators
Regular pencil

Procedure

1.   Give each pair of students two copies of Worksheet 4–2b, an index card, a centimeter ruler, one red and one blue marker, and a calculator. Guide students through the steps provided for each shape on the worksheet.

2.   For Shape I on Worksheet 4–2b, students should select a longer side of the parallelogram and draw a red bar along that entire side. They should then place an edge of the index card against the red bar and use the card's adjacent edge to draw a blue bar that connects perpendicularly from the red bar to the opposite side of the shape.

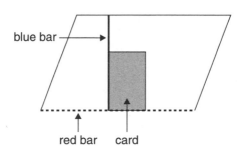

3.   The red and blue bars should be measured in centimeters to the nearest tenth and then labeled. These measures (the dimensions for area) should be multiplied to find the area of the parallelogram. Have students round their product to the nearest tenth and then write an equation below Shape I on Worksheet 4–2b to show their results (numbers may vary): "Area of parallelogram = $10.1 \times 7.2 = 72.72 \approx 72.7$ sq cm."

4.   Now have students draw a diagonal on Shape I. Two triangles will be formed. Ask students how the areas of the triangles compare to each other and to the area of the related parallelogram. They should notice that the triangles are congruent, so their areas are equivalent. Consequently, each triangle's area is equal to half the area of the related parallelogram. Using their own value found for the parallelogram's area, have students write another equation below Shape I like the following: "Area of triangle = $\left(\frac{1}{2}\right)(72.7)$ $= 36.35 \approx 36.4$ sq cm."

5.   Consider Shape II on Worksheet 4–2b. Two segments should be drawn parallel to two sides of the triangle, respectively, to show a parallelogram that contains two of the given triangle. Parallel segments may be drawn by aligning the ruler with a side of the triangle and carefully sliding over the ruler, without rotating it, until it touches the vertex

opposite to the aligning side. A red and a blue bar should be drawn similarly to those on Shape I. The following diagram shows the changes to Shape II:

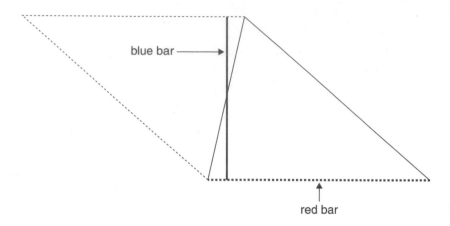

The blue bar drawn perpendicular to the red bar along the parallelogram's side or the triangle's side might also be drawn so that it lies completely in the interior of the triangle and intersects a vertex of the triangle. Discuss this idea with the students.

6. As done with Shape I, the red and blue bars on Shape II should be measured in centimeters to the nearest tenth and then labeled. These measures should be multiplied to find the area of the parallelogram. Have students round their product to the nearest tenth and then write an equation below Shape II on Worksheet 4–2b to show their results (numbers may vary): "Area of parallelogram = 5.9 × 8.2 = 48.38 ≈ 48.4 sq cm." Another equation should be written to show the area of the related triangle: "Area of triangle = $\left(\frac{1}{2}\right)$(48.4) = 24.2 sq cm."

7. Remind students that rectangles are members of the parallelogram family and that finding the area of a <u>rectangle</u> is equivalent to finding the area of a <u>parallelogram</u>: the length of one side of the rectangle is multiplied by the perpendicular distance from that side to its opposite parallel side; the perpendicular distance corresponds to the length of the side of the rectangle adjacent to the first side measured. *Perpendicular* measures are always needed to find area. As with all other parallelograms, the diagonal of a rectangle will form two congruent triangles.

Answer Key for Worksheet 4–2b
See the text for details; numbers may vary.

Worksheet 4–2b   Name _____

Measuring Parallelograms and   Date _____
Triangles to Find Area

Follow the teacher's instructions to measure each shape and find its area.

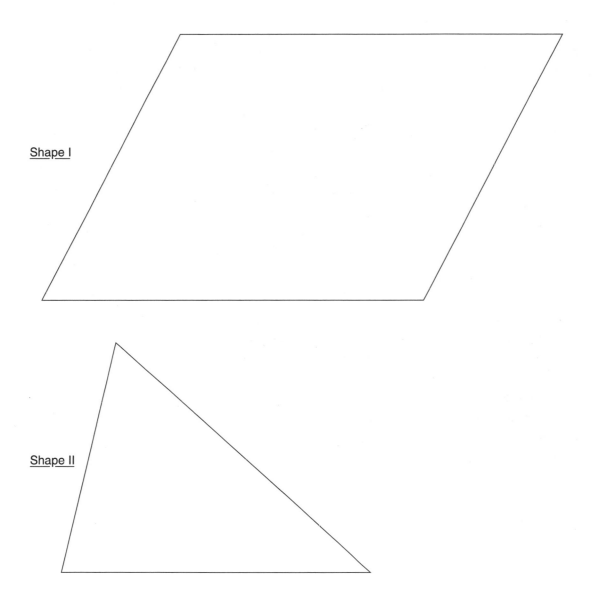

Shape I

Shape II

Activity 3

Independent Practice

Materials

> Worksheet 4–2c
> Regular pencil
> Calculators

Procedure

Give each student a copy of Worksheet 4–2c and a calculator. Remind students that every triangle is part of some related parallelogram. Also, every rectangle is a parallelogram. Encourage students to draw and label diagrams when solving word problems. After everyone has completed the worksheet, have various students share their results with the entire class.

Answer Key for Worksheet 4–2c

1. C

2. B

3. A

4. C

5. D

Possible Testing Errors That May Occur for This Objective

- When finding the area of a parallelogram, students multiply the lengths of two adjacent sides that are not perpendicular to each other.

- To find a triangle's area, students find the area of the related rectangle or parallelogram, but fail to take half of that product for the triangle's area.

- Students find the perimeter of a parallelogram instead of finding the area required by the problem.

Worksheet 4-2c

Name _____

Applying the Areas of
Parallelograms and Triangles

Date _____

Solve the exercises provided.

1. The two shorter sides of a right triangle are 8 inches and 5 inches long. What is the area of the triangle?

    A. 89 sq. in.   B. 40 sq. in.   C. 20 sq. in.   D. 13 sq. in.

2. A lawn design has flower beds around two sides of the lawn. The largest section has only grass, as shown in the diagram. How many square meters are in the area of the grass section?

    A. 1200 sq m

    B. 884 sq m

    C. 180 sq m

    D. 160 sq m

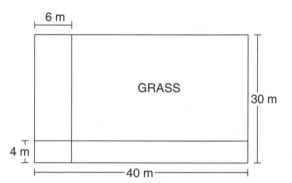

3. The total area of the floor of a parallelogram-shaped room is 405 square yards. If the length of one edge of the floor is 27 yards, what is the perpendicular distance from that edge across to the opposite edge of the floor?

    A. 15 yd.   B. 27 yd.   C. 54 yd.   D. Not here

4. Find the area, to the nearest tenth, of the shaded triangle shown in the diagram. The outer shape containing the triangle is a parallelogram.

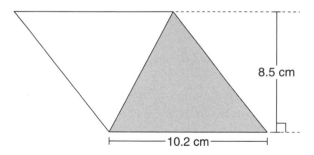

    A. 86.7 sq cm   B. 80.0 sq cm   C. 43.4 sq cm   D. 18.7 sq cm

5. A square platform has an area of 900 square feet. What is the perimeter of the platform?

    A. 900 ft.   B. 300 ft.   C. 225 ft.   D. 120 ft.

Objective 3: Apply Special Angle and Shape Properties to Solve a Real-World Problem Involving Variables

Special angles, which are formed when a transversal cuts across parallel lines, are often encountered in geometric situations. These angles are sometimes found in combination with the interior angles of a polygon. A study of these types of angles may be based on pairs of supplementary angles or on straight angles. The following activities provide experience with various angle relationships. It is assumed that students are familiar with the definitions of *supplementary, complementary,* and *vertical* angles, but each type will be reviewed as needed in the activities.

Activity 1
Manipulative Stage

Materials

Building Mat 4–3a
Worksheet 4–3a
Worksheet 4–3b
Scissors
Transparent tape (1 roll per two students)
Colored pencils (1 red and 1 blue pencil per two students)
Unlined paper (8.5 inches × 11 inches)
Index cards (3 inches × 5 inches)
Ruler or straightedge
Regular pencil and paper

Procedure

1. This activity consists of two parts. Part A deals with the interior angles of polygons, and Part B with transversals of parallel line segments. The two parts may be done at different class times or in any order. Each part may also be done consecutively with its corresponding part in Activity 2.

Part A: Interior Angles of Polygons

2. Give each pair of students two copies of Worksheet 4–3a (record sheet), one copy of Worksheet 4–3b (patterns for polygons), two copies of Building Mat 4–3a, scissors, transparent tape, and a red pencil. Worksheet 4–3a will also be used in Activity 2, Part A.

3. Have students cut out the polygons provided on Worksheet 4–3b. They should draw a large dot with red pencil near each vertex in the interior of each polygon.

4. Working with only one polygon at a time, students should first identify the specific name of the polygon and locate its row on the table on Worksheet 4–3a. They should record the polygon's number of sides in the appropriate column of the table.

5. Students should then tear off each corner (that is, a vertex with some of the angle's interior) of the cutout polygon, keeping a radius of about 0.75 inch from the vertex. This will prevent corner pieces from being too small and difficult to handle.

6. When all corner pieces have been removed from the polygon, students should label the next available row of two lines on Building Mat 4–3a with the specific name of the polygon. Then they should begin placing the pieces above one of the lines on the mat,

so that the vertex of each piece touches the point on the line. The red dots will help identify the vertex in each corner piece. The pieces should not overlap, but should be touching at their sides (parts of the polygon's sides). The pieces should not extend below the line on the mat. When a set of corner pieces is complete for a line, students should carefully tape the pieces in place, then move to the next line on the mat if necessary.

7. For the triangle, all three corners should fit exactly above one line. Here is a possible placement of a triangle's corners on a line on the building mat:

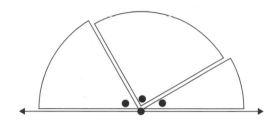

The other polygons will require more than one line, and some corners may need to be cut into two smaller pieces, starting at the vertex with the red dot, so that one smaller piece is placed on one line and the other smaller piece is placed on another line. (A possible arrangement of the pentagon's corner pieces will be provided in a later discussion.)

8. The corner pieces combined above a single line represent a subset of a polygon's angles, which correspond to a *straight* angle. That is, the total angle measure from these corner pieces will equal 180 degrees. Therefore, the number of lines on the building mat, which are needed to mount all the corner pieces for a particular polygon, indicate how many groups of 180 degrees will equal the total measure of the interior angles of the polygon. When students discover the number of lines needed for a polygon, they should record this information as a product with 180 degrees on the row for that polygon in the table on Worksheet 4–3a. Using this product, students should compute the total angle measure for the polygon and record that amount in the last column of the table.

9. After students have finished working with one polygon, they should repeat the process with a new polygon from Worksheet 4–3b.

10. When the first four rows of the table have been completed, ask students to compare the number of sides of each polygon to the number of groups of 180 degrees that were found, using that polygon's corner pieces. They should notice that there are two fewer groups of 180 degrees than there are sides for each polygon. Do not have students record a statement below the table on Worksheet 4–3a at this time. The recording will be done in Activity 2, Part A.

11. Discuss the 5-sided polygon from Worksheet 4–3b before allowing students to work with their partners.

Consider the 5-sided polygon from Worksheet 4–3b. Since a 5-sided polygon is a *pentagon*, have students locate the row for a pentagon in the table of Worksheet 4–3a, and record "5" for the number of sides in the second column.

Students should draw a red dot in each corner of the pentagon on Worksheet 4–3b and then cut out the shape. The five corner pieces should be torn off the cutout shape, care being taken not to make the pieces too small to handle easily. Have students find the next available row of two lines on Building Mat 4–3a and write "pentagon" in the left margin beside the lines. The labeling will help students identify which lines were used for each polygon after they finish the activity.

Students should begin arranging their five corner pieces above one or more lines on the building mat to find which pieces might fit together on the same line. For the pentagon, three lines will be needed in all. The red dots of pieces should be placed near the dot on a line, and the pieces should be touching but not overlapping. Some corner pieces may need to be cut into smaller pieces so they will fit on a line with other pieces; however, students should minimize the number of extra cuts they make. Following is a possible arrangement for the corner pieces of the pentagon. The bold solid segments are the original sides of the corner pieces, and the thin broken segments represent the cutting edge when a corner piece had to be cut into smaller pieces.

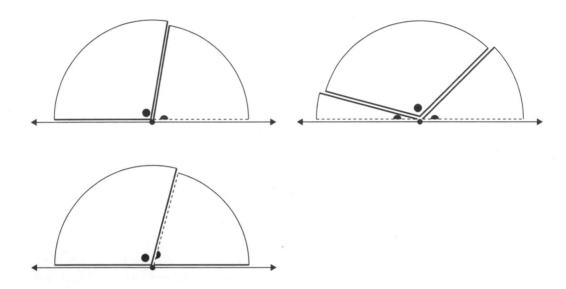

Students need to be closely supervised during this process. Some are not careful with detailed work like this, and they will leave large gaps between corner pieces or allow pieces to overlap. Such accumulated errors may cause some students to place pieces from the pentagon on a fourth line of the building mat when only three lines are actually required. This will interfere with the pattern they need to find in their completed table.

Part B: Transversals of Parallel Line Segments

12. Give each pair of students two sheets of unlined paper, an index card, a ruler, and one red and one blue colored pencil.

13. Using the ruler, students should draw a segment from the upper left corner to the lower right corner on one sheet of unlined paper. On the second sheet of paper, they should draw another segment from the upper right corner to the lower left corner. The two segments should have different degrees of steepness. Have students label the first sheet as Sheet A and the second sheet as Sheet B.

14. On Sheet A, have students place the index card near the top of the sheet of paper so that the card overlaps the line segment. Aligning the ruler with the line

segment, they should trace the line segment onto the card. The card and paper will appear as shown:

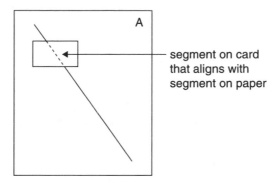

15. Have students draw along the top edge of the index card, then slide the card down the line segment, keeping the segment on the card aligned with the line segment on the paper. In a new position, students should trace along the top edge of the card again. Repeat the sliding and tracing process until three segments have been traced, thereby creating three *parallel* segments on Sheet A. The original line segment drawn on Sheet A now becomes a *transversal* of the three parallel segments. Here is a possible completed sheet A after the index card has been slid along the original line segment:

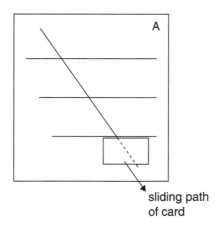

16. Discuss the idea that the line segments drawn on Sheet A have three different intersection points. The configuration of angles at each intersection point is the same as the other configurations. At the top intersection point are two sizes of angle measures. Have students draw an arc in red pencil to show the smaller angles and an arc in blue pencil to show the larger angles. The angles marked with the same color (red-red or blue-blue) are *vertical* angles, and each red-blue pair of angles will be *supplementary* angles.

17. Have students repeat the coloring process on the angles at the other two intersection points. Discuss the idea that all angles marked in red pencil on Sheet A are congruent and have the same angle measure, and all angles marked in blue pencil are

congruent with the same measure. This is an intuitive approach to the transversal concept, so do not stress vocabulary, such as *opposite interior angles* or *corresponding angles* unless students are receptive to a more in-depth study. Here is an example of the marked angles on Sheet A:

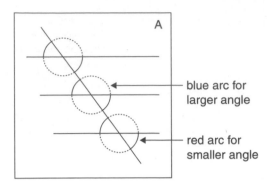

18. Now have students repeat the process of drawing parallel segments and coloring angles on Sheet B. They should use the other side of the index card when tracing a new segment on the card. Stress the idea that the configurations at all the intersection points on the transversal are congruent. Encourage students to notice which angles are congruent within a configuration and between configurations located at different intersection points.

Answer Key for Worksheet 4–3b
The following are the table entries:

Triangle; 3 sides; 1 × 180°; 180°

Quadrilateral; 4 sides; 2 × 180°; 360°

Pentagon; 5 sides; 3 × 180°; 540°

Hexagon; 6 sides; 4 × 180°; 720°

Building Mat 4–3a

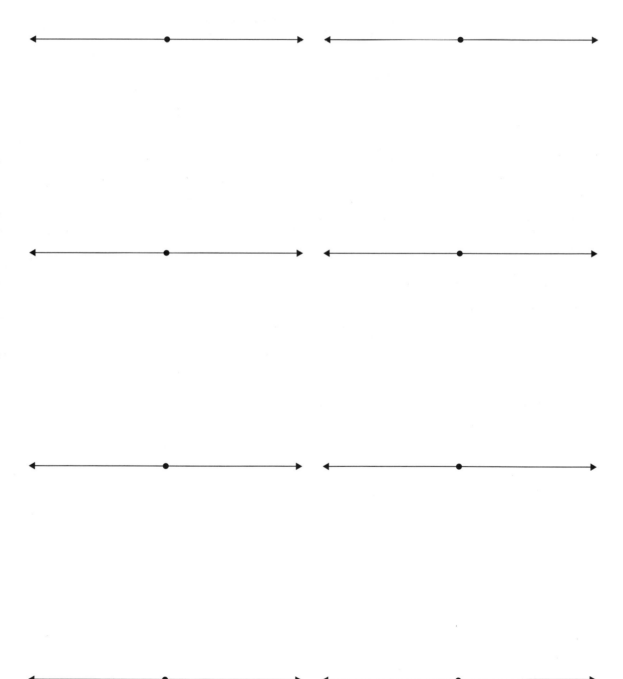

Worksheet 4–3a

Record Sheet for the Interior
Angles of Polygons

Name _____

Date _____

Record your results from Activity 1 and Activity 2 on the table provided. Do you see a relationship between the number of sides of a polygon and the number of groups of 180 degrees the polygon has? Write a statement about the relationship below the table.

Polygon	How many sides?	How many 180° groups?	Total Degrees
Triangle			
Quadrilateral			
Pentagon			
Hexagon			
Heptagon			
Octagon			
Nonagon			
Decagon			

What numerical relationship do you see?

Worksheet 4–3b

**Building Sums for the Interior
Angles of Polygons**

Name _____

Date _____

Cut out each polygon. For each polygon, draw a large dot inside the polygon near each vertex. Follow the teacher's instructions to build sums on Building Mat 4–3a. Record the results on Worksheet 4–3a.

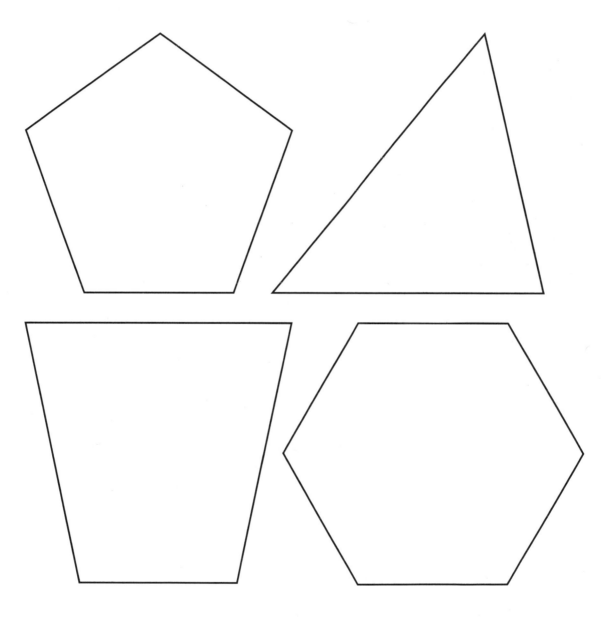

Activity 2
Pictorial Stage

Materials

Worksheet 4–3a (from Activity 1)
Worksheet 4–3c
Worksheet 4–3d
Ruler or straightedge
Colored pencils (1 red and 1 blue per two students)
Regular pencil

Procedure

1. This activity consists of two parts. Part A deals with the interior angles of polygons and Part B with transversals of parallel line segments. The two parts may be done at different class times or in any order. Each part may also be done consecutively with its corresponding part in Activity 1.

Part A: Interior Angles of Polygons

2. Give each pair of students two copies of Worksheet 4–3c, one red pencil and one blue pencil, and a ruler or straightedge. They will also need their copies of Worksheet 4–3a, which was partially completed in Activity 1.

3. For each polygon on Worksheet 4–3c, have students write the polygon's name beside the drawing. Then have students select one vertex of the polygon from which to draw possible diagonals to other vertices of the polygon, using a regular pencil. All diagonals drawn must lie in the interior of the polygon, so the initial vertex must be chosen carefully. The diagonals should form triangles whose combined interiors cover the entire interior of the polygon and whose vertices correspond to the vertices of the polygon. The triangles will be disjoint in that their interiors do not overlap; only their sides will be shared with other triangles.

4. Have students draw an arc in red pencil in the interior of each angle of every triangle within a polygon. Then have them draw an arc in blue pencil in the interior of each angle of the polygon. The arcs represent the *measures* of the respective angles. Guide students to observe that the total red arcs within a polygon correspond to the total blue arcs for the same polygon. That is, the total angle measure from all the disjoint triangles within a polygon equals the total angle measure of the polygon itself.

5. Have students write "180°" inside each triangle of every polygon on Worksheet 4–3c. They should count how many groups of 180 degrees appear in each polygon and record the results in the table on Worksheet 4–3a. Using the groups of 180 degrees, they should also find the total degrees for the interior angles of each polygon, since the two amounts are equal, and record that information in the last column of the table.

6. When the table is complete, ask students to compare the number of sides of a polygon to the number of groups of 180 degrees found for that polygon. A statement should be recorded below the table on Worksheet 4–3a that summarizes the relationship found. The preferred observation is that there are two fewer triangles formed inside a

polygon than the number of sides of the polygon. So if a polygon has N sides, there will be $(N - 2)$ triangles formed, yielding $(N - 2) \times 180°$ for the total interior angle measure for the polygon.

7.   Discuss the 9-sided polygon on Worksheet 4–3c with the entire class before allowing students to work on their own.

Consider the 9-sided polygon on Worksheet 4–3c. Students should first label the polygon with its specific name: *nonagon*.

In order to have all diagonals from a single vertex lie in the interior of the polygon so that disjoint triangles are formed within the polygon, the *indented* vertex is the best choice in this case. After triangles have been formed, students should draw arcs to represent the different angle measures involved. Red arcs (shown solid here) should be drawn to show the angle measures for each triangle, and blue arcs (shown dotted here) should be drawn to indicate angle measures for the polygon. The subdivided diagram of the nonagon will appear as shown:

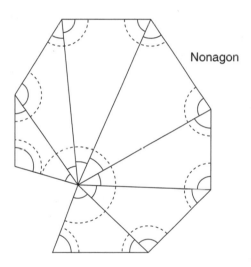

Nonagon

Discuss the idea that the measure of all the red arcs combined will equal the measure of all the blue arcs combined. So the total interior angle measure from each triangle may be used to find the total interior angle measure for the polygon. Have students write "180°" inside each disjoint triangle formed.

Each triangle contributes 180 degrees of interior angle measure to the polygon. For the nonagon, 7 triangles were drawn. Therefore, the total interior angle measure for the nonagon will equal $7 \times 180°$, or 1,260 degrees. On the row of the nonagon in the table on Worksheet 4–3a, students should record, in order, the following: 9 sides; $7 \times 180°$; and 1,260°.

Part B: Transversals of Parallel Line Segments

8.   Give each pair of students two copies of Worksheet 4–3d and a red pencil and a blue pencil.

9.   For each exercise on Worksheet 4–3d, have students draw an arc for each angle formed by a transversal. Draw red arcs for the smaller angles involved and blue arcs for the larger angles. Discuss the idea that all red angles are congruent to each other and all blue angles are congruent to each other. If a third angle size occurs, draw its arc in regular pencil.

10. In Exercise 2, since two angles from different transversals are given to be congruent, only two sizes of angles will be formed. Therefore, only two colors will be needed to draw the arcs of the angles. Students should discover this relationship as they identify and mark each angle. In Exercise 3, a right angle is marked. Students should identify the other right angles on the diagram in regular pencil. In the right triangle, the upper angle will equal 60 degrees. An arc should be drawn for this angle in regular pencil.

11. Discuss Exercise 1 with the entire class to demonstrate the coloring process.

Consider the diagram in Exercise 1. Since line a is parallel to line b, the transversal will form various pairs of congruent angles. Have students draw arcs with red pencil to mark the smaller angles and draw blue arcs to mark the larger angles. Discuss the idea that all red angles are congruent and all blue angles are congruent. Any pair of a red angle with a blue angle will be supplementary angles, whose measures total 180 degrees. Guide students to notice the positions of any angles that are congruent to each other. Here is a completed diagram for Exercise 1 (solid arcs represent red arcs and dotted arcs represent blue arcs):

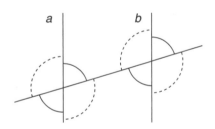

Answer Key for Worksheet 4–3c
The following are the table entries:

Heptagon; 7 sides; 5 × 180°; 900°

Octagon; 8 sides; 6 × 180°; 1,080°

Nonagon; 9 sides; 7 × 180°; 1,260°

Decagon; 10 sides; 8 × 180°; 1,440°

Answer Key for Worksheet 4–3d

1. [See the diagram in the text.]

2. [Arcs are not marked except given arcs; only angle measures are shown.]

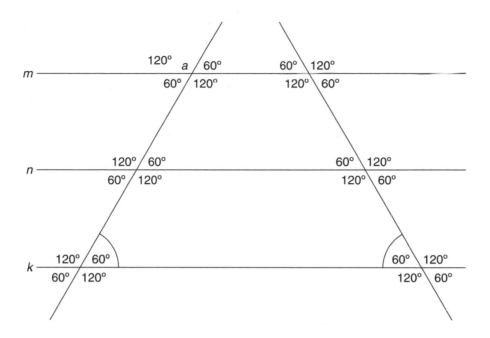

3. [Some arcs are shown to clarify certain angles; measures are shown; boxes indicate 90° angle measures.]

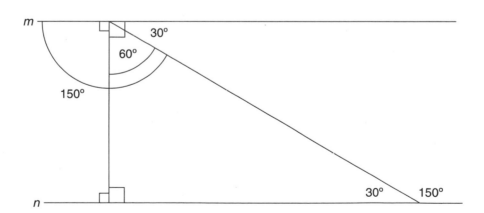

276

Worksheet 4–3c

Finding Sums for the Interior
Angles of Polygons

Name _____

Date _____

Write the name beside each polygon. Draw diagonals from one vertex to form disjoint triangles *inside* the polygon. Follow the teacher's instructions to find sums and record the
results on Worksheet 4–3a.

Worksheet 4-3d

Name _____

Finding Angles Formed by a
Transversal with Parallel Segments

Date _____

In each diagram, mark congruent angles with the same color. When given an angle measure, find the missing angle measures in the same diagram.

1. Line *a* is parallel to line *b*.

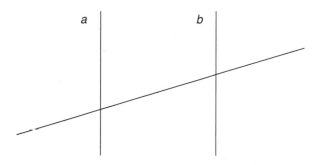

2. Lines *m*, *n*, and *k* are parallel to each other. The two angles already marked with arcs are congruent to each other. If the measure of $\angle a = 120°$, find and label the measures of the other angles.

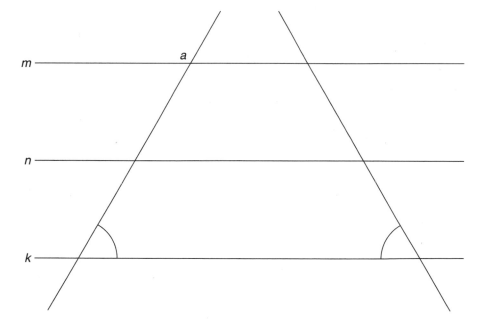

Worksheet 4–3d Continued

Name _____

Date _____

3. Line *m* is parallel to line *n*. If the given angle measures 30 degrees, find and label the measures of any other angles you can determine.

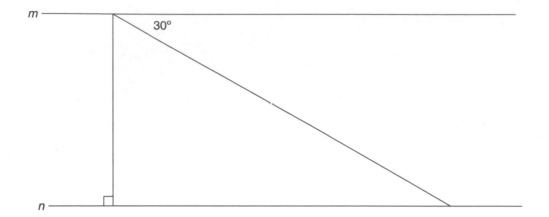

Activity 3
Independent Practice

Materials
    Worksheet 4–3e
    Regular pencil

Procedure
Give each student a copy of Worksheet 4–3e to complete. Encourage students to mark any known information directly on a given diagram. Remind students to identify all congruent angles on a diagram and label the angle measures on the diagram. Students should also label any other angle measures they can infer from data given in a problem. Exercises on the worksheet cover more general concepts involving angles and polygons, as well as sums of interior angle measures of polygons and transversals of parallel lines. Also remind students that in a 30°-60°-90° triangle, the length of the hypotenuse is twice the length of the side opposite the 30° angle. When everyone has finished the worksheet, ask several students to share their reasoning and their answers with the entire class.

Answer Key for Worksheet 4–3e
    1. B

    2. A

    3. D

    4. B

    5. C

    6. A

Possible Testing Errors That May Occur for This Objective
*   Students do not know the relationships among angles formed by a transversal with parallel lines.

*   Students do not know how to subdivide a polygon into several triangles in order to find the sum of the interior angle measures of the polygon, or they use the wrong formula to find the sum.

*   Students fail to use all geometric information provided in a problem and draw the wrong conclusion as a result.

Worksheet 4–3e   Name _____

Using Angle Relationships   Date _____
to Solve Problems

Solve each exercise provided. Be ready to share your reasoning and your answers with the entire class.

1. *Given:* Two angles are supplementary. The measure of one angle is 30° more than the measure of the other angle. *Conclusion:* The measures of the two angles are 60° and 90°. This conclusion:

   A. Is verified by the first statement given.

   B. Is contradicted by the first statement given.

   C. Is invalid because a 90° angle cannot be supplementary to another angle.

   D. Is valid because 90° is 30° more than 60°.

2. In the concave pentagon shown below, side *BC* is parallel to side *AE*, and side *CD* is perpendicular to side *BC*. The measure of ∠*CDE*, when made on the inside of the pentagon, is 200°. What is the measure of the interior angle, ∠*DEA*, in degrees?

   A. 70°   C. 270°

   B. 160°   D. 360°

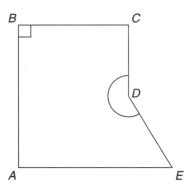

3. A city parks department plans to convert a triangular plot of land into an urban rock garden. The plot has sides that measure 23 feet, 30 feet, and 18 feet. If a special boulder is to be placed in the corner with the smallest angle, where should it be placed?

   A. In the center of the triangular plot

   B. In the corner opposite the side that is 30 feet

   C. In the corner opposite the side that is 23 feet

   D. In the corner opposite the side that is 18 feet

Worksheet 4–3e Continued

Name _____

Date _____

4. A triangular plot of land is shaded on the given street map. Avenue A and Avenue B are parallel. What are the measures of the three interior angles of the triangular plot?

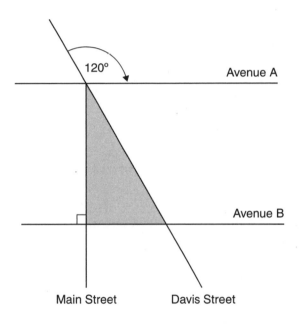

A. 90°, 65°, 25°

B. 90°, 60°, 30°

C. 90°, 50°, 40°

D. 120°, 40°, 20°

282

Name _____

Date _____

5. A pilot is flying her plane at an altitude of 2,500 feet. She sees the end of a runway at an angle of depression of 30 degrees. What is the approximate horizontal distance of the plane from the runway at this point?

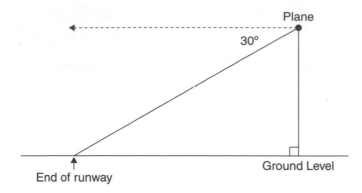

A. 1,250 feet

B. 2,500 feet

C. 4,330 feet

D. 5,000 feet

6. What will be the sum of the interior angle measures of a decagon or 10-sided polygon?

A. 1,440°   B. 1,080°   C. 720°   D. 360°

Objective 4: Apply the Pythagorean Theorem to Solve Geometric Problems With or Without Variables

To fully understand the Pythagorean Theorem, students need to explore both right and nonright triangles and the relationships among their three sides. The following activities provide such opportunities and will lead students to discover the famous theorem for themselves.

Activity 1
Manipulative Stage

Materials

Worksheet 4–4a (recording sheet)

Large 1-inch grids (approximately 14 inches by 16 inches; 1 grid per pair of students)

Packets of 100 1-inch paper squares (1 packet per student)

Long bamboo skewers (1 per pair of students)

Transparent tape (1 roll per pair of students)

Regular pencil

Procedure

1. Give each pair of students a large grid sheet, 2 packets of 100 paper squares (1 inch × 1 inch), a bamboo skewer, two copies of Worksheet 4–4a, and a roll of transparent tape. The grid may be drawn off on heavy bulletin board or butcher paper to form approximately a 14-inch × 16-inch grid (unit length of 1 inch), or a grid may be drawn on two sheets of 8.5-inch × 14-inch paper, which can then be taped together at their longer edges to make the larger grid that is needed. Laminating the final grids will make them more durable. Worksheet 4–4a should have at least 10 lines for recording the data.

2. In Activity 1, students will work only with right triangles. In the next activity, the Pictorial Stage, they will investigate other triangles in order to determine which conditions of the theorem are really necessary. Allow students to find patterns for themselves. The same recording table, Worksheet 4–4a, will be used for both activities.

3. The large grid should be positioned so that the longer edge appears like a horizontal axis and the shorter edge appears like a vertical axis on the left. Students will arrange paper squares as square regions at the left and the bottom edges of the grid. The sizes of these two square regions are shown on Worksheet 4–4a for the first three exercises. The grid edge from each of these two square regions together will form the legs of a right triangle. Students will then try to build a square region, whose edge will be the hypotenuse of the same triangle.

4. For each exercise, after the assigned pair of square regions is in place along the two adjacent grid edges, have students place the bamboo skewer on the large grid so that it touches the corner of the top paper square along the left edge of the grid and the corner of the right-most paper square along the bottom edge of the grid. The skewer will form a right triangle with the left edge portion and bottom edge portion of the grid bounded by the skewer. Students should tape the ends of the skewer in place on the grid to keep it from moving during the exercise.

5. Now ask students if all the paper squares forming the two regions touching the large grid will be enough to form another square region along the skewer, or longer side of the triangle. Students should move all the paper squares from the two regions onto the grid and try to form a new square region. A square region will be possible each time because of the assigned lengths used for the shorter sides of the triangle.

6. The edge of the new square region will coincide with the hypotenuse (skewer segment) of the right triangle. Students should record their results on the appropriate line of the table on Worksheet 4–4a. The question in the right-most column of the table simply asks whether the combined paper squares from the first two square regions were enough to make the third square region. It will be possible for all exercises in Activity 1.

7. Follow the above procedure for each pair of side lengths shown in Exercises 1 to 3 on Worksheet 4–4a. Record the results in the table each time. Students will continue to use this same table during the Pictorial Stage.

8. Guide students through Exercise 1 from Worksheet 4–4a before allowing them to work the other two exercises on their own.

For Exercise 1, students will use the side lengths of 3 inches and 4 inches to build their first pair of square regions on the grid. Have students place 3 paper squares along the shorter edge of the large inch grid, starting from the lower left corner of the grid. Then have them place 4 paper squares along the longer edge of the grid, starting from the same corner as the 3 paper squares. Ask them to use more paper squares to build a square region (3 inches × 3 inches) that has the first 3 paper squares along one side; repeat the process with the 4 paper squares. Now have students place the bamboo skewer on the large grid so that it touches the corner of the top paper square along the left edge of the grid and the corner of the right-most paper square along the bottom edge of the grid. The skewer now forms a right triangle with the left edge portion (3 inches) and bottom edge portion (4 inches) of the grid bounded by the skewer. Tape the skewer in place. Here is an example of the finished square regions and the skewer on the grid:

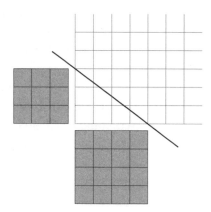

Now ask students if all the paper squares forming the 3 × 3 region and the 4 × 4 region touching the large grid will be enough to form another square region along the skewer, or longer side of the triangle. Students should move the 9 paper squares and the 16 paper squares onto the grid and form a new square region that is 5 inches × 5 inches in size. The new square region is shown here.

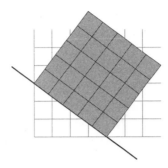

The 5-inch edge of the new square region will coincide with the hypotenuse (skewer segment) of the right triangle. Students should now record their results on the first line of their table in the following order: "right, 3 in., 4 in., 5 in., 9 sq. in., 16 sq. in., 25 sq. in., yes." The question in the right-most column of the table simply asks whether the combined paper squares from the first two square regions were enough to make the third square region. It was possible for this exercise, and will also be possible for Exercises 2 and 3.

Note: Alternative materials for this activity might be commercial colored square tiles, along with a large sheet of paper containing an L-frame (14-inch vertical bar with 16-inch horizontal bar) with no grid lines shown. The bamboo skewer would still be used in the described manner. The previous illustrations would remain the same, just without markings on the large grid.

Answer Key for Worksheet 4–4a
Answers are given for the first three exercises only.

1. right, 3 in., 4 in., 5 in., 9 sq. in., 16 sq. in., 25 sq. in., yes

2. right, 6 in., 8 in., 10 in., 36 sq. in., 64 sq. in., 100 sq. in., yes

3. right, 5 in., 12 in., 13 in., 25 sq. in., 144 sq. in., 169 sq. in., yes

286

Worksheet 4–4a

Modeling the Pythagorean
Theorem with Triangles

Name _____

Date _____

Build square regions with 1-inch paper squares on a grid or with cutout grid shapes.
Follow the teacher's instructions to make different triangles. Record your results in the
table. Side lengths for Exercises 1 to 3 are shown.

Type of Triangle	Edge Lengths			Areas			Area 1 + Area 2 = Area 3? Yes/No
	Short Side 1	Short Side 2	Long Side 3	Short Side 1	Short Side 2	Long Side 3	
1. right	3	4					
2. right	6	8					
3. right	5	12					
4.							
5.							
6.							
7.							
8.							
9.							
10.							

Activity 2
Pictorial Stage

Materials
Worksheet 4–4a (from Activity 1)
5-millimeter grid paper
Small index cards (1 per pair of students)
Scissors (1 per pair of students)
Transparent tape (1 roll per pair of students)
Plain paper
Regular pencil

Procedure

1. Give each pair of students 3 sheets of 5-millimeter grid paper, 4 sheets of plain paper, a small index card, scissors, and a roll of transparent tape. They will continue to use the recording table on Worksheet 4–4a from the Manipulative Stage.

2. In Activity 2 students will cut various square regions from the grid paper. They will form new triangles by arranging three selected square regions, so that only their vertices or corners touch in a prescribed way (see the illustration). The edge between each pair of touching vertices will form a side of the new triangle. The paper regions will then be taped down on a plain sheet of paper, carefully preserving the triangle that has been formed.

3. The index card should be used to test the triangle's three angles for a possible right angle. The triangle should be identified as *obtuse*, *acute*, or *right*, and the triangle's side lengths and the areas of the corresponding paper grid squares recorded on a line of the table on Worksheet 4–4a. Students should also answer the question about the areas in the right-most column.

4. For Exercises 4 to 10 on Worksheet 4–4a, use the following sets of side lengths for the paper squares. The type of triangle the side lengths will produce is also given.

4. 5, 5, 8—obtuse triangle   8. 4, 4, 4—acute triangle
5. 6, 6, 6—acute triangle   9. 10, 10, 12—acute triangle
6. 9, 12, 15—right triangle   10. 12, 16, 20—right triangle
7. 5, 8, 10—obtuse triangle

5. After the table on Worksheet 4–4a is completed for all 10 triangles (3 from the Manipulative Stage and 7 from the Pictorial Stage), ask the students to notice which types of triangles have "yes" in the right-most column of the table. Only the right triangles should have "yes." Have students write a statement below their table stating that "only for *right* triangles does the sum of the squares of the shorter two side lengths equal the square of the longest side length" (or some similar wording).

6. Before allowing students to work on their own, discuss Exercise 4 with the class.

Consider Exercise 4. The side lengths are 5, 5, and 8 units. Students should make cutouts of two 5×5 squares and one 8×8 square from their 5-millimeter grid paper. A triangle should be formed with the 3 paper squares and then the paper squares taped down on a sheet of plain paper. The corner of the index card will not fit *exactly* into any angle (therefore, no right angle exists), and one angle of the triangle opens wider than the corner of the index card, indicating an *obtuse* angle. So the triangle formed will be an *obtuse* triangle with side lengths 5, 5, and 8 units, with corresponding areas 25, 25, and 64 square units, all to be recorded in line 4 of the table on Worksheet 4–4a. Since (25 + 25) does not equal 64, the word "no" will be written in the right-most column. Have students write the side lengths and the triangle name below the taped-down paper squares.

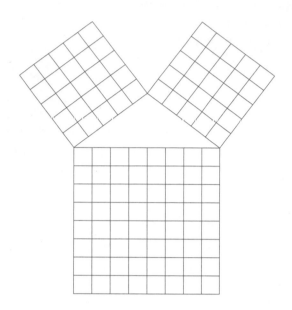

Answer Key for Worksheet 4–4a

1. right, 3 in., 4 in., 5 in., 9 sq. in., 16 sq. in., 25 sq. in., yes

2. right, 6 in., 8 in., 10 in., 36 sq. in., 64 sq. in., 100 sq. in., yes

3. right, 5 in., 12 in., 13 in., 25 sq. in., 144 sq. in., 169 sq. in., yes

4. obtuse, 5 units, 5 units, 8 units, 25 sq. units, 25 sq. units, 64 sq. units, no

5. acute, 6 units, 6 units, 6 units, 36 sq. units, 36 sq. units, 36 sq. units, no

6. right, 9 units, 12 units, 15 units, 81 sq. units, 144 sq. units, 225 sq. units, yes

7. obtuse, 5 units, 8 units, 10 units, 25 sq. units, 64 sq. units, 100 sq. units, no

8. acute, 4 units, 4 units, 4 units, 16 sq. units, 16 sq. units, 16 sq. units., no

9. acute, 10 units, 10 units, 12 units, 100 sq. units, 100 sq. units, 144 sq. units, no

10. right, 12 units, 16 units, 20 units, 144 sq. units, 256 sq. units, 400 sq. units, yes

Activity 3
Independent Practice

Materials

Worksheet 4–4b

Regular pencil

Procedure

Give each student a copy of Worksheet 4–4b to complete. Encourage students to draw and label diagrams to help them solve the word problems. After everyone has finished, have several students share their answers with the entire class.

Answer Key for Worksheet 4–4b

1. B

2. D

3. D

4. B

5. C

6. A

Possible Testing Errors That May Occur for This Objective

- Students will find the <u>mean</u> of the two given side lengths of the triangle instead of finding the needed length of the hypotenuse. The hypotenuse must be longer than either of the two legs of the triangle.

- Students will find the sum of the two given side lengths of the triangle instead of correctly finding the length of the hypotenuse. If the hypotenuse were to equal the sum of the lengths of the two shorter sides, a triangle would not be possible.

- When the lengths of the hypotenuse and a leg of the triangle are given and the length of the other leg of the triangle is sought, students will add the squares of the two given lengths, instead of subtracting to find the square of the missing leg of the triangle.

Worksheet 4–4b   Name _____

Solving Word Problems with   Date _____
the Pythagorean Theorem

Complete each exercise provided. Draw and label diagrams to solve the problems, if needed. A calculator may be helpful.

1. Josh drove 20 miles due north from Akron to Timberline, then drove 21 miles due east to Ft. Davis. If he drove the shortest distance from Akron northeast to Ft. Davis without going through Timberline, how far would he drive?

    A. 41 mi.   B. 29 mi.   C. 18 mi.   D. 10 mi.

2. A rectangular garden has a 10-meter-long side and an 18-meter-long diagonal. About how many meters of fencing are needed to enclose the garden?

    A. 15 m   B. 25 m   C. 28 m   D. 50 m

3. Which figure best represents a triangle with side lengths a, b, and c in which the relationship $a^2 + b^2 = c^2$ is always true?

    A.
    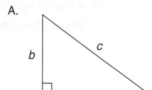

    C.
    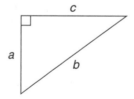

    B.
    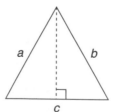

    D.
    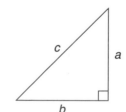

Worksheet 4–4b Continued

Name _____

Date _____

4. A guidewire connects from the top of a vertical pole to the ground and forms a 45-degree angle with the ground. If the guidewire is 110 feet long, about how tall is the pole?

A. 155 ft.   B. 78 ft.   C. 55 ft.   D. 11 ft.

5. Kate walked diagonally across a rectangular lawn that measured 50 feet wide by 75 feet long. Which expression determines how far Kate walked?

A. $\dfrac{(50)(75)}{2}$ B. $\sqrt{50} + \sqrt{75}$ C. $\sqrt{(50)^2 + (75)^2}$ D. $2(50 + 75)$

6. A wooden pole was broken during a windstorm. The original height of the pole above the ground was 14 meters. After the pole broke, the top of the pole touched the ground 6 meters from the base of the pole. How tall was the part of the pole that was left standing?

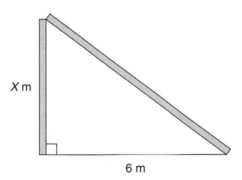

X m

6 m

A. 5.7 m   B. 8 m   C. 12.6 m   D. Not here

Objective 5: Find Missing Measures Using Similar Two-Dimensional Shapes

Students have great difficulty understanding that as side measures of polygons increase by a constant factor, the perimeter increases proportionately by the same factor. This proportional change is a characteristic of dilations or the process of forming similar shapes by enlargement or reduction. For example, if all sides are doubled (a factor of 2), the perimeter will also double (a factor of 2). For an extension of this characteristic, when the side measures increase, the area of the polygon increases by the square of the factor used to change the side lengths. That is, if the side lengths are tripled (a factor of 3), the area is multiplied by 3×3, or 9. The activities described below will help students understand the special relationship between the sides of a polygon and the perimeter of the polygon when a similar polygon is generated by a dilation.

Activity 1

Manipulative Stage

Materials

Packets of 1-inch flat straw pieces (100 pieces per packet per pair of students)

Rectangular pieces of felt material (approximately 12 inches by 18 inches; one per pair of students)

Worksheet 4–5a (recording sheet)

Regular pencil

Procedure

1. Give each pair of students a packet of 100 1-inch pieces cut from flat plastic straws or coffee stirrers, a piece of felt for a building mat, and a copy of Worksheet 4–5a as a recording sheet. This activity involves similar shapes. It is assumed that students already know the basic definition of *similar polygons*: two polygons that have the same shape and same corresponding angle measures but whose corresponding sides taken pairwise form equivalent ratios. Dilations and similarity will be connected in this activity.

2. Consider a single straw piece as the unit of measure (approximately 1 inch) for building polygons. Have students work on a piece of felt material so that the straw pieces do not move around too freely during the building process.

3. For each initial polygon (A) built according to the directions on the worksheet, students should record on Worksheet 4–5a the number of straw units used to make each side. They should then count all the unit pieces used to make the shape in order to find the perimeter of the polygon. The perimeter should also be recorded on Worksheet 4–5a.

4. After students have built an initial polygon and recorded its measures, have them build another larger polygon (B) with the same shape as the first one (the first shape will be *dilated* to form a larger, similar shape) by doubling [2×], tripling [3×], or otherwise expanding all the original sides as indicated on Worksheet 4–5a. The side lengths and perimeter of the new shape should then be found by counting the straw pieces, and these new measures should be recorded in the appropriate spaces on Worksheet 4–5a.

5.   Repeat the above process for each new initial polygon built. After four pairs (A and B) of polygons have been built and their measures recorded, ask students to look for patterns among the side lengths and perimeters of each pair of polygons built. The hope is that they will discover that as all side lengths are changed, so also is the perimeter changed in the same way. Have students record their ideas at the bottom of Worksheet 4–5a.

6.   Discuss Exercise 1 on Worksheet 4–5a with the class before allowing the students to work the other exercises involving pentagons, quadrilaterals, and triangles.

For Exercise 1 on Worksheet 4–5a, students are asked to build a small <u>hexagon</u> (preferably an *irregular* hexagon) with their straw pieces, then record the different side lengths and the perimeter on the worksheet in the row for 1A. For row 1B, students are directed to build a larger <u>hexagon</u> by <u>doubling</u> [2×] each side length of the first hexagon. That is, if 3 straw pieces were used for one side, then 2 × 3, or 6, straw pieces must be used for the corresponding side in the larger hexagon.

Once the larger hexagon is built, each of its side lengths and its perimeter should be recorded in row 1B of Worksheet 4–5a. Here is a sample of a pair of hexagons where the side lengths of the first hexagon have been <u>doubled</u> to make the second, larger hexagon. The side lengths and perimeters of the two hexagons would be recorded on their respective rows, 1A and 1B, on Worksheet 4–5a.

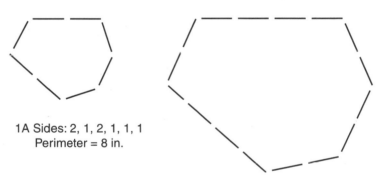

1A Sides: 2, 1, 2, 1, 1, 1
Perimeter = 8 in.

1B Sides: 4, 2, 4, 2, 2, 2
Perimeter = 16 in.

Answer Key for Worksheet 4–5a
Entries in the table will vary depending on how students build their required polygons. The final results, however, should be the same: whatever factor is used to enlarge the sides of a polygon will also be used to enlarge the perimeter.

294

Worksheet 4–5a

Name _____

Building Similar Polygons and
Comparing Their Perimeters

Date _____

As you build the required polygons with your straw pieces, record their measurements on
the table provided. Not all <u>side</u> columns will be needed for every polygon.

Polygon	Side 1	Side 2	Side 3	Side 4	Side 5	Side 6	Perimeter
1A Hexagon							
1B [2×]							
2A Pentagon							
2B [3×]							
3A Quadri-lateral							
3B [4×]							
4A Triangle							
4B [5×]							

As the side lengths of polygon A change to make the new *similar* polygon B, how
does the perimeter of polygon A compare to the perimeter of polygon B?

Activity 2
Pictorial Stage

Materials

Worksheet 4–5b
Regular pencil

Procedure

1. Give each pair of students two copies of Worksheet 4–5b.

2. For each polygon on Worksheet 4–5b, have students draw a *similar* polygon according to the dilating instructions provided. Two shapes will be enlarged and two shapes reduced. The amount of change required will be stated as a scale factor. The horizontal or vertical distance between adjacent dots on a worksheet grid will be 1 unit of length. The diagonal distance between two dots is greater than 1 unit in length.

3. For each polygon on Worksheet 4–5b, both those provided and those drawn, students should label each side with its length and record the perimeter inside the shape.

4. After the required polygons have been drawn and all polygons have been labeled and their perimeters found, ask students to describe in their own words how changing all side lengths in a polygon by the same scale factor, thereby obtaining another *similar* polygon, will affect the original perimeter. Have them write a statement on the back of the worksheet telling what they have discovered. Have some students share their statements with the entire class.

5. Discuss Exercise 1 with the class before allowing students to work the other exercises on their own.

Consider Exercise 1 on Worksheet 4–5b. Students must apply a scale factor of $\frac{1}{2}$ to dilate the polygon and form a new similar polygon. That is, they must find half of each original side length in order to draw the new shape. Since the scale factor is less than 1, the new shape will be a *reduction* of the original shape. The side lengths of the original polygon are 6, 4, 2, 2, 4, and 2 units, respectively. These measures should be labeled on their corresponding sides of the figure on the worksheet. The perimeter should be recorded inside the figure as "p = 20 units." Be sure that students count the spaces between adjacent dots as units and not the dots themselves.

When the new side lengths are found, their measures will be 3, 2, 1, 1, 2, and 1 unit, respectively. The new perimeter will be 10 units, which should be recorded inside the newly drawn polygon. Here is an example of the original shape and the new shape with their perimeters recorded. The original shape is shown with a solid line and the new shape is shown with a broken line. The side measures are not shown in the illustration.

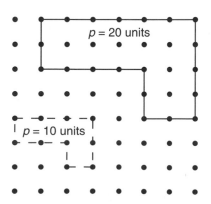

Answer Key for Worksheet 4–5b

1. Original: 6, 4, 2, 2, 4, and 2 units; p = 20 units

   New: 3, 2, 1, 1, 2, and 1 units; p = 10 units

2. Original: 3, 1, 1, 1, 1, 1, 1, and 1 units; p = 10 units

   New: 6, 2, 2, 2, 2, 2, 2, and 2 units; p = 20 units

3. Original: 1, 2, 1, and 2 units; p = 6 units

   New: 3, 6, 3, and 6 units; p = 18 units

4. Original: 4, 2, 2, 2, 2, and 4 units; p = 16 units

   New: 1, $\frac{1}{2}$, $\frac{1}{2}$, $\frac{1}{2}$, $\frac{1}{2}$, and 1 units; p = 4 units

Worksheet 4–5b

Name _____

Drawing Similar Polygons and
Comparing Their Perimeters

Date _____

Draw the required polygons. Record the side measures and perimeter of each polygon on the drawing.

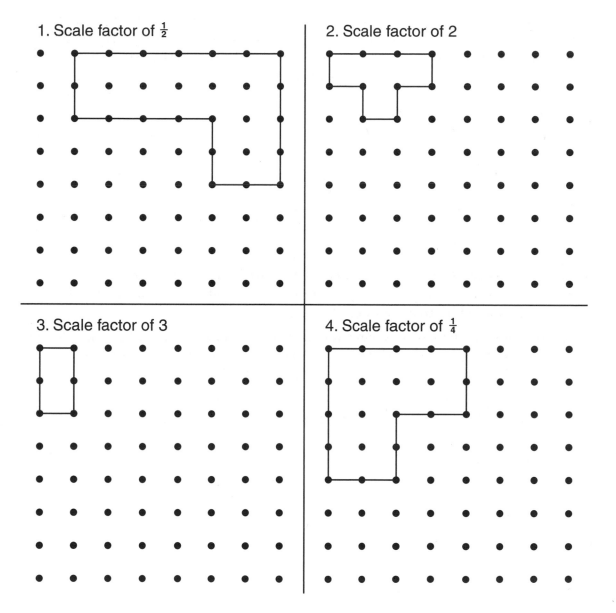

1. Scale factor of $\frac{1}{2}$

2. Scale factor of 2

3. Scale factor of 3

4. Scale factor of $\frac{1}{4}$

Activity 3
Independent Practice

Materials
> Worksheet 4–5c
> Regular pencil

Procedure
Give each student a copy of Worksheet 4–5c. Encourage students to draw and label shapes to help them solve the problems on the worksheet that do not provide illustrations. When all have completed the worksheet, have various students share their reasoning and their answers for each of the exercises.

Answer Key for Worksheet 4–5c
1. C

2. B

3. A

4. C

Possible Testing Errors That May Occur for This Objective
- Students view the change between corresponding side lengths of similar shapes as addition rather than multiplication.

- When finding the new measures for an enlargement, students will multiply to find one new side length but divide to find another side length for the same new shape. They do not change all side lengths the same way.

- Students fail to realize that in a dilation (enlargement or reduction) the side lengths and the perimeter change by the same scale factor.

Worksheet 4–5c

Name _____

Dilation: Reducing and Enlarging
Polygons

Date _____

Complete the exercises provided. If helpful, draw diagrams to solve the problems.

1. A rectangle has a length of 5 feet and a perimeter of 16 feet. What is the perimeter of a similar rectangle with a width of 12 feet?

   A. 32 ft.   B. 36 ft.   C. 64 ft.   D. 80 ft.

2. $\triangle ABC$ is similar to $\triangle FGH$. Find the length of side AC.

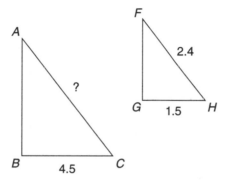

   A. 6.0 units

   B. 7.2 units

   C. 8.4 units

   D. 9.0 units

3. The larger quadrilateral was dilated to form the smaller quadrilateral. Two corresponding side lengths are shown. What was the scale factor used to change the larger into the smaller shape?

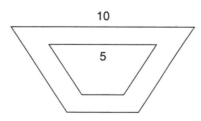

   A. $\frac{1}{2}$ B. $\frac{1}{4}$ C. 2   D. 3

4. Rectangle A is similar to rectangle B. The longer side length of rectangle A is 5 inches. The longer side length of rectangle B is 20 inches, and its area is 240 square inches. Find the area of rectangle A.

   A. 3 sq. in.   B. 12 sq. in.   C. 15 sq. in.   D. 25 sq. in.

Objective 6: Apply Ratio and Proportion to Solve Geometric Problems
Many real-world problems involve geometric properties in some way. Often these properties must be applied in order to set up appropriate proportions by which to solve for an unknown value. The following activities provide experience with central angles and their corresponding arc lengths on a circle. In addition, the ratios of side segments formed when a triangle's two sides are cut by a line parallel to the third side of the triangle are studied.

Activity 1
Manipulative Stage

Materials

Building Mat 4–6a
Worksheet 4–6a
Worksheet 4–6b
Scissors
Inch rulers (1 per pair of students)
Colored pencils (1 red and 1 blue per pair of students)
Regular pencil

Procedure

1. This activity consists of two parts. Part A deals with the central angles of a circle and Part B with parallel lines intersecting a triangle under certain conditions. The two parts may be done at different class times or in any order. Each part may also be done consecutively with its corresponding part in Activity 2.

Part A: Central Angles of a Circle

2. Give each pair of students one copy of Worksheet 4–6a, two copies of Worksheet 4–6b, and one pair of scissors.

3. Have partners cut apart the sectors of the circle on Worksheet 4–6a. Have them place sector A on top of sector B to find how many of sector A will cover sector B. Ask them how many measures of the central angle *A* equal the measure of the central angle *B* (2), and how many of arc length *a* of sector A equal the arc length *b* of sector B (2). Repeat the process with sector C versus sector B. Four of sector C will cover sector B. Four of the measure of central angle *C* will equal the measure of central angle *B*, and four of the arc length *c* of sector C will equal the arc length *b* of sector B. Here is an illustration of sector C being placed on sector B and counted.

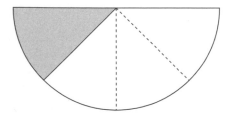

4. Have students trace sector A onto the first circle shown on Worksheet 4–6b, and sector C onto the second circle shown on Worksheet 4–6b. Four of sector A will cover the first circle, and eight of sector C will cover the second circle. Students should label each central angle formed and mark its corresponding arc length on the circle. Here is an example of sector A's tracing onto the first circle, the labeling of the central angle A, and the marking off of its arc length a:

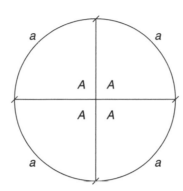

5. Beside the first completed circle on Worksheet 4–6b, students should record the following results for sector A:

4 of $m\angle A = 360°$, so $\dfrac{m\angle A}{360°} = \dfrac{1}{4}$;

4 of arc length a = circumference C, so $\dfrac{a}{C} = \dfrac{1}{4}$.

Beside the second completed circle on Worksheet 4–6b, students should record the following for sector C:

8 of $m\angle C = 360°$, so $\dfrac{m\angle C}{360°} = \dfrac{1}{8}$;

8 of arc length c = circumference C, so $\dfrac{c}{C} = \dfrac{1}{8}$.

6. Guide students to observe that in a circle, a central angle's measure compared to a full revolution equals the same ratio as the central angle's arc length compared to the circumference of the circle.

Part B: Triangles Cut by Parallel Lines

7. Give each pair of students two copies of Building Mat 4–6a, a red pencil and a blue pencil, and an inch ruler. The building mat should be positioned so that the points are above the lines and the two lines go from left to right. A triangle will be built and drawn in red pencil from point A on the mat, and another triangle will be built and drawn in blue pencil from point B.

8. For the triangle from point A, have students align the 0-mark on the inch ruler with point A. Then the other end of the ruler should be rotated to the left until the 2-mark intersects line m and the 4-mark intersects line n. A line segment should be drawn in red along the edge of the ruler from point A to the intersection point on line n. The lengths of the two disjoint segments forming the red segment should be labeled while the ruler is still in position (2 inches and 2 inches). The end of the ruler should then be rotated to

the right until the 2.5-mark intersects line m and the 5-mark intersects line n. Another line segment should be drawn in red in this new position from point A to the intersection point on line n. Its disjoint segments should also be labeled (2.5 inches and 2.5 inches). Here is an illustration of the completed red triangle (not drawn to scale):

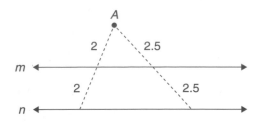

9. On each red side of the triangle, have students compare the length from point A to line m to the total length from point A to line n. In the upper left corner of the building mat, students should record the ratios for the sides of the red triangle as follows: Red (A)—$\frac{2}{4} = \frac{1}{2} = 0.5$ and $\frac{2.5}{5} = \frac{1}{2} = 0.5$. Observe that the ratios for the red sides are equal.

10. Now repeat the process to build a blue triangle from point B on the mat. Have students place the 0-mark of the inch ruler at point B, then rotate the other end of the ruler to the left until the 3.5-mark intersects line m and the 5.25-mark intersects line n. A blue segment should be drawn along the edge of the ruler from point B to the intersection point on line n. The lengths of the two disjoint segments forming the blue segment should be labeled while the ruler is still in position (3.5 inches and 1.75 inches). The end of the ruler should then be rotated to the right until the 4-mark intersects line m and the 6-mark intersects line n. Another line segment should be drawn in blue in this new position from point B to the intersection point on line n. Its disjoint segments should also be labeled (4 inches and 2 inches).

11. On each blue side of the triangle, have students compare the length from point B to line m to the total length from point B to line n. In the upper right corner of the building mat, students should record the ratios for the sides of the blue triangle as follows: Blue (B)—$\frac{3.5}{5.25} = \frac{2}{3} = 0.\overline{6}$ and $\frac{4}{6} = \frac{2}{3} = 0.\overline{6}$. Observe that the ratios for the blue sides are also equal.

12. Discuss the idea that the ratios of segment lengths were found using two parallel lines, where one line coincided with the third side of the triangle being built and the other line passed through the interior of the triangle. If time allows more exploration, have students draw two lines on the back of Building Mat 4–6a that are *almost* parallel lines and mark a point C above the two lines. They should then draw two sides from point C to the bottom line. Since these measurements will not be as carefully controlled as the others were, have students measure with a centimeter ruler instead of an inch ruler. They should set up the same ratios for the two sides as done previously, but the decimal values of the simplified ratios will not be equal.

Answer Key for Worksheet 4–6b
The details are given in the text.

Building Mat 4–6a

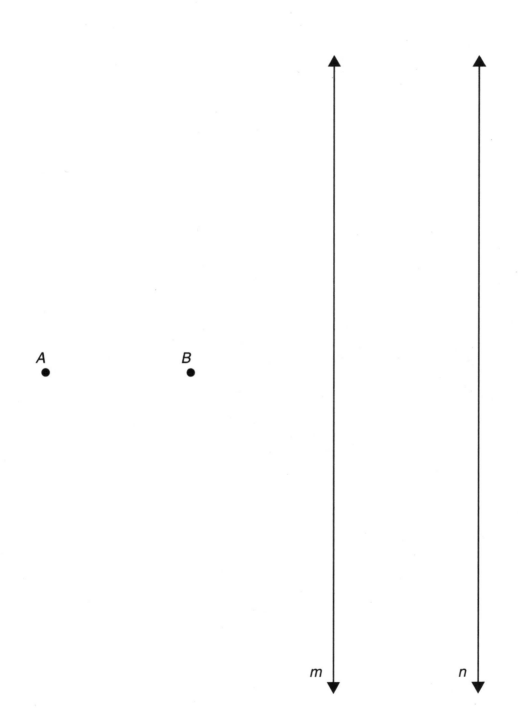

304

Worksheet 4–6a
Pattern for Sectors of a Circle

Cut the sectors apart and use sectors A, B, and C with Worksheet 4–6b.

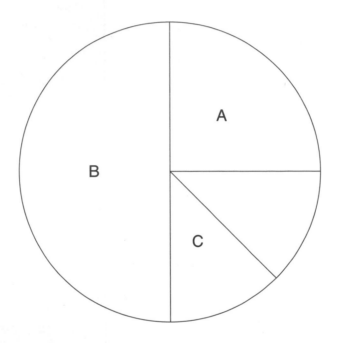

Worksheet 4–6b

Comparing Sectors of a Circle

Name _____

Date _____

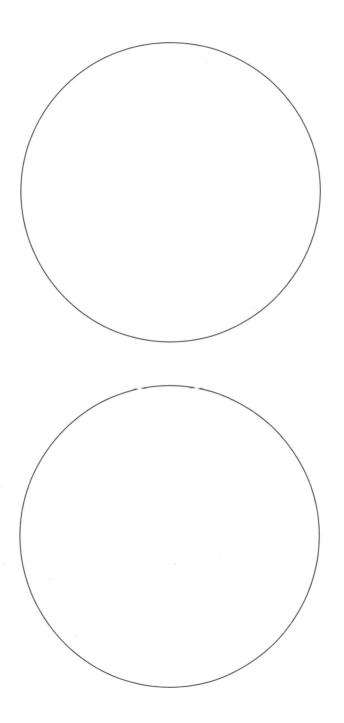

Activity 2
Pictorial Stage

Materials

       Worksheet 4–6c
       Worksheet 4–6d
       Centimeter rulers (1 per pair of students)
       Colored pencils (1 red and 1 blue per pair of students)
       Calculators (1 per pair of students)
       Regular pencil

Procedure

    1.   This activity consists of two parts. Part A deals with the central angles of a circle and Part B with parallel lines intersecting a triangle under certain conditions. The two parts may be done at different class times or in any order. Each part may also be done consecutively with its corresponding part in Activity 1.

Part A: Central Angles of a Circle

    2.   Give each pair of students two copies of Worksheet 4–6c. It is assumed that students have mastered the formula for the circumference of a circle, but the formula should be reviewed before students apply it in this activity.

    3.   Have students use the diagram on Worksheet 4–6c to answer the questions provided on the worksheet. Guide them to write a statement about the relationship between a central angle's measure and its corresponding arc length.

    4.   Discuss angle A and its arc length a with the entire class. Then have partners find the answers for angle B.

    Consider angle A, a central angle of the circle on Worksheet 4–6c. A complete revolution equals 360 degrees. Since the measure of angle A is 1 out of 10 equal parts of 360 degrees, the measure of angle A equals $\frac{1}{10} \times 360°$, or 36 degrees. Below Exercise 1, students should record the following equation: $m \angle A = \frac{1}{10} \times 360° = 36°$.

    Since the radius of the circle is 2 inches, have students compute the circumference: $C = 2\pi r \approx 2(3.14)(2) = 12.56$ inches. The arc length a is 1 out of 10 equal parts of the circumference, so the arc length equals $\frac{1}{10} \times 12.56$, or 1.256 inches. Below Exercise 2, students should record the following equation: $a = \frac{1}{10} \times C = \frac{1}{10} \times 12.56 = 1.256$ inches.

    After students complete Exercises 3 and 4, discuss the ratios involved with each angle. For angle A, the central angle measure involved a ratio of 1:10, and so did the arc length. For angle B, each involved a ratio of 3:10. A possible statement for Exercise 5 might be as follows: "In a circle, the ratio of a central angle's measure to 360° equals the ratio of the angle's corresponding arc length to the circumference of the circle."

Part B: Triangles Cut by Parallel Lines

    5.   For Part B, give each pair of students two copies of Worksheet 4–6d, a centimeter ruler, and a calculator. Encourage students to be accurate when measuring with the ruler. Each measurement should be to the nearest tenth of a centimeter.

6. For each figure on Worksheet 4–6d, have students measure the required segments and compute the given ratios. Round each ratio value to the nearest tenth. In Exercise 2, also have students apply a ratio to predict a value for *MW*. Then confirm the length by actually measuring the segment on the figure.

7. After students have completed the worksheet, discuss the idea that the ratios for the two sides of a triangle, which are cut by the same parallel lines, are equal. When computed and rounded, the ratios for Exercise 1 should be equal, and the ratios for Exercise 2 should be equal.

Measurements made by students for the segments will vary, but here are sample measurements for Exercise 1 to show the process to be followed. Suppose $AB = 2.4$ cm, $AC = 6.9$ cm, $AD = 2.2$ cm, and $AE = 6.3$ cm. Then the computed and rounded ratios will be as follows: $\frac{AB}{AC} = \frac{2.4}{6.9} = 0.347 \approx 0.3$ and $\frac{AD}{AE} = \frac{2.2}{6.3} = 0.349 \approx 0.3$. Since the two sides of the larger triangle, $\triangle CAE$, are cut by the same pair of parallel lines, where one line coincides with the third side of the triangle, the ratios for the two sides will be equal. Rounding is used with the ratios to compensate for inaccuracies in measuring.

Answer Key for Worksheet 4–6c

1. [See the text.]

2. [See the text.]

3. $m\angle B = \frac{3}{10} \times 360° = 108°$

4. $b = \frac{3}{10} \times C = \frac{3}{10} \times 12.56 = 3.768$ inches

5. [See the text.]

Answer Key for Worksheet 4–6d

Actual measurements will vary slightly, but rounded ratios in the same exercise should be equal. In Exercise 2, the *predicted* length, *MW*, should be found by multiplying the common ratio value found by the length *MZ*.

308

The diagram shows a circle divided into 10 congruent sectors. Use the diagram to answer the questions below about central angles *A* and *B*, and their respective arc lengths *a* and *b*. Assume that the circle has a radius of 2 inches.

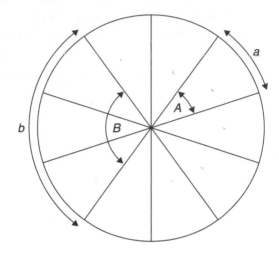

1. How much of one revolution of 360 degrees does the measure of angle *A* represent?

2. How much of the circumference does the arc length *a* represent?

3. How much of one revolution of 360 degrees does the measure of angle *B* represent?

4. How much of the circumference does the arc length *b* represent?

Worksheet 4–6d   Name _____

Triangles Cut by Parallel Lines   Date _____

In the figures, line m is parallel to line n, and line k is parallel to line h. Use a centimeter ruler to measure the required segments to the nearest tenth, and label the segments with their measures. Find the ratios. Round each ratio value to the nearest tenth.

1.

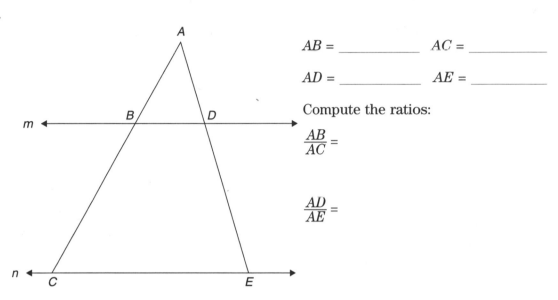

$AB =$ _____ $AC =$ _____

$AD =$ _____ $AE =$ _____

Compute the ratios:

$$\frac{AB}{AC} =$$

$$\frac{AD}{AE} =$$

2.

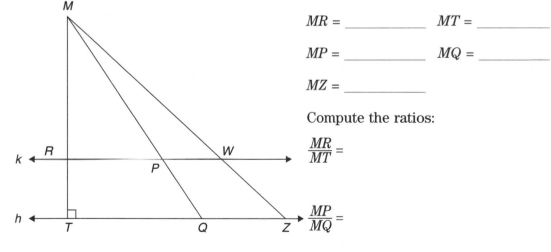

$MR =$ _____ $MT =$ _____

$MP =$ _____ $MQ =$ _____

$MZ =$ _____

Compute the ratios:

$$\frac{MR}{MT} =$$

$$\frac{MP}{MQ} =$$

Use the ratios to predict MW. Then measure MW to confirm the predicted value. How close was your prediction?

Activity 3
Independent Practice

Materials
> Worksheet 4–6e
> Regular pencil
> Calculator

Procedure
Give each student a copy of Worksheet 4–6e and a calculator. Remind students that if two ratios are equal, the ratios may be set up as a *proportion* in order to find a missing term of the proportion. Stress the labeling of diagrams with any new information that is found while solving a problem. After everyone has finished the worksheet, ask various students to share their reasoning and their answers with the entire class.

Answer Key for Worksheet 4–6e
1. D

2. A

3. B [Hint: Central angle measures of sectors are compared to the *values* represented by the sectors, not to the arc lengths of the sectors.]

4. C

5. B [Hint: Consider the triangle's proportion, AM to AB = AN to AC.]

Possible Testing Errors That May Occur for This Objective
- When using a proportion to compare central angle measures and arc lengths of a circle, students compute missing angle measures or the circumference incorrectly.

- Students try to apply a proportion to the sides of a triangle cut by two lines, which are not parallel. They do not confirm the existence of the necessary parallel condition.

- When setting up a proportion to solve a problem, students do not keep the same order for the ratios involved. For example, they might use $\frac{m\angle A}{360°} = \frac{C}{a}$, where C is the circumference of the circle and a is the arc length for the central angle A, instead of $\frac{m\angle A}{360°} = \frac{a}{C}$.

Worksheet 4–6e

Applying Ratios in
Geometric Situations

Solve each exercise provided. Be ready to share your reasoning and your answers with the entire class.

1. A circular game spinner with a diameter of 6 inches is divided into 3 sections. The central angle is 200 degrees for the green sector and 110 degrees for the blue sector. What is the approximate length of the arc of the red sector?

    A. 5.2 inches

    B. 4.5 inches

    C. 3.9 inches

    D. 2.6 inches

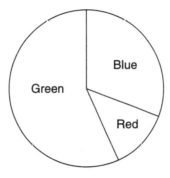

2. In Devonshire, Avenue A, Avenue B, and Avenue C are parallel streets. Each of these streets is perpendicular to Highway 78. Davis Street intersects all four of these streets, as shown on the map. If all streets are straight line segments, how long is Davis Street between Avenue A and Avenue B?

    A. 6,600 ft.

    B. 9,800 ft.

    C. 14,500 ft.

    D. 19,800 ft.

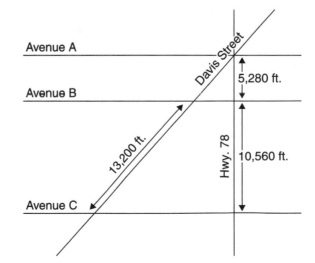

312

Name _____

Date _____

3. The manager of the school cafeteria wants to make a circle graph showing the types of meals sold on Thursday. The table summarizes these data:

Meals Sold on Thursday

Hamburgers	156
Pizza	210
Salads	84
Other	50

Approximately what size of the central angle should the manager use for the section of the graph representing the salads?

A. 36.0°   B. 60.5°   C. 116.7°   D. 151.2°

4. If diagram A is transformed to diagram B, which proportion might be used to solve for length x on diagram B?

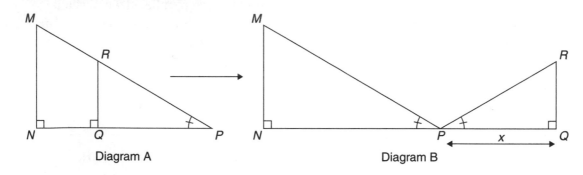

Diagram A   Diagram B

A. $\dfrac{RP}{MP} = \dfrac{QP}{NQ}$ B. $\dfrac{RP}{QP} = \dfrac{MP}{NQ}$ C. $\dfrac{QP}{NP} = \dfrac{RP}{MP}$ D. $\dfrac{RQ}{MN} = \dfrac{QP}{NP}$

Worksheet 4–6e Continued

Name _____

Date _____

5. A coordinate grid is placed over a map. City A is located at (–2, –1), City B is at (3, 3.5), and City C is at (3, –1). If $\overline{MN} \parallel \overline{BC}$ and $\overline{AC} \parallel \overline{MP}$, what is the location of City M, which is halfway between City A and City B?

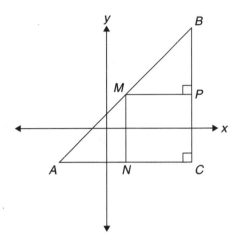

A. (0.5, –1)   C. (3, 1.25)

B. (0.5, 1.25)   D. (–2, 3.5)

Objective 7: Find the Area of a Composite Two-Dimensional Shape by Using Rectangles and Triangles

The area of an *irregular shape* cannot be found with a single standard area formula. Therefore, students need practice with various methods of finding the areas of such shapes. Basic <u>counting</u> of grid squares and parts of grid squares is a good place to start. Partial grid squares bounded by invisible triangles within the irregular shape might be combined to make "whole" grid squares, or a triangular portion of the original shape might be viewed as half of a rectangular region and its area then computed from the area of that associated rectangle. Unless students have been trained to see the triangle-rectangle relationship, however, they will most likely try to visually "glue" parts of grid squares together to make whole ones. Practice in subdividing an irregular shape into familiar standard shapes is necessary, but students need a strong conceptual understanding of the area of a rectangle in order to use this method effectively.

Activity 1
Manipulative Stage

Materials

Worksheet 4–7a
Scissors (1 per pair of students)
Transparent tape (1 roll per pair of students)
Regular paper and regular pencils

Procedure

1. Give each pair of students a copy of Worksheet 4–7a, a pair of scissors, and a roll of transparent tape.

2. Students should study the irregular shape shown on Worksheet 4–7a, then decide where to cut it in order to form smaller familiar shapes like triangles or rectangles. They should mark off in pencil the boundaries of new shapes they plan to make. Some new shapes may be extensions from the original shape's boundary. For example, if a triangular shape is seen as half of a rectangle, one-half of the rectangle may lie outside the original irregular shape.

3. Once they have decided what shapes to make, partners should cut apart the original shape into the new shapes, including any extensions.

4. Students should determine the area in square units (grid squares) of each new shape and write the area inside the shape. Areas may be found by just counting the grid squares inside the shape; this may be especially true when finding areas of triangles. The areas of rectangles may be computed as the product of two adjacent sides. All new shapes should then be taped onto a blank sheet of paper.

5. All the required areas should finally be added together to find the total area of the original irregular shape. A number sentence expressing this sum should be recorded on the same sheet of paper below the new shapes.

6. When all pairs of students have finished, have different students show how they subdivided the irregular shape and tell which areas they used to find the total area.

7. Discuss the example shown below with students before allowing them to cut out and subdivide the shape on Worksheet 4–7a.

Here is an example of an irregular shape that has been subdivided in two different ways. The triangular portion needed will be half of the extended rectangle.

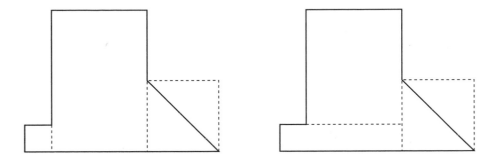

Answer Key for Worksheet 4–7a

Two triangles exist and have areas of 2 square units and 3 square units. Various rectangles are possible for the rest of the shape. The total area will be 70 square units.

Worksheet 4–7a

Subdividing an Irregular Shape

Name _____

Date _____

Subdivide the given shape into small rectangles. Follow the teacher's instructions to cut apart the rectangles and find their areas. Remember that each triangle is just half of a rectangle, so cut out the entire rectangle at first.

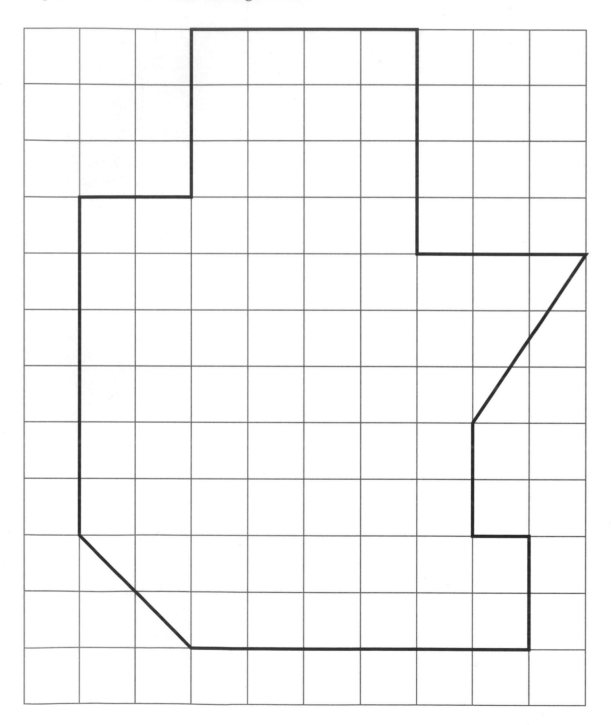

Activity 2
Pictorial Stage

Materials
    Worksheet 4–7b
    Regular pencils

Procedure
    1. Give each pair of students two copies of Worksheet 4–7b. Partners will estimate the area of *irregular* shapes by counting the square units in different ways or by finding areas of parts of the original shape, then adding those smaller areas together for the entire shape. Some shapes will have grids. Other shapes will have side measures shown with which students must reason to find the needed areas. If no grid is given, assume that all angles are right angles.
    2. Have students label the sides and subdivide each shape into rectangles. When grids are given, they should count the area square units inside the shape to confirm the total area they <u>compute</u>.
    3. Have different students share the ways they found their total areas.
    4. Discuss Exercise 1 with the class before allowing students to work on their own.

    Here is an example of the shape for Exercise 1 being subdivided and labeled to show adjacent sides of each rectangle formed. Other subdivisions are possible.

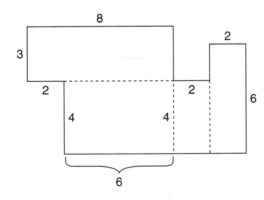

$3 \times 8 = 24$
$4 \times 6 = 24$
$2 \times 4 = 8$
$2 \times 6 = 12$
_____

        68 sq. units
        for total area

Answer Key for Worksheet 4–7b

1. Possible subdivision shown in text; total area = 68 sq. units

2. Possible subdivision shown below:

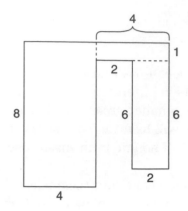

$$8 \times 4 = 32$$
$$4 \times 1 = 4$$
$$6 \times 2 = \underline{12}$$
$$48 \text{ sq. units}$$
for total area

3. Total area = 28 sq. units

4. Total area = 31 sq. units

Worksheet 4–7b   Name _____

Finding Areas Using Diagrams   Date _____

Subdivide each irregular shape into small rectangular shapes. Label two adjacent side lengths for each rectangle formed. Use the areas of the smaller shapes to find the total area of the irregular shape. Use "units" for side lengths and "square units" for areas.

1.

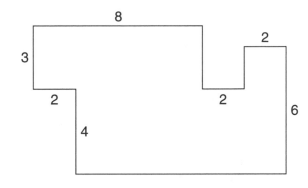

2.

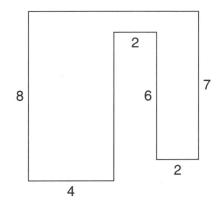

3.

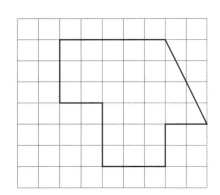

4.

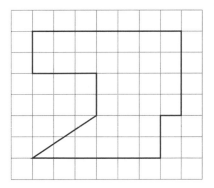

Activity 3
Independent Practice

Materials

Worksheet 4–7c

Regular pencils

Procedure

Give each student a copy of Worksheet 4–7c to complete independently. When all are finished, have various students describe their methods for finding the different areas.

Answer Key for Worksheet 4–7c

1. A   2. C   3. A   4. D

Possible Testing Errors That May Occur for This Objective

- If a triangle is included in the irregular shape, students will use the area of the entire rectangle, which contains the triangle, in the total area, instead of using half of the rectangle's area.

- Students will find the area of the largest rectangle contained <u>within</u> the shaded region, whose area is required. They do not adjust for the additional areas of the other sections (triangles, smaller rectangles) attached to that rectangle.

- If a grid is provided, students will miscount the square units inside the given region or will use an incorrect multiplication fact when computing the area of a smaller rectangle within the region.

Worksheet 4–7c   Name _____

Finding Areas of Irregular Shapes   Date _____

Answer each exercise below. Be ready to share your reasoning and your answers with the entire class.

1. Anna tore a design (shaded part) out of grid paper. Which is the best estimate of the area of the design?

   A. 31 sq. units

   B. 39 sq. units

   C. 42 sq. units

   D. 48 sq. units

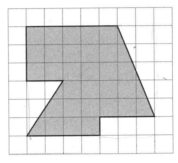

2. The total area of the trapezoid is 60 square inches. What is the approximate length of *d*?

   A. 11.5 in.

   B. 10.7 in.

   C. 8.5 in.

   D. 8.0 in.

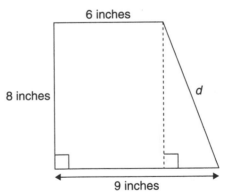

322

Name _____

Date _____

3. Find the equation that can be used to determine the total area of the composite figure shown here.

A. $A = bc + \frac{1}{2}ac + \frac{1}{2}c^2$

B. $A = bc + ac + c^2$

C. $A = 2b + 2c + ac + c^2$

D. $A = ac + b^2 + c^2$

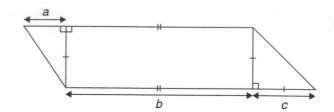

4. The lengths of the bases of an isosceles trapezoid are shown here. If the perimeter of this trapezoid is 38 units, what is its area?

A. 180 sq. units

B. 95 sq. units

C. 54 sq. units

D. 42 sq. units

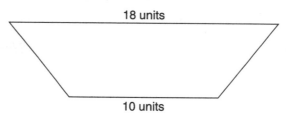

18 units

10 units

Objective 8: Recognize Characteristics of Three-Dimensional Shapes (Cylinders, Prisms, Pyramids, and Cones)

Students need much experience with solid or three-dimensional (3D) shapes. Commercial sets of "solids" are available that contain a variety of prisms, pyramids, cones, cylinders, and spheres. The shapes are wooden or plastic and come in several sizes. Everyday containers are also abundant, and the students could collect some. Students need experience just describing in their own words how each 3D shape looks; descriptions may be given either orally or in written form. In addition to working directly with the solids, they need exposure to perspective drawings of such objects so that they can predict which parts of the real object are not shown in the drawing.

Activity 1
Manipulative Stage

Materials

> Small plastic 3D objects (solids)
> Water-based paint, ink, or poster paint
> Large sheets of art paper
> Colored markers

Procedure

1.   Give each pair of students a small plastic solid, a small bowl of washable colored paint or ink, and a large sheet of art paper that will not absorb too much paint. Ink pads, or small sponges in saucers with washable ink or paint poured on the top surface of the sponge, will also work.

2.   Students should take each surface of their solid and press or dip it into the paint, then press the painted surface onto the sheet of paper ink blotter-style. For curved surfaces as on cones or cylinders, the entire surface should be covered in paint, then carefully *rolled* on the paper without being picked up or shifted. A sphere might be randomly rolled in several directions on the paper to create an irregular path of paint.

3.   With a colored marker, students should write "curved surface" below each impression of a curved surface. Each paper should be titled according to the solid used, for example, "Surfaces of My Cone."

4.   Have partners show their particular solid and its surface impressions to the entire class, as well as describe the solid in their own words. Focus on the idea that most solid shapes consist of more than one surface, but the impression of each flat surface might look like a circle, rectangle, triangle, or other polygon, and the impression of a curved surface will be a "rolled-out" shape of some kind.

Sample Surface Impressions of a Cone and a Sphere

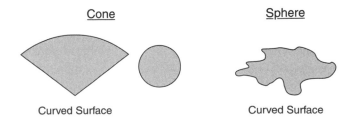

Cone	Sphere
Curved Surface	Curved Surface

Activity 2

Pictorial Stage

Materials

Worksheet 4–8a

Sets of geometric solids (same as those shown on worksheet plus extras)

Regular pencils

Procedure

1. After students have had experience touching and describing a variety of solids, they need to practice recognizing the perspective drawings of the solids. Give each student a copy of Worksheet 4–8a. This worksheet shows some of the solids typically studied in the first or left-most column, that is, a square prism, a cylinder, a cone, and a triangular prism. Two rows on the worksheet have been left blank for you to add other solids, such as pyramids or spheres, that will be in the student sets for this activity.

2. Have students work in groups of 3 to 4 students each, but each student will complete his or her own worksheet. Give each group a set of solids containing the solids on the worksheet, as well as a few solids not shown on the worksheet.

3. From their set, group members must select the solid that matches to each perspective drawing on their worksheets, then use the solid to count how many of each surface type the solid has and record the number on the worksheet.

4. Monitor the group work closely to make sure students are correctly matching each object with its drawing and accurately identifying and counting the different surfaces.

5. When everyone has finished the worksheet, discuss the answers with the entire class.

6. For additional practice, have students tell how many edges or how many vertices each solid on Worksheet 4–8a has.

Answer Key for Worksheet 4–8a

Partially completed worksheet:

Solid Shape	Flat Surfaces				Curved Surfaces
	▢	◯	△	▭	
(square prism)	2	0	0	4	0
(cylinder)	0	2	0	0	1
(cone)	0	1	0	0	1
(triangular prism)	0	0	2	3	0

Worksheet 4–8a

Name _____

Exploring the Solids

Date _____

Examine each object in your set of solids. Find the ones that are listed on the chart below and record how many of each type of surface each object has.

	Flat Surfaces				
Solid Shape	▢	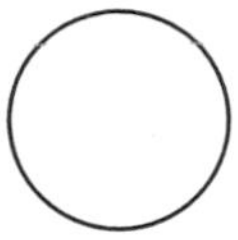 ◯	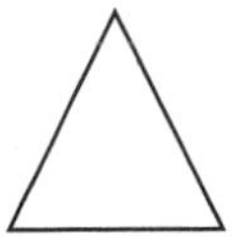 △	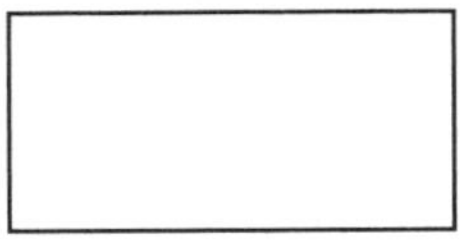 ▭	Curved Surfaces
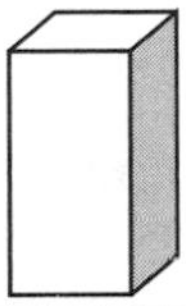					
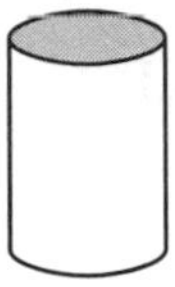					
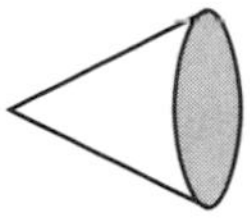					
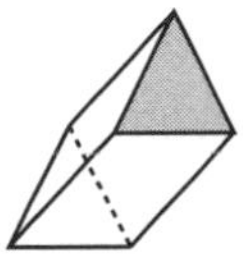					

Activity 3
Independent Practice

Materials
Worksheet 4–8b
Regular pencils

Procedure
Give each student a copy of Worksheet 4–8b to complete independently. When all have finished, have them share their answers with their group from Activity 2 or with the entire class.

Answer Key for Worksheet 4–8b
1. C   2. B   3. A   4. C   5. D   6. A

Possible Testing Errors That May Occur for This Objective
- Students miscount the faces or edges of a solid that is illustrated in the test item because they do not realize that some parts are hidden in a perspective drawing; that is, they count only what they can see directly.

- If a solid's name is given in the test item but an illustration is not provided, students do not know which solid is intended, so they select incorrect responses concerning the solid's characteristics. For example, if the test item requires the number of faces of a square pyramid, students might choose "six" because they are thinking of a square prism instead.

- Students have difficulty interpreting certain parts of perspective drawings as "curved surfaces." They view the drawn parts as "flat surfaces," because the parts are drawn on flat paper. Students cannot visualize the 3D form represented by the two-dimensional drawing.

- Students often confuse the definitions of *edge*, *vertex*, and *face*, which causes them to select incorrect responses.

Worksheet 4–8b   Name _____

Exploring the Solids   Date _____

Complete the exercises below. Be ready to share your answers with other students.

1. Which figure has exactly 4 faces?

2. Which characteristics belong to a cylinder?

    A. Only a curved surface

    B. 2 flat surfaces and 1 curved surface

    C. 6 flat surfaces

    D. 1 flat surface and 1 curved surface

3. Which solid has only rectangular faces?

    A. Cube   B. Cone   C. Pyramid   D. Sphere

4. Which figure represents a solid that does NOT have a curved surface?

A.   B.   C.   D.

5. How many edges and faces does a square pyramid have?

    A. 6 edges and 4 faces   C. 6 edges and 5 faces

    B. 12 edges and 6 faces   D. 8 edges and 5 faces

6. Which two 3D figures have the same number of faces?

    A. A triangular prism and a square pyramid

    B. A triangular pyramid and a rectangular prism

    C. A triangular prism and a rectangular prism

    D. A triangular pyramid and a square pyramid

Objective 9: Apply the Volume of Prisms or Cylinders to Solve Real-World Problems

Students have great difficulty comprehending the multiplicative nature of volume. They substitute values into formulas without any understanding as to why the formulas work. The following activities develop the "repeated sets" idea that eventually evolves into the formulas for volume.

Activity 1

Manipulative Stage

Materials

Worksheet 4–9a

Connectable centimeter cubes (50 to 60 per two students)

Cosmetic sponge rounds (the type used to apply or remove makeup about 5.5 centimeters in diameter and 1 centimeter thick; other diameters are available)

Centimeter rulers

Calculators (1 per pair of students)

Regular pencil and paper

Procedure

1. Give each pair of students a centimeter ruler, two copies of Worksheet 4–9a, a set of at least 50 connectable centimeter cubes, four cosmetic sponge rounds, and a calculator. If sponges are not readily available, other round disks that are 1 centimeter thick may be substituted.

2. *Prisms:* Have each pair of students build three different rectangular prisms with the connectable cubes. They will build one prism at a time. The dimensions for each prism are listed on Worksheet 4–9a.

3. After each prism is built, students should record the volume (total cubes used) of the prism in the appropriate space of the table on Worksheet 4–9a. Once the volume measure is recorded, students should dismantle the cubes and proceed to build the next prism.

4. *Cylinders:* After the three prisms are built, discuss the idea that each cosmetic sponge round is actually a cylinder. Confirm that each sponge is 1 centimeter high. Have students trace around one cosmetic sponge on a sheet of paper. Have them place as many centimeter cubes inside the circular outline as possible. Some cube corners may be outside the circle. Since the sponge equals the height of the single layer of cubes, the number of cubes filling the circular outline approximates the volume of one sponge. This is the volume of 1 unit layer of a cylinder and should be recorded in the table as the volume for cylinder #1.

5. Have students measure the diameter of one sponge. They should then use that measure to compute the radius and area of the circular outline of the sponge. These measures should be recorded in the table on Worksheet 4–9a for the cylinder having a height of 1 centimeter, or cylinder #1.

6. Now have students build other cylinders by stacking several sponges together. For two sponges, encourage students to build two layers of cubes inside the circular outline to find the volume. For three or four sponges stacked, encourage students to reason through how many cubes it might take to represent each stack. These measures should

also be recorded in the table on Worksheet 4–9a. Every cylinder in the table should have the same base radius and base area. Only the heights and volumes will differ.

7. After all prisms and cylinders have been built, ask students to compare the dimensions to the volume of each prism. Have students write a statement about their discovery at the bottom of Worksheet 4–9a. A possible statement might be as follows: "The product of the three dimensions equals the volume."

8. To check their observations further, ask each team to select its own dimensions for a fourth prism (keep the numbers small) and record the dimensions as prism #4 on the table on Worksheet 4–9a. If possible, teams might build their fourth prism to confirm the volume measure expected.

9. Repeat the discussion with the cylinders. Ask students to compare the computed area of the circular outline (the cylinder's base) and height of each cylinder to the estimated volume in cubes. Because the cubes do not fit completely inside the circular outline of the sponge, the volume counted in cubes will not be equal to the actual product of the circle's area and the cylinder's height, but the values will be close enough to justify multiplication as the needed operation. A possible statement for students to write at the bottom of the worksheet might be the following: "The product of the base area and the height equals the volume of the cylinder."

10. Discuss the procedure for building prism #1 and cylinder #1 before allowing teams to work on their own.

Consider prism #1 on Worksheet 4–9a. Its dimensions for the base are 2 centimeters and 5 centimeters, and its height dimension is 3 centimeters.

Each pair of students should first build the 2 cm × 5 cm base with their cubes. The *base* represents their *first* or *bottom* level of cubes. There should be 2 rows of 5 cubes each, or 10 cubes, in the base. Students should then build additional levels like the first level until they have 3 levels in all, which is the height of prism #1. The total number of cubes used to build prism #1 equals the volume of prism #1. Thus, the volume of 30 cubes (or 30 cubic centimeters) should be recorded in the "volume" column of the row for prism #1.

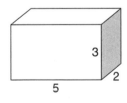

30 cubes used

Now consider cylinder #1, which requires only one sponge with a height of 1 centimeter. Students should trace around the sponge on a sheet of paper to form a circle. They should try to fill the circle with centimeter cubes. There will be some unfilled spaces and some cube corners may extend beyond the circle, but approximately 23 cubes will be used. This amount should be recorded in the table as the estimated volume for cylinder #1.

Assume that the diameter of the sponge is about 5.5 centimeters. Then the radius is 2.75 centimeters and the area of the circular outline is about 23.75 square centimeters. The radius and area measures should also be recorded in the table for cylinder #1.

In the illustration shown here, the four shaded parts represent cubes that overlap the circle. Only half of each part lies inside the circle. If cubes are placed in these positions, they would add 4 halves or 2 more whole cubes to the 21 cubes already inside the circle. This yields a volume of 23 cubes for the single sponge. Students will later observe that the product of 23.75 × 1 is relatively close to this estimated volume of 23 cubes.

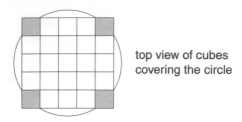

top view of cubes
covering the circle

Answer Key for Worksheet 4–9a
The cylinder answers assume the cylinder has a diameter of 5.5 centimeters.

Prism #1: 2; 5; 3; volume = 30 cubes

Prism #2: 4; 3; 2; volume = 24 cubes

Prism #3: 3; 3; 4; volume = 36 cubes

Prism #4: Answers will vary.

Cylinder #1: 2.75; 23.75; 1; volume ≈ 23 cubes

Cylinder #2: 2.75; 23.75; 2; volume ≈ 46 cubes

Cylinder #3: 2.75; 23.75; 3; volume ≈ 69 cubes

Cylinder #4: 2.75; 23.75; 4; volume ≈ 92 cubes

Worksheet 4–9a   Name _____

Building Prisms and Cylinders   Date _____

Build different solid prisms and cylinders. Record their dimensions and other measures with their volumes in the table.

PRISM	BASE SIDE 1 (cm)	BASE SIDE 2 (cm)	HEIGHT (cm)	VOLUME (number of cubes)
#1	2	5	3	
#2	4	3	2	
#3	3	3	4	
#4				
CYLIN-DER	RADIUS OF BASE (cm)	AREA OF BASE (sq cm)	HEIGHT (cm)	VOLUME (number of cubes)
#1			1	
#2			2	
#3			3	
#4			4	

How are the dimensions of a prism related to the prism's volume?

How are the dimensions of a cylinder related to the cylinder's volume?

Activity 2
Pictorial Stage

Materials

Worksheet 4–9b
Straightedge (1 per pair of students)
Calculators
Regular pencil

Procedure

1. Give each pair of students two copies of Worksheet 4–9b, a straightedge, and a calculator. The worksheet contains a partial frame of a prism viewed from one corner with its three dimensions marked on the frame in unit lengths. The worksheet also contains an outline of a cylinder with its dimensions marked off.

2. Students should complete the prism by drawing its missing edges on the frame. This should be done by sliding the straightedge from the given edge lengths to other parallel positions to draw the remaining edges of the prism. The diagram of the completed prism will be a perspective view of the prism.

3. Students should now write the dimensions on appropriate segments of the prism's diagram. Beside the prism, they should also write equations for the prism's top layer volume and the prism's total volume. The total volume is found by multiplying the top layer volume by the number of layers that form the shape.

4. Similarly, students should draw the layers of the cylinder, using the height markings as guidelines. They will write equations for the cylinder's top layer volume and total volume.

5. Here is a discussion of the prism exercise on Worksheet 4–9b.

The prism on Worksheet 4–9b is shown from a perspective view and has the dimensions of 5, 6, and 3 units marked on three intersecting edges.

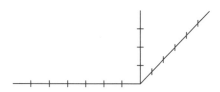

Students should use the straightedge to draw additional segments as edges to complete the perspective view of the prism. Each new edge should be parallel to one of the three dimensions already marked on the given frame. Students should also draw segments on the side faces of the prism to indicate the separate layers. Each layer is 1 unit tall. Here is a completed diagram of the prism with its three dimensions labeled on the top layer and on the vertical edge. Three layers are indicated on the diagram also.

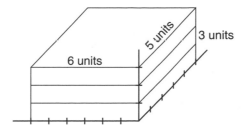

On Worksheet 4–9b, have students record the following equations on or near the completed diagram for the prism: top layer volume = 6 × 5 × 1 = 30 cubic units, and total prism volume = 3 layers × 30 cubic units = 90 cubic units.

The completed diagram for the cylinder is also provided here.

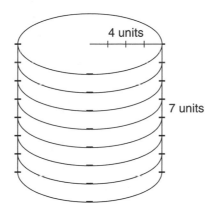

Answer Key for Worksheet 4–9b

Prism

Top layer volume = 6 × 5 × 1 = 30 cubic units

Total prism volume = 3 layers × 30 cubic units = 90 cubic units

Cylinder

Top layer volume = 3.14 × 4 × 4 × 1 – 50.24 cubic units

Total cylinder volume = 7 layers × 50.24 cubic units = 351.68 cubic units

334

Worksheet 4–9b

Name _____

Drawing Cylinders and
Rectangular Prisms

Date _____

For the prism, use a straightedge to draw opposite, parallel edges to complete the prism.
Label the dimensions on the completed prism. Similarly, complete and label the drawing
of the cylinder. For each shape, find the volume in cubic units of the top layer and of the
total shape.

Prism

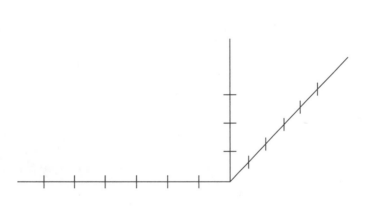

Cylinder

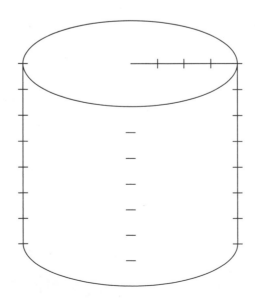

Activity 3
Independent Practice

Materials
Worksheet 4–9c
Calculators
Regular pencil

Procedure
Give each student a copy of Worksheet 4–9c and a calculator. Encourage students to make free-hand sketches of any described prisms and cylinders. Use 3.14 to approximate pi. Students should label all known or inferred measurements on any diagrams being used. When all have completed the worksheet, have several students explain the steps they used to solve the exercises.

Answer Key for Worksheet 4–9c
1. A

2. C

3. D

4. C

5. A

6. A

7. D

Possible Testing Errors That May Occur for This Objective
- To find the volume of a prism or a cylinder, students add the dimension measures together instead of multiplying them.

- When students are asked to find the volume of a cylinder when given the radius of the base of the cylinder, they do not square the radius before multiplying by pi and the height.

- When the volume and two dimensions of a prism are known, students find the missing dimension by multiplying the volume and the two given dimensions together instead of dividing the volume by the product of the two dimensions.

Worksheet 4–9c

Name _____

Applying the Volume of
a Prism or a Cylinder

Date _____

Solve the exercises provided.

1. A box with rectangular faces is 48 inches long, 24 inches wide, and 12 inches high. Which is closest to the volume of the box in cubic feet?

   A. 8 cu. ft.   B. 14 cu. ft.   C. 18 cu. ft.   D. 24 cu. ft.

2. A soup can has a diameter of 3 inches and is 4 inches tall. Find the can's volume to the nearest tenth in cubic inches.

   A. 113.0 in.^{3} B. 37.7 in.^{3} C. 28.3 in.^{3} D. Not here

3. The volume of a cylinder is 1,413 cubic centimeters and its height is 18 centimeters. Find the radius measure for the cylinder's base.

   A. 76 cm   B. 25 cm   C. 10 cm   D. 5 cm

4. The volume of a rectangular prism is 280 cubic meters. If the base measures 5 meters by 7 meters, what is the height or third dimension of this prism?

   A. 40 m   B. 10 m   C. 8 m   D. Not here

5. The water level in an aquarium is 2.5 feet high when the aquarium is full. The area of the base of the aquarium is 6 square feet. If the water drains out until the water level is only 2 feet high, what volume of water has been drained out of the aquarium?

   A. 3 ft.^{3} B. 6 ft.^{3} C. 15 ft.^{3} D. 30 ft.^{3}

6. Carrie has a cylindrical candle mold that has a diameter of 8.6 centimeters and a height of 10 centimeters. She plans to melt a rectangular block of wax to pour into the mold. About how many candles can she make if the block of wax measures 10 centimeters by 16 centimeters by 12 centimeters?

   A. 3   B. 7   C. 12   D. 18

7. How many 2-inch cubes can fill a box completely if the box is 10 inches long, 6 inches wide, and 4 inches tall?

   A. 240   B. 120   C. 60   D. 30

Objective 10: Find Dimensions or Other Measures of a Right Rectangular Prism That Correspond to Dimensions or Measures of a Similar Given Prism

When studying dilations as transformations, students work with reductions or enlargements of planar shapes and discover that the changes in dimensions produce equivalent changes in perimeter. Area measures change according to the square of the dimensional change. Experiences with changes in volume are also needed. In the following activities, students discover the relationship between the change in dimensions and the change in the volume of a rectangular prism. It is assumed that students have already mastered the formula for the volume of a prism.

Activity 1
Manipulative Stage

Materials

>   Worksheet 4–10a
>   Connectable centimeter cubes (270 cubes per four students)
>   Calculators (1 per team of students)
>   Regular pencil

Procedure

1.   Give each team of four students four copies of Worksheet 4–10a, a set of at least 270 connectable centimeter cubes, and a calculator.

2.   Have each team of students build three different rectangular prisms with the connectable cubes. They will build three prisms one at a time. When each prism is built, that prism will be left intact while a specified enlargement of that prism is also built with cubes. The dimensions for each original prism, as well as its required enlargement, are listed on Worksheet 4–10a.

3.   After an original prism and its enlargement are built, students should record the volume (total cubes used) of the original prism and also the dimensions and volume of the enlarged prism in the appropriate spaces of the table on Worksheet 4–10a. Once that pair of prisms is recorded, students should dismantle the cubes and proceed to build the next original prism and its enlargement.

4.   After all three pairs of prisms have been built, ask students to compare the change in dimensions to the change in volume for each pair of prisms. Have students write a statement about their discovery at the bottom of Worksheet 4–10a. A possible statement might be as follows: "The product of the size changes in the three dimensions equals the size change in volume." For example, if each dimension is multiplied by 3, the original volume will multiply by $3 \times 3 \times 3$, or 27.

5.   To check their observations further, ask each team to select their own dimensions for a fourth prism (keep the numbers small) and record the dimensions as prism #4 on the table on Worksheet 4–10a. Students should then record what the new dimensions would be if their fourth prism were enlarged by a factor of 5 and also predict and record what the new volume would be. The volume of the enlargement will be high for this fourth prism. If enough cubes are available, one team might build the enlargement of their fourth prism to show to the class and thereby confirm their predicted volume.

6.   Discuss the procedure for building prism #1 before allowing teams to work on their own.

Consider prism #1 on Worksheet 4–10a. Its dimensions for the base are 2 centimeters and 5 centimeters, and its height dimension is 3 centimeters, assuming that centimeter cubes are being used. If centimeter cubes are not used, then each edge length of a cube should be called a "unit" and the volumes will be in "cubic units."

Each team of four students should first build the 2 cm × 5 cm base with their cubes. The *base* represents their *first* or *bottom* level of cubes. There should be 2 rows of 5 cubes each, or 10 cubes, in the base. Students should then build additional levels like the first level until they have 3 levels in all, which is the height of prism #1. The total number of cubes used to build prism #1 equals the volume of prism #1. Thus, the volume of 30 cubes (or 30 cubic centimeters or 30 cubic units) should be recorded in the "volume" column of the row for prism #1.

The second row of the table indicates that prism #1 should be doubled (2×); that is, each <u>dimension</u> of prism #1 should be <u>multiplied by 2</u> in order to create an enlargement of prism #1. On the row for "(2×) #1" on the table, students should record the new dimensions: 4, 10, and 6, respectively.

Leaving prism #1 intact, teams should use additional cubes to build a new base (first level) that is 4 centimeters by 10 centimeters. This first level of 4 rows of 10 cubes each, or 40 cubes, should then be repeated until there are 6 levels total, the height of the new prism. Students should use some type of counting strategy, such as 40 + 40 + 40 + 40 + 40 + 40 or 6(40), to find the volume of the new or enlarged prism. Such a strategy eventually evolves into a formula for volume. A volume of 240 cubes should be recorded in the "volume" column of the row for "(2×) #1" in the table on Worksheet 4–10a.

Ask students to compare the original volume of 30 cubes to the enlarged volume of 240 cubes. They should notice that 8 × 30 = 240. Have them write "8×" to the right of the "volume" column, but vertically between the 30 and the 240 entries. Ask students to reflect on how multiplying each dimension by 2 might be connected to a volume being multiplied by 8. They will need to combine their thoughts on prism #1 with their ideas for the other prisms in order to answer the question at the bottom of Worksheet 4–10a.

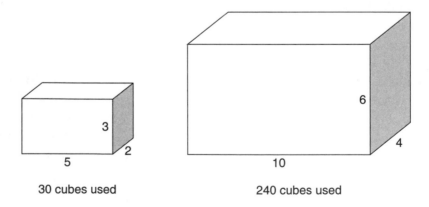

30 cubes used   240 cubes used

Answer Key for Worksheet 4–10a

Prism #1: $2 \times 5 \times 3$, volume = 30 cubes

(2×) #1: $4 \times 10 \times 6$, volume = 240 cubes

Prism #2: $2 \times 2 \times 2 = 8$ cubes

(3×) #2: $6 \times 6 \times 6 = 216$ cubes

Prism #3: $2 \times 2 \times 1 = 4$ cubes

(4×) #3: $8 \times 8 \times 4 = 256$ cubes

Prism #4: Numbers will vary.

(5×) #4: Numbers will vary.

340

Worksheet 4–10a

Name _____

Building Similar Prisms

Date _____

Build different solid prisms with small cubes. Record their dimensions and volumes in the table.

PRISM	BASE SIDE 1	BASE SIDE 2	HEIGHT	VOLUME (number of cubes)
#1	2	5	3	
(2×) #1				
#2	2	2	2	
(3×) #2				
#3	2	2	1	
(4×) #3				
#4				
(5×) #4				

As the dimensions of a prism change to form a new similar prism, how does the original volume change?

Activity 2
Pictorial Stage

Materials

Worksheet 4–10b
Straightedge (1 per pair of students)
Calculators
Regular pencil

Procedure

1. Give each pair of students two copies of Worksheet 4–10b, a straightedge, and a calculator. The worksheet contains diagrams of two prisms drawn in perspective with their three dimensions labeled on the diagrams.

2. For each original prism, students should draw its specified enlargement on the new frame, which consists of three segments sharing a common vertex. This should be done by marking off on a straightedge each labeled segment on the original prism (actual measuring is not needed here) and transferring the required copies of that segment to its corresponding segment on the new frame.

3. When all three segments have been copied the required number of times on the new frame, have students slide the straightedge from those new segments to other parallel positions to draw the remaining edges of the new enlarged prism. The diagram of the new prism will be a perspective view of the prism.

4. Students should now write the new dimensions on appropriate segments of the new prism's diagram. Beside the pair of prisms, they should write equations for the following: the original prism's volume, the product of the three dimension changes, the new prism's volume based on its new dimensions, and the new prism's volume based on the original prism's volume. The last two volumes, of course, should be equivalent.

5. Here is a discussion of the first exercise on Worksheet 4–10b, using prism #1.

Prism #1 on Worksheet 4–10b is shown from a perspective view and has the dimensions of 5, 7, and 3 units labeled on three intersecting edges. Another set of intersecting edges is shown at the right. This second set will be used to draw a corresponding perspective view of an enlargement of prism #1.

The new prism must be drawn, based on a 2.5 enlargement factor. That is, each dimension of prism #1 must be multiplied by 2.5 to find its corresponding dimension for the new prism. Students should notice, however, that the prism is not drawn to scale. Therefore, to do a free-hand sketch of the enlargement, students merely need to copy on a straightedge (a ruler or an edge of a sheet of paper) each segment that represents an edge of prism #1, then mark off that distance twice, followed by half the distance, onto the corresponding segment on the new frame. Here is an illustration of the straightedge being applied to copy prism #1's dimension segment of 5 units onto the new frame. The dimension segment of 7 units has already been copied 2.5 times onto the new frame.

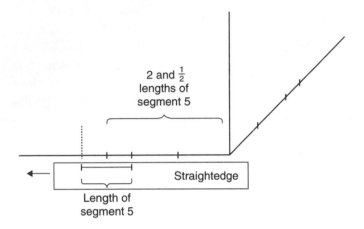

After each of the three dimensions of prism #1 has been copied 2.5 times on the new frame, students should use the straightedge to draw additional segments as edges to complete the perspective view of the enlarged prism. Each new edge should be parallel to one of the three dimensions already marked on the new frame. Here is a completed diagram of the enlarged prism with its three dimensions labeled:

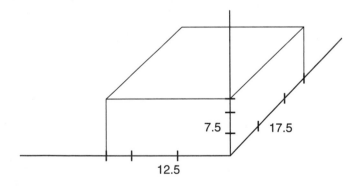

On Worksheet 4–10b, have students record the following equations on or near the completed diagram for prism #1: the original prism's volume, the product of the three dimension changes, the new enlarged prism's volume based on its new dimensions, and the new prism's volume based on the original prism's volume. For prism #1, here are the respective equations:

$5 \times 7 \times 3 = 105$ cubic units, volume of prism #1
$2.5 \times 2.5 \times 2.5 = 15.625$, the change factor for volume
$12.5 \times 17.5 \times 7.5 = 1,640.625$ cubic units, enlarged volume
$15.625 \times 105 = 1,640.625$ cubic units, enlarged volume

Answer Key for Worksheet 4–10b

Prism #1

$5 \times 7 \times 3 = 105$ cubic units, volume of prism #1

$2.5 \times 2.5 \times 2.5 = 15.625$, the change factor for volume

$12.5 \times 17.5 \times 7.5 = 1,640.625$ cubic units, enlarged volume

$15.625 \times 105 = 1,640.625$ cubic units, enlarged volume

Prism #2

$13 \times 6 \times 12 = 936$ cubic units, volume of prism #2

$3 \times 3 \times 3 = 27$, the change factor for volume

$39 \times 18 \times 36 = 25,272$ cubic units, enlarged volume

$27 \times 936 = 25,272$ cubic units, enlarged volume

344

Worksheet 4–10b

**Drawing Enlargements of
Rectangular Prisms**

Name _____

Date _____

For each original prism, use a straightedge to mark off multiple copies of the original
edge lengths on the new frame. Extend the frame if needed. Draw opposite, parallel
edges to complete the enlarged prism. Label the dimensions on the new prism. Find the
volume of the original prism and its enlarged prism. Original prisms are not drawn to
scale. Computations should be based on numbers shown on the diagrams, not on actual
measurements.

Prism #1

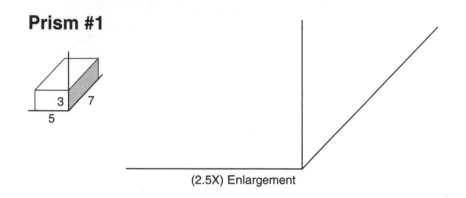

(2.5X) Enlargement

Prism #2

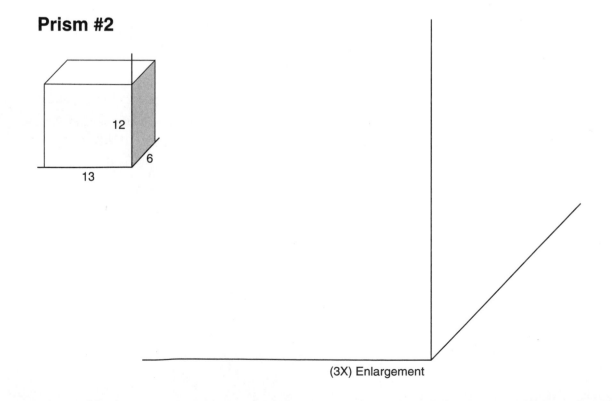

(3X) Enlargement

Activity 3
Independent Practice

Materials
> Worksheet 4–10c
> Calculators
> Regular pencil

Procedure
Give each student a copy of Worksheet 4–10c and a calculator. Remind students of how dimension changes affect the volume of a rectangular prism. Encourage them to make free-hand sketches of any described prisms and their enlargements. Students should also label all known or inferred measurements on any diagrams being used. When all have completed the worksheet, have several students explain the steps they used to solve the exercises.

Answer Key for Worksheet 4–10c

1. B

2. D

3. C

4. D

5. A

6. B

Possible Testing Errors That May Occur for This Objective

- When a prism has been enlarged by multiplying each of its dimensions by the same constant, students incorrectly find the volume of the enlarged prism by multiplying the original volume by that same constant.

- When the volume and two dimensions of a prism are known, students find the missing dimension by multiplying the volume and the two given dimensions together, instead of dividing the volume by the product of the two dimensions.

346

Enlarging the Volume of a
Rectangular Prism

Solve the exercises provided.

1. Which set of dimensions corresponds to a rectangular prism similar to a prism whose base measures 12 feet by 9 feet and whose height measures 18 feet?

   A. 2 ft. × 1 ft. × 6 ft.   C. 4 ft. × 2 ft. × 8 ft.

   B. 4 ft. × 3 ft. × 6 ft.   D. 2 ft. × 3 ft. × 4 ft.

2. A small cube has a volume of 64 cubic centimeters. If the small cube is enlarged by tripling its dimensions, what will be the volume of the new cube?

   A. 192 cu cm   B. 576 cu cm   C. 1,024 cu cm   D. 1,728 cu cm

3. If the surface area of a cube is increased by a factor of 9, what is the change in the length of each side of the cube?

   A. The length is 6 times the original length.

   B. The length is 18 times the original length.

   C. The length is 3 times the original length.

   D. The length is 9 times the original length.

4. A rectangular solid has a volume of 40 cubic decimeters. If the length, width, and height are all changed to one-half their original size, what will be the new volume of the rectangular solid?

   A. 20 cu dm   B. 10 cu dm   C. 8 cu dm   D. 5 cu dm

5. Marion wants to build a small rectangular box similar to a 24-inch by 36-inch by 20-inch container. His design shows a 6-inch by 12-inch by 5-inch box. What correction is needed in the design so that the box and the container will be similar?

   A. Decrease 12 in. to 9 in.   C. Increase 6 in. to 12 in.

   B. Increase 5 in. to 10 in.   D. Decrease 12 in. to 6 in.

6. A rectangular prism has a height of 10 centimeters and a volume of 200 cubic centimeters. When the prism is enlarged by increasing all dimensions proportionally, the new volume will be 1,600 cubic centimeters. What will be the height of the new prism?

   A. 10 cm   B. 20 cm   C. 40 cm   D. 80 cm

Objective 11: Find the Volume of a Composite Three-Dimensional Shape by Applying Perspectives and Side Views of Rectangular Prisms

The volume of an *irregular shape* cannot be found with a single standard volume formula. Therefore, students need practice with various methods of finding the volumes of such shapes. Practice in subdividing an irregular shape into familiar standard shapes like prisms is necessary, but students need a strong conceptual understanding of the volume of a prism in order to use this method effectively. The activities provided here require students to connect side views with perspectives in order to identify dimensions needed to find different volumes of the prisms forming the original shape. It is assumed that students have already had experience with perspective views and side views of three-dimensional shapes; lessons on these concepts may be found in *Math Essentials, Middle School Level* in this same series.

Activity 1

Manipulative Stage

Materials

Connectable cubes (0.75-inch or 1-inch size preferred; 15 cubes per pair of students)

Regular pencil and paper

Procedure

1. Give each pair of students 15 connectable cubes.

2. Students should build a free-form or irregular structure using various stacks of eight or more total of the connectable cubes. The structure should not be a single prism; it should have various appendages in its design and two or more levels of cubes involved in some way. The structure will be a composite of several rectangular prisms joined together.

3. Have students draw the top, front, back, left-side, and right-side views of their connectable cube structure. It will be helpful when drawing the cube structure if students place the structure on a sheet of paper with its edges labeled as "front," "back," "left side," and "right side." Then the paper may be easily rotated to change the viewpoint and the drawings may be labeled with the corresponding titles.

4. In addition, students should draw a perspective view of their cube structure. This requires them to look at the structure from one of its corners rather than from a direct side or orthogonal view. Have them record the number of cubes used in the initial structure below the perspective drawing. This represents the total volume of the initial structure.

5. After the initial perspective view is drawn, students should separate their original irregular structure into two or more rectangular prisms. They should minimize the number of prisms used by forming the largest prisms possible and trying to avoid having individual cubes serve as prisms.

6. Have students draw a perspective view for each new prism formed. Below each perspective drawing, they should record the volume in cubes used for that particular prism.

7. Finally, below all the drawings for the initial structure, students should record a number sentence or equation that shows the sum of the separate prism volumes to be equal to the total volume of the initial structure.

8. Have students repeat steps 2 through 7 with one or two more irregular cube structures.

9. Discuss an example of a cube structure with the class before allowing students to work on their own.

Here are examples of a perspective view and three samples of side or orthogonal views for a 10-cube structure. The total volume of the structure has been recorded below the perspective drawing of the initial structure.

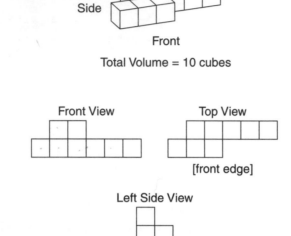

Total Volume = 10 cubes

Front View   Top View

[front edge]

Left Side View

The initial structure may be separated into smaller prisms in various ways. One example is shown here with the separate prism volumes and the final total volume equation recorded below the perspective drawings of the prisms.

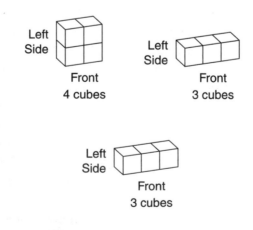

4 cubes

3 cubes

3 cubes

Total Volume = 4 + 3 + 3 = 10 cubes

Activity 2
Pictorial Stage

Materials
Worksheet 4–11a

Connectable cubes (0.75-inch or 1-inch size preferred; 15 cubes per pair of students)

Red and blue pencils (1 red and 1 blue pencil per pair of students)

Regular pencil and paper

Procedure
1. Give each pair of students two copies of Worksheet 4–11a, 15 connectable cubes, and one red and one blue pencil.

2. For each exercise on the worksheet, partners must build a cube structure that corresponds to the views shown in the exercise, using 15 or fewer cubes. Each exercise consists of three orthogonal views. A given side view may be for the left or for the right side; students must determine which side will lead to a solution. When students complete a structure, inspect the structure for its agreement with the provided views. Have students make changes where necessary. It is possible for several different structures to have the same set of orthogonal views. Several students who have already demonstrated strength in this type of visualization may serve as "class inspectors" in order to save time.

3. When students have found a cube structure that satisfies the three views of an exercise, they should label the squares of the top view with the number of cubes in the stack represented by that square. Labeling the diagram in this manner will allow students to compare their cube structures to those of other students even after the actual structures are dismantled.

4. After a cube structure is built, have students make a perspective drawing of the structure. They should decide on how to subdivide the structure into a minimal number of smaller prisms. For each prism selected, on the perspective drawing students should select one vertex and outline the three edges extending from the vertex in either red or blue pencil. Use different colors for two vertices whose marked edges might intersect.

5. Students should find the volumes of the selected prisms using the three dimensions that have been marked from a vertex in each prism. The total volume of the initial structure should then be recorded as an equation below the perspective drawing. The equation should reflect the separate volumes of the prisms involved.

6. Have different students share their results with the entire class when the worksheets are completed. For each exercise on Worksheet 4–11a, one pair of students might show their particular cube structure for that exercise, along with the equation for the volumes of the selected prisms. If another pair of students has a different structure for the same exercise, ask that pair to share their structure as well. Their total volumes may or may not be equal, depending on how the initial structures vary.

7. Discuss Exercise 1 with the class before allowing students to work independently.

For Exercise 1 on Worksheet 4–11a, one possible cube structure will have the following top view where a number indicates the number of cubes used in that particular stack. A blank square indicates only 1 cube in that position.

[front edge]

Top View

A perspective drawing for this structure might be shown as follows:

Front

A possible subdivision of the structure into four prisms *A, B, C,* and *D* might be shown, with arrows marking edge lengths, whose measures contribute to a particular prism's volume. Solid arrows are in red pencil and dotted arrows are in blue pencil to help separate the different prisms formed.

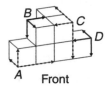

An equation that represents the total volume of the initial structure should be recorded below the perspective drawing marked with arrows. Here is a possible equation to use:

$$\text{Total volume } (A + B + C + D) = (1 \times 2 \times 1) + (1 \times 1 \times 1) + (1 \times 2 \times 2) + (1 \times 1 \times 1)$$
$$= 2 + 1 + 4 + 1 = 8 \text{ cubes}$$

If students have built a different cube structure for Exercise 1 from the one discussed here, their volume equation may differ from this equation.

Answer Key for Worksheet 4–11a

Possible structures are shown using top views with the number 2 or 3 inside squares to indicate the amount of cubes in each stack. Blank squares indicate only one cube in the stack. Other structures may be possible. For each structure, a corresponding perspective view is shown and selected prisms, for example, *A, B,* and *C,* are marked. An equation is given for the sum of the prism volumes.

1.

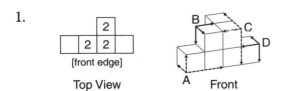

Total Volume (A + B + C + D) =
(1 x 2 x 1) + (1 x 1 x 1) + (1 x 2 x 2) + (1 x 1 x 1) =
2 + 1 + 4 + 1 = 8 cubes

2.

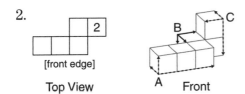

Total Volume (A + B + C) =
(1 x 3 x 1) + (1 x 1 x 1) + (1 x 1 x 2) =
3 + 1 + 2 = 6 cubes

3.

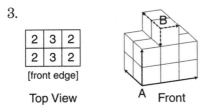

Total Volume (A + B) =
(2 x 3 x 2) + (1 x 2 x 1) =
12 + 2 = 14 cubes

4.

Total Volume (A + B + C) =
(1 x 1 x 1) + (2 x 2 x 1) + (3 x 3 x 1) =
1 + 4 + 9 = 14 cubes

Worksheet 4–11a

Finding Volumes of Irregular
Cube Structures

Name _____

Date _____

For each exercise, build a cube structure that matches the three orthogonal views provided. Show each completed structure to your teacher. Label each top view as instructed. Draw a perspective view of each structure built. Divide each structure into prisms by identifying the selected prisms on the perspective view with sets of arrows. Find the volume of each structure, using the prisms.

1.

Side View

Front View

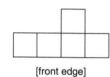

[front edge]

Top View

2.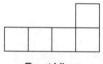

Front View

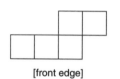

[front edge]

Top View

Side View

3.

Front View

[front edge]

Top View

Side View

4.

Side View

Front View

[front edge]

Top View

Activity 3
Independent Practice

Materials
    Worksheet 4–11b
    Regular pencil

Procedure
Give each student a copy of Worksheet 4–11b. After students have completed the worksheet, have different students share their answers with the entire class.

Answer Key for Worksheet 4–11b
  1. C

  2. B

  3. D

  4. B

  5. A

Possible Testing Errors That May Occur for This Objective

- Students will multiply all given measurements of an irregular shape in order to find the shape's volume, not realizing that the shape is not a prism or that the measurements may not all belong to the same prism.

- When subdividing an irregular 3D shape into several prisms, students fail to use disjoint prisms. Portions of two or more prisms will overlap, causing a larger total volume to be found for the original shape.

- When given several side views of a required shape, students incorrectly visualize the corresponding 3D shape. This leads to their using the wrong prisms and therefore finding the wrong prism volumes necessary for computing the total volume of the original irregular shape.

Worksheet 4–11b   Name _____

Finding Volumes of   Date _____
Irregular Shapes

Complete each exercise.

1. Which expression below represents the sum of the volumes of disjoint rectangular prisms, which together form the cube structure shown here?

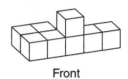

Front

   A. $(1 \times 5 \times 1) + (1 \times 2 \times 1) + (1 \times 1 \times 2)$

   B. $(2 \times 5 \times 1) + (1 \times 1 \times 1) + (1 \times 1 \times 2)$

   C. $(2 \times 2 \times 1) + (1 \times 1 \times 2) + (1 \times 2 \times 1)$

   D. $(2 \times 2 \times 1) + (1 \times 3 \times 1) + (1 \times 2 \times 1)$

2. A solid 3D block of concrete has the following orthogonal views with related measures and edges indicated. All angles are right angles. What is the volume of the block?

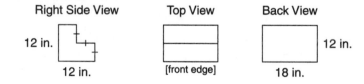

Right Side View   Top View   Back View

12 in.   12 in.

12 in.   [front edge]   18 in.

   A. 2,592 cu. in.   C. 1,296 cu. in.

   B. 1,944 cu. in.   D. 648 cu. in.

3. A cube-shaped box is made of wood and has no lid. If each outer edge is 30 centimeters long and each side and bottom of the box is 2 centimeters thick, about how many cubic centimeters of wood form the box itself?

   A. 2,000 cu cm   C. 6,000 cu cm

   B. 4,000 cu cm   D. 8,000 cu cm

Name _____

Date _____

4. What is the least number of prisms needed to find the total volume of this solid irregular shape? Mark off the selected prisms on the shape itself.

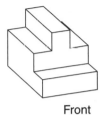

Front

A. 2   C. 4

B. 3   D. 5

5. A concrete wall is 2 feet thick and 5 feet high. On the outside of the wall each section is 10 feet long. Each corner of the wall forms a right angle. How many cubic feet of concrete were used to make the wall?

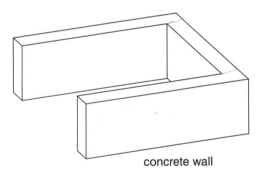

concrete wall

A. 260 cu. ft.

B. 200 cu. ft.

C. 160 cu. ft.

D. 100 cu. ft.

Name _____

Date _____

GEOMETRY AND MEASUREMENT WITH APPLICATIONS PRACTICE TEST ANSWER SHEET

1. ○ A ○ B ○ C ○ D   12. ○ A ○ B ○ C ○ D

2. ○ A ○ B ○ C ○ D   13. ○ A ○ B ○ C ○ D

3. ○ A ○ B ○ C ○ D   14. ○ A ○ B ○ C ○ D

4. ○ A ○ B ○ C ○ D   15. ○ A ○ B ○ C ○ D

5. ○ A ○ B ○ C ○ D   16. ○ A ○ B ○ C ○ D

6. ○ A ○ B ○ C ○ D   17. ○ A ○ B ○ C ○ D

7. ○ A ○ B ○ C ○ D   18. ○ A ○ B ○ C ○ D

8. ○ A ○ B ○ C ○ D   19. ○ A ○ B ○ C ○ D

9. ○ A ○ B ○ C ○ D   20. ○ A ○ B ○ C ○ D

10. ○ A ○ B ○ C ○ D   21. ○ A ○ B ○ C ○ D

11. ○ A ○ B ○ C ○ D   22. ○ A ○ B ○ C ○ D

Section 4 Practice Test

1. A 5.0-centimeter square is inscribed in a circle with a radius of approximately 3.5 centimeters. What is the approximate area of the shaded region to the nearest tenth?

    A. 13.5 sq cm   C. 25.0 sq cm

    B. 19.3 sq cm   D. 38.5 sq cm

2. The White House had a circular garden with a radius of 30 feet. All of the fencing around the garden was removed and used to enclose a new square garden. What was the approximate side length of the square garden?

    A. 188 ft.   B. 95 ft.   C. 47 ft.   D. 30 ft.

3. A lawn design has flower beds around two sides of the lawn. The largest section has only grass, as shown in the diagram. How many square meters are in the area of the grass section?

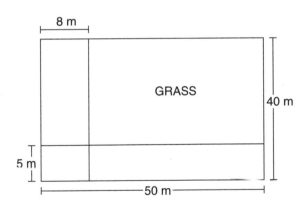

    A. 2,000 sq m

    B. 1,750 sq m

    C. 1,680 sq m

    D. 1,470 sq m

Section 4 Practice Test (Continued)

4. The total area of the floor of a parallelogram-shaped room is 532 square yards. If the length of one edge of the floor is 28 yards, what is the perpendicular distance from that edge across to the opposite edge of the floor?

   A. 12 yd.   B. 19 yd.   C. 28 yd.   D. Not here

5. In the concave pentagon shown below, side BC is parallel to side AE, and side CD is perpendicular to side BC. The measure of ∠CDE, when made on the inside of the pentagon, is 210 degrees. What is the measure of the interior angle, ∠DEA, in degrees?

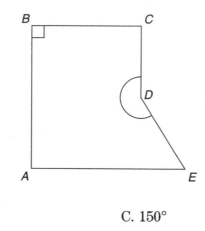

   A. 480°   C. 150°

   B. 360°   D. 60°

6. A pilot is flying her plane at an altitude of 3,000 feet. She sees the end of a runway at an angle of depression of 30 degrees. What is the approximate horizontal distance of the plane from the runway at this point?

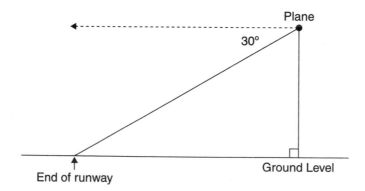

   A. 1,500 ft.

   B. 3,000 ft.

   C. 5,200 ft.

   D. 6,000 ft.

Section 4 Practice Test (Continued)

7. A rectangular garden has a 12-meter-long side and a 20-meter-long diagonal. About how many meters of fencing are needed to enclose the garden?

   A. 56 m   B. 32 m   C. 28 m   D. 16 m

8. A guidewire connects from the top of a vertical pole to the ground and forms a 45-degree angle with the ground. If the guidewire is 150 feet long, about how tall is the pole?

   A. 84 ft.   B. 106 ft.   C. 150 ft.   D. 195 ft.

9. A rectangle has a length of 6 feet and a perimeter of 20 feet. What is the perimeter of a similar rectangle with a width of 12 feet?

   A. 26 ft.   B. 48 ft.   C. 60 ft.   D. 120 ft.

10. The larger quadrilateral was dilated to form the smaller quadrilateral. Two corresponding side lengths are shown. What was the scale factor used to change the larger into the smaller shape?

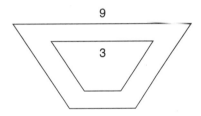

   A. $\frac{1}{6}$ B. $\frac{1}{3}$ C. 3   D. 6

11. A circular game spinner with a diameter of 7 inches is divided into 3 sections. The central angle is 200 degrees for the green sector and 50 degrees for the red sector. What is the approximate length of the arc of the blue sector?

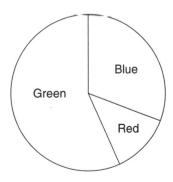

   A. 13.4 in.   C. 6.7 in.

   B. 10.5 in.   D. 3.1 in.

Section 4 Practice Test (Continued)

12. A coordinate grid is placed over a map. City A is located at (–3, –2), City B is at (6, 4), and City C is at (6, –2). If $\overline{MN} \parallel \overline{BC}$ and $\overline{AC} \parallel \overline{MP}$, what is the location of City M, which is halfway between City A and City B? [Not drawn to scale.]

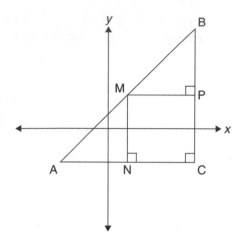

A. (1.5, –2)

C. (–3, 4)

B. (6, 1)

D. (1.5, 1)

13. Find the equation that can be used to determine the total area of the composite figure shown here.

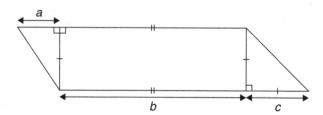

A. $A = bc + \dfrac{1}{2}ac + \dfrac{1}{2}c^2$

B. $A = bc + ac + c^2$

C. $A = 2b + 2c + ac + c^2$

D. $A = ac + b^2 + c^2$

Section 4 Practice Test (Continued)

14. The lengths of the bases of an isosceles trapezoid are shown here. If the perimeter of this trapezoid is 42 units, what is its area?

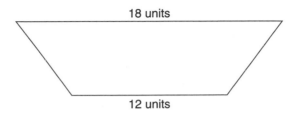

18 units

12 units

    A. 216 square units

    B. 108 square units

    C. 78 square units

    D. 60 square units

15. Which figure represents a solid that does NOT have a flat surface?

    A.   B.   C.   D.

16. Which two three-dimensional figures have the same number of faces?

    A. A triangular prism and a square pyramid

    B. A triangular pyramid and a rectangular prism

    C. A triangular prism and a rectangular prism

    D. A triangular pyramid and a square pyramid

17. The water level in an aquarium is 3 feet high when the aquarium is full. The area of the base of the aquarium is 12 square feet. If the water drains out until the water level is only 2.5 feet high, what volume of water has been drained out of the aquarium?

    A. 6 ft.^{3} B. 15 ft.^{3} C. 30 ft.^{3} D. 36 ft.^{3}

362

Section 4 Practice Test (Continued)

18. Lynn has a cylindrical candle mold that has a diameter of 9.4 centimeters and a height of 12 centimeters. She plans to melt a rectangular block of wax to pour into the mold. About how many candles can she make if the block of wax measures 10 centimeters by 16 centimeters by 12 centimeters?

   A. 12   B. 8   C. 5   D. 2

19. A rectangular solid has a volume of 56 cubic decimeters. If the length, width, and height are all changed to one-half their original size, what will be the new volume of the rectangular solid?

   A. 28 cu dm³   B. 14 cu dm³   C. 7 cu dm³   D. 5 cu dm³

20. Marcus wants to build a small rectangular box similar to a 24-inch by 48-inch by 20-inch container. His design shows a 6-inch by 12-inch by 8-inch box. What correction is needed in the design so that the box and the container will be similar?

   A. Decrease 12 in. to 9 in.   C. Increase 6 in. to 12 in.

   B. Increase 8 in. to 10 in.   D. Decrease 8 in. to 5 in.

21. A cube-shaped box is made of wood and has no lid. If each outer edge is 20 centimeters long and each side and bottom of the box is 2 centimeters thick, about how many cubic centimeters of wood form the box itself?

   A. 2,000 cu cm   C. 6,400 cu cm

   B. 3,400 cu cm   D. 8,000 cu cm

22. A solid 3D block of concrete has the following orthogonal views with related measures and edges indicated. All angles are right angles. What is the volume of the block?

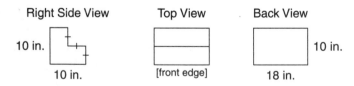

   A. 1,800 cu. in.   C. 1,100 cu. in.

   B. 1,350 cu. in.   D. 850 cu. in.

Answer Key

The objective being tested is shown in brackets beside the answer.

1. A [1]	12. D [6]
2. C [1]	13. A [7]
3. D [2]	14. C [7]
4. B [2]	15. B [8]
5. D [3]	16. A [8]
6. C [3]	17. A [9]
7. A [4]	18. D [9]
8. B [4]	19. C [10]
9. C [5]	20. D [10]
10. B [5]	21. B [11]
11. C [6]	22. B [11]

Math Essentials, Middle School Level: Lessons and Activities for Test Preparation

Frances M. Thompson, Ed.D.

Paper/ 368 pages

ISBN: 0-7879-6602-9

Math Essentials, Middle School Level gives middle school math teachers the tools they need to help prepare all types of students (including gifted and learning disabled) for mathematics testing and the National Council of Teachers of Mathematics (NCTM) standards. *Math Essentials* highlights Dr. Thompson's proven approach by incorporating manipulatives, diagrams, and independent practice. This dynamic book covers thirty key objectives arranged in four sections. Each objective includes three activities (two developmental lessons and one independent practice) and a list of commonly made errors related to the objective.

The book's activities are designed to be flexible and can be used as a connected set or taught separately, depending on the learning needs of your students. Most activities and problems also include a worksheet and an answer key and each of the four sections contains a practice test with an answer key.

Hands-On Algebra: Ready-To-Use Games & Activities For Grades 7-12

Frances M. Thompson, Ed.D.

Paper/ 640 pages

ISBN: 0-87628-386-5

For grades 7-12 teachers, here's an extensive collection of 159 ready-to-use games and activities to make algebra meaningful and fun for kids of all ability levels!

Through a unique three-step approach, students gain mastery over algebra concepts and skills one activity at a time:

- Activity 1 offers **physical models** (using available materials) and easy-to-follow instructions to help learners seek patterns.
- Activity 2 uses **pictorial models** like diagrams, tables, and graphs to further help students retain and test what they have learned.
- Activity 3 encourages **exploration** and **application** of newly learned concepts and skills through cooperative games, puzzles, problems, and graphic calculator or computer activities.

Ready-to-Use
Math Proficiency
Lessons and Activities
4th Grade Level

Frances M. Thompson, Ed.D.

Paper/ 400 pages
ISBN: 0-7879-6596-0

Ready-to-Use Math Proficiency Lessons and Activities 4th Grade Level offers teachers a collection of 40 key objectives that help students master the standard mathematics curriculum that they are expected to have learned in grades 1 to 4. Each of these objectives includes three developmental activities.

- Activity 1 provides physical models and the materials that are described in detail, including pattern sheets, building mats, and worksheets with answer keys.
- Activity 2 uses pictorial models such as pictures or diagrams that help students retain and assess what they have learned.
- Activity 3 encourages exploration and application of newly learned lessons. Worksheet items for this third stage give students more opportunities to prepare for the testing experience.

Hands-On Math:
Ready-To-Use
Games & Activities
For Grades 4-8

Frances M. Thompson, Ed.D.

Paper/ 544 pages
ISBN: 0-7879-6740-8

Here's a super treasury of 279 exciting math games and activities that help students learn by engaging both their minds and their bodies. Dispensing with tired "rote" learning and memorization, *Hands-On Math!* uses fun-filled exercises that encourage your students to think and reason mathematically.

In line with NCTM guidelines, this invaluable teacher's aid develops basic and advanced math skills through an effective combination of three components for each lesson: a concrete exercise (manipulatives), a pictorial model, and a cooperative learning experience.

Organized into eight sections, each covering concepts from a different area of mathematics, *Hands-On Math!* provides scores of reproducible record sheets, workmats and other student handouts to use as often as needed.

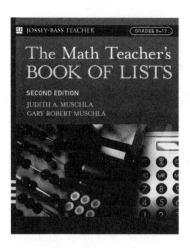

The Math Teacher's Book Of Lists, 2nd Edition

Judith A. Muschla and Gary Robert Muschla

Paper/ 250 pages
ISBN: 0-7879-7398-X

The Math Teacher's Book of Lists, 2nd Edition is a one-stop math resource with exciting, challenging, and quick reference materials, all supporting NCTM standards. It includes comprehensive and updated content from general mathematics through algebra, geometry, trigonometry, and calculus, useful in 5-12 classrooms as well as community college classes.

Part I contains nine sections of reproducible lists and offers essential, time-saving and relevant information on over 300 topics. Part II contains a variety of reproducible teaching aids and activities to support the instructional program.

The original lists have been substantially updated; a new section, "Lists for Student Reference," has been added, along with approximately twelve new lists, including "Fractals," "Topics in Discrete Math," "Math Websites for Students," and "Math Websites for Teachers."

This new edition, like the original, is designed for easy implementation. Each list is written in clear, simple-to-read language, stands alone, and may be used with students of various grades and abilities; materials can be customized to your needs. These lists are linked through cross references and can serve as the basis for developing supplementary materials for the classroom, expanding topics in the curriculum, or extending lessons with related topics.

The Math Teacher's Book of Lists provides:

- An invaluable resource for effective mathematics instruction.
- An imaginative way to help students understand the grand scope, practicality and intriguing intricacies of mathematics.

The Authors

Judith A. Muschla has taught middle and high school mathematics in South River, NJ, for the last 27 years, and received the governor's Teacher Recognition Program Award in New Jersey. **Gary Robert Muschla** taught reading and writing for more than 25 years in Spotswood, NJ. This is their eighth co-authored mathematics book.

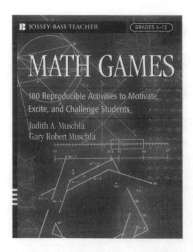

Math Games:
180 Reproducible Activities to Motivate, Excite, and Challenge Students, Grades 6-12

Judith A. Muschla, Gary Robert Muschla

Paper/ 240 pages

ISBN: 0-7879-7081-6

This is a dynamic collection of 180 reproducible activity sheets to stimulate and challenge your students in all areas of math from whole numbers to data analysis while emphasizing problem solving, critical thinking, and the use of technology for today's curriculum.

Each of the book's activities can help you teach students in grades 6 through 12 how to think with numbers, recognize relationships, and make connections between mathematical concepts. You pick the activity appropriate for their needs, encourage the use of a calculator, or provide further challenges with activities that have multiple answers.

Designed to be user friendly, all of the ready-to-use activities are organized into seven convenient sections and printed in a lay-flat format for ease of photocopying as many times as needed.

Hands-On Math Projects With Real-Life Applications: Ready To Use Lessons and Materials For Grades 6-12

Judith A. Muschla, Gary Robert Muschla

Paper/ 384 pages

ISBN: 0-13-032015-3

Help students apply math concepts and skills to everyday problems found across the curriculum, in sports, and in daily life with this outstanding collection of 60 hands-on investigations. These tested projects stress cooperative learning, group sharing, and writing as they build skills in problem solving, critical thinking, decision-making and computation. What's more, you get tested guidelines techniques and tools for managing the classroom during project activities and assessing students' performance.

Other Books of Interest

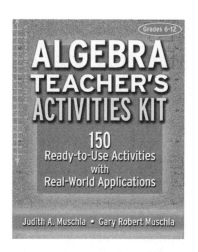

Algebra Teacher's Activities Kit: 150 Ready-to-Use Activities with Real-World Applications

By Judith A. Muschla and Gary R. Muschla

Paper/ 325 pages

ISBN: 0-7879-6598-7

A unique resource that provides 150 ready-to-use algebra activities designed to help students in grades 6-12 master pre-algebra, Algebra I, and Algebra II. The book covers the skills typically included in an algebra curriculum. Developed to motivate and challenge students, many of the activities focus on real-life applications. Each of the book's ten sections contains teaching suggestions that provide teachers with strategies for implementing activities and are accompanied by helpful answer keys. The activities supply students with quick feedback, and many of the answers are self-correcting.

Each activity stands alone and can be applied in the manner that best fits your particular teaching program. *Algebra Teacher's Activities Kit* can be used as a supplement to your instructional program, to reinforce skills and concepts you've previously taught, for extra credit assignments, or to assist substitute teachers.

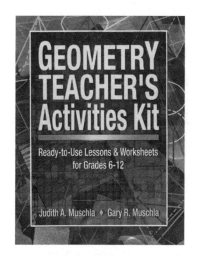

Geometry Teacher's Activities Kit: Ready-To-Use Lessons & Worksheets For Grades 6-12

Judith A. Muschla, Gary Robert Muschla

Paper/ 384 pages

ISBN: 0-13-060038-5

This unique resource provides 130 detailed lessons with reproducible worksheets to help students understand geometry concepts and recognize and interpret geometry's relationship to the real world. The lessons and worksheets are organized into seven sections, each covering one major area of geometry and presented in a consistent and easy-to-follow format, including a learning objective, special materials (if any), teaching notes with step-by-step directions, answer key, and reproducible student activity sheets. Activities in sections 1-6 are presented in order of difficulty within each section while those in Part 7, "A Potpourri of Geometry," are open-ended and may be used with most middle and high school classes. Many activities throughout the book may be used with calculators and computers in line with the NCTM's recommendations.

Algebra Out Loud:
Learning Mathematics Through Reading and Writing Activities

Pat Mower, Ph.D.

Paper/ 256 pages
ISBN: 0-7879-6898-6

Algebra Out Loud is a unique resource designed for mathematics instructors who are teaching Algebra I and II. This easy-to-use guide is filled with illustrative examples, strategies, activities, and lessons that will help students more easily understand mathematical text and learn the skills they need to effectively communicate mathematical concepts.

Algebra Out Loud gives teachers the tools they need to help their students learn how to communicate about math ideas between student and teacher, student and peers, and student and the wider world. The book offers proven writing activities that will engage the students in writing about algebraic vocabulary, processes, theorems, definitions, and graphs. The strategies and activities in Algebra Out Loud will give students the edge in learning how to summarize, analyze, present, utilize, and retain mathematical content.

The Author

Pat Mower, Ph.D., is an associate professor in the Department of Mathematics and Statistics at Washburn University in Topeka, Kansas. Dr. Mower prepares preservice teachers to teach mathematics in elementary, middle, and secondary schools. Her interests include reading and writing in mathematics and alternative methods for the teaching and learning of mathematics.

Forthcoming 2006:
Geometry Out Loud:
Learning Mathematics Through Reading and Writing Activities

Pat Mower, Ph.D.

Paper/ 300 pages (est.)
ISBN: 0-7879-7601-6

This book offers intriguing activities, strategies, and ideas to foster math communication-and with it, an understanding of geometric principles. *Geometry Out Loud* addresses a wide range of topics including reading, writing, and project-based learning in geometry, and it supports the NCTM standards on teaching mathematical communication. The book's flexible design allows teachers to select individual lessons and suggests strategies that are applicable to a variety of mathematical problem tasks.